ALSO BY CYNTHIA D. BERTELSEN

MUSHROOM: A Global History

A HASTINESS OF COOKS:
A Practical Handbook for Use in Deciphering the Mysteries of
Historic Recipes and Cookbooks

IN THE SHADOW OF RAVENS: A Novel

WISDOM SOAKED IN PALM OIL:
Journeying Through the Food and Flavors of Africa

MEATBALLS & LEFSE:
Memories and Recipes from a
Scandinavian-American Farming Life

STOVES & SUITCASES
Searching for Home in the World's Kitchens

CYNTHIA D. BERTELSEN

Turquoise Moon Press

Stoves & Suitcases:
Searching for Home in the World's Kitchens

©2021 Cynthia D. Bertelsen

Cover photo: Massonstock

Title page illustration: Alexander Pokusay

Cover and book design: Cathy Gibbons Reedy

1. Biography and Autobiography 2. Cooking 3. Gastronomy 4. Travel
ISBN: 978-1-7345579-2-3

Printed in the United States of America

Turquoise Moon Press
Gainesville, FL

turquoisemoonpress.com

For Erik, who lived the journey too

TABLE OF CONTENTS

The happy childhood is hardly worth your while.
~ Frank McCourt

A nomad I will remain for life, in love with
distant and uncharted places.
~ Isabelle Eberhardt

Life itself is an exile. The way home is not the way back.
~ Colin Wilson

Choosing a Path

A Few Words about Memory

I wanted to capture time through how food and I were getting along at any given moment. That necessitated writing some dark stuff, some sad stuff, and a lot of painful memories, because my life has often been dark, sad, and painful. I didn't want to sugarcoat anything.

~ Kate Christensen

Memory is a funny thing.

Memory is perplexing.

Memory is "otherworldly."

Memory is the stuff of fabulists.

Trying to remember what happened last week, much less fifty or seventy years in the past, challenges a memoirist more than I thought possible. This truth struck a chord as I dove into writing this book. The more I remembered, the more I realized what I did not. My memories did not always tally with those who'd been there at the same time.

Skepticism of historical memory stretches far back into time, despite oral histories carefully preserved in various cultures around the world. I began to distrust my own memory, and in doing so, I found a like-minded soul.

Only this particular soul lived nearly 2,500 years ago.

Greek historian Thucydides complained in his *History of the Peloponnesian War* that "different eye-witnesses give different accounts of the same events, speaking out of partiality for one side or the other or else from imperfect memories." He chastised people—implying Herodotus—for their uncritical acceptance of the words of the ancients, as one author called it, "hearsay history."

Despite memory being the frail and delicate shell game it is, the memoir now enjoys explosive popularity because everyone believes their life story to be unique, fueled in the wake of Twitter- and Facebook-generated narcissism. Consider all those foodie memoirs clogging publishing lists a few years back. Memoirists work with memory, a fluid concept at best but decidedly non-static in the river of time.

Unlike autobiography, memoir tends to portray the intangible.

Feelings. Emotions. Time.

But the passage of time filters these building blocks of memory in the same way a sieve keeps out big chunks of bone when a cook strains meat broth.

Something is always left behind.

And, like Thucydides, I tend to be wary when someone bases a truth entirely on that slippery, half-there ingredient—memory.

Indeed, memory is a funny thing, similar to passing sieve-like through a door into another world, one filled with ghosts and illusions and partial truths.

Memory goes thin over time.

Was all that time only a shadow, fleeting, disappearing like mist when the sun burst forth through the billowy white clouds?

I leave you here with the bones in the sieve.

How it All Began: Searching for Home

So, here you are. Too foreign for home, too foreign for here.
Never enough for both.
~ Ijeoma Umebinyuo

"We don't worry too much about these little ones," the delivery-room nurse told Mom as she cradled my tiny head in the palm of her hand. "They usually don't live very long."

Those were the first words I heard spoken. Of course, I don't remember a thing.

Weeks and weeks too early, way before Mom's due date. Leaving the warm rosy safety of the womb for the cold confines of an incubator in Sacramento, my lungs unprepared for the warm California air surrounding me, I languished, pumped full of life-giving oxygen. Six weeks in that incubator isolated me from all human touch, except the cool, rubber-gloved hands of nurses and doctors fighting to keep me alive.

When I weighed as much as a five-pound bag of flour, my young and inexperienced parents carried me home, joyous at my survival. They named me Cynthia Diane, "Cindy," for short. Both names refer indirectly to the Roman and Greek goddesses of the moon.

But unbeknownst to my parents, those days and weeks in that oxygen-rich incubator damaged my hearing and my vision.

With that, I became an exile, in a way. As another Cindy—Puerto Rican poet Cindy Jiménez-Vera—put it, "Being born is the first exile."

What does it mean to be exiled?

"Exile" conjures up visions of Napoleon languishing on Elba or Leonardo da Vinci in the Château du Clos Lucé, near Amboise, France, yearning for his native Italy.

Yet exile takes various forms under different circumstances. Exile generally includes two different concepts. Both stem from ancient Roman culture.

There's the outright political form, as in the cases of Napoleon and

Leonardo. Banishment describes their fate. Then there's self-exile, as in the case of The Lost Generation in Paris in the 1920s. The Roman concept of *fuga* at work.

In between these two, things get a little less black and white, taking on hues of murky grey.

Exile.

Nomad.

Refugee.

Pilgrim.

All words defining my life at one time or another.

Hearing loss like mine isolates a person from others. At first glance, it's an invisible disability. But it makes itself known when a person with that disability begins to move about in community, in social interactions. Forming community becomes more fraught for the hearing-impaired.

People with disabilities often experience something termed "internal exile."

Until I was thirty years old, I never heard a bird sing. I learned to read lips at age five. At the same age, I wore a patch over my right eye in order to increase the sight in my left. And I always sat in the front row in school, straining to hear. I missed the jokes, the song lyrics, the whispers, the giggles at sleepovers. All things children with normal hearing do.

Like many children, I often wondered if I'd been switched at birth, if perhaps out there in the wider world my real family loved and cared for a kid who truly belonged in my house, to these people who called themselves my family. But when I began to see some similarities between my smile and Daddy's, I realized the truth: this was my family.

Deafness brings out a cruel streak in some people, who tease and poke fun. In my case, such treatment further increased sensations of exile in my own home. Or at least a sense of being "Other," of not belonging. Feelings of trauma, primarily emotional, cradled me most days, due to the incessant humiliation and name-calling heaped upon me.

But a strange thing happened because of all that.

To cope, once I learned to read, I turned first to books, aided and abetted by my maternal grandmother, whom I named Teeny Grandma. My paternal grandmother, I called Big Grandma not because she was fat but because she stood a foot taller than Teeny, all of four feet eleven inches in height. Through books, I explored the world, forgetting albeit briefly my life as a hearing-impaired person. Teeny gave me an unforgettable book for Christmas the year I turned nine. Walt Disney's *People & Places* still sits on a bookshelf in my house. It's traveled with me every time I've moved. Twenty-two times I've packed up my belongings and left a place for good. Some places I returned to, but only on short visits of days or weeks.

Later, another coping mechanism presented itself: cooking.

Tasked with meal preparation for my natal family of six after Mom enrolled in graduate school, I discovered the Time-Life Foods of the World series at the public library. With that treasure, for such it seemed to me, I felt less like a turkey crowded in with a flock of peacocks or shredded like carrion under a vulture's talons, mouth frozen in a silent scream, Edvard Munch-style.

For me, stoves became something akin to altars, something almost holy, places of communion where I could prepare meals and share the fruits of my labors with others. Although some culinary efforts resulted in burnt offerings, despite my best intentions!

Travel became yet another coping mechanism for me.

Dr. Seuss's *Oh, the Places You'll Go!* got it right.

Oh, the places I went! And lived!

- Pullman, Washington
- Gainesville, St. Petersburg, Cedar Key, Florida
- Puebla, Mexico
- Ponce, Puerto Rico
- Fram, Paraguay
- Holmen and Milwaukee, Wisconsin
- La Lima, El Zamorano, and San Pedro Sula, Honduras
- Port-au-Prince, Haiti
- Rabat, Morocco
- Ouagadougou, Burkina Faso
- Paris, France
- Blacksburg, Virginia
- Manado, Indonesia

I count myself among the transients, pilgrims, gypsies, tourists, explorers, adventurers, and expatriates of the world. Place attachment is not easy for me.

By wandering, the question of what to eat came up. Every day. That's where roaming the world became even more fascinating, the discoveries endless.

Stoves & Suitcases is not about my hearing and visual disabilities. Rather, it's a story of how my life unfolded despite those things. Through vignettes—also called flash memoir—I weave a tale of how a kid with an iffy start in life embraced the world and its food, with all the sadness and splendor and warts and beauty therein.

> *But from the minute I could read, I was not "separated" but whole,*
> *of a piece, and not only with other people but my own self.*
> ~ M.F.K. Fisher

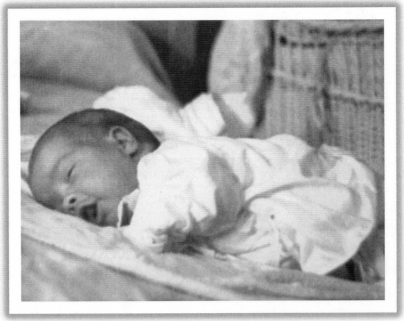

Author at 2 months, weighing 5 pounds

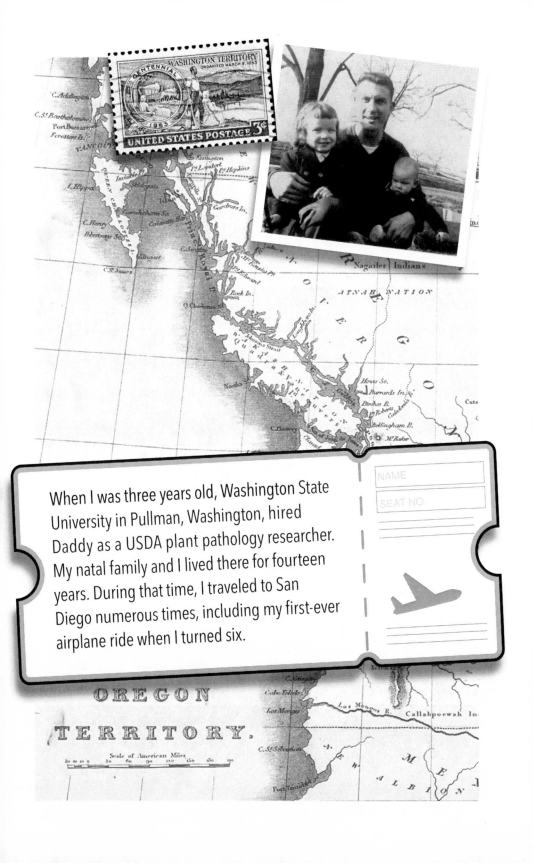

When I was three years old, Washington State University in Pullman, Washington, hired Daddy as a USDA plant pathology researcher. My natal family and I lived there for fourteen years. During that time, I traveled to San Diego numerous times, including my first-ever airplane ride when I turned six.

Wheat

Garlic Bread

There is always one moment in childhood
when the door opens and lets the future in.
~ Graham Greene

That year, winter passed into a rather reluctant spring. A few scraggly lime-green leaves still hung on the lilac bush after a freak frost killed all the aromatic little purple flowers. I always loved to smell those tiny odes to pleasure as I raced out the door of our sad little apartment in Pullman, Washington. Wheat country. That's where I moved when I was three years old once Daddy earned his Ph.D. in plant pathology at the University of California-Davis. Named after George Pullman of train and good travel food fame, Pullman was home to Washington State College. Daddy worked there as a wheat disease scientist, researching cures for what ailed the wheat growing in the surrounding hills and fields.

Daddy cooked well. Quite well, as a matter of fact. Better than Mom. Truth be told, his vegetable beef soup became my favorite dish (see page 51). Most days, he didn't cook, although we kids often wished he did. Mom's kitchen repertoire reminded me later in my life of days-of-the-week underwear: If it's Monday, it must be creamed-tuna-on-rice day, that sort of thing.

But Daddy didn't always grab a saucepan or soup pot.

One month before my fifth birthday, my baby brother Tim appeared several weeks early, arriving red-faced and skinny on a cold, snowy February day. Mom stayed in the hospital with him for four days, a standard protocol for new mothers in those days.

I guess it was the third day, when fish begin to stink, as the adage goes, and Jesus rose from the dead.

Daddy came home early from work, bundled my brother Jeff and me up in our snowsuits, and hustled us into the black 1949 Pontiac he later sold to a graduate student for one dollar.

"We're going to the Fischers' house for dinner tonight," Daddy told me as he gunned the cold motor to life. He'd apparently tired of cooking for children. His boss, George Fischer, and his wife Geneva, never had any children, so Geneva loved having us over for dinner or picnics on their farm. It overlooked rolling hills full of yellowing wheat, the air pungent with the odor of manure from the docile black-and-white dairy cows whose soft noses I loved to pet. Lewis and Clark passed through Palouse country on their way west in 1805, forty-six miles west of Pullman. Meriwether Clark wrote in his diary:

> … *little river in a Stard. bend, imediately below a long bad rapid in which the water is Confined in a Chanel of about 20 yards between rugid rocks for the distance of a mile and a half and a rapid rockey Chanel for 2 miles above. This must be a verry bad place in high water, here is a great fishing place, the timbers of Several houses piled up, and a number of wholes of fish, and the bottom appears to have been made use of as a place of deposit for their fish for ages past, here two Indians from the upper forks over took us and continued on down on horse back.*

"Palouse" comes from the name of a Native American tribe, the Palus, who'd lived in those rolling hills for thousands of years.

Although I'd been to the Fischers' farm many times, it seemed as if we drove forever. Maybe the darkness made the road seem unfamiliar. I kept asking Daddy every few minutes, "Are we there yet? Why not? When?"

In answer to my questions, he pulled into the Fischers' long rutted driveway. We bounced along in the darkness, no light save that of our headlights, for about a quarter-mile until we saw lamps glowing on the porch of the Fischers' old plankboard farmhouse. Geneva Fischer, rotund with the plumpness of middle age, stood on the sagging porch, waving. I scrambled down from the front seat and ran toward her as Daddy picked Jeff up like a football. None of us wore seatbelts. They hadn't been invented yet.

"George is waiting for you in the shop," she said as she hugged me and tweaked my red nose.

"You're a regular little Rudolf," she joked as I turned and darted to the big red barn where George's magical world of shiny gemstones and other rocks dazzled me.

I spied George standing next to the workbench where he polished the stones he found or bought on his many trips around the West.

"Hey there, kiddo, how are you doin'?"

He turned toward me, holding a gleaming gold stone in his outstretched hand.

"I'm finishing up this special little rock just for you."

I held out my hand, and he laid the shimmering stone on my cold palm.

"A tiger's eye!" I yelled. "Thank you, Dr. Fischer, thank you!"

"Yes, a piece of tiger eye," he chuckled. "Glad you like it."

Back at the house, Geneva yelled, "Come and get it," ringing the big clapper bell on the porch to make sure we received the message. I raced across the yard to the house and lined up at the sink to wash my hands.

The house smelled of spaghetti, like the spaghetti bake that Daddy's mother made whenever we visited my grandparents in San Diego. When Geneva removed the foil cover, I exclaimed, "Daddy, that's Point Loma Special!" He grinned at me and winked at Geneva.

"Yes, Geneva asked me what I wanted for dinner, and I told her."

The bread, soft, buttery, tasted of something utterly unfamiliar to me. I ate three big pieces as the grown-ups talked. Mostly about wheat diseases, or smut talk, as Daddy joked. He and George were seeking cures for wheat smuts caused by fungi.

Mrs. Fischer prepared her garlic bread by cutting a "French loaf" or baguette into neat slices. Then she buttered each piece on both sides with melted butter infused with minced garlic. Wrapped tightly in aluminum foil, baked at 350°F until heated through, the soft, moist crumb nearly melted in my mouth when I ate it.

Jeff and I soon began nodding off. The warm room and the good food and the lull of soft voices did that.

Daddy tucked us into the front seat, me next to the passenger door, as the Fischers said goodbye. As we pulled out of the driveway, I asked, "What was that bread, Daddy? I liked it."

He glanced at me and said, "Well, that was garlic bread."

"Why don't we eat it in our house?"

"Well, Mom doesn't like garlic," he replied as we turned onto the two-lane highway.

"Well, I do!" I said.

"So do I, so do I," he laughed.

Many Americans like Mom associated eating garlic with being low-class or poor, immigrants and other outsiders, eating things like *bruschetta*. And the belief that it caused bad breath hovered in the background as well. Eating garlic seemed to define people as "Other."

That was my first lesson in how people often use food habits to label certain groups of people as different.

Bruschetta

6 large slices country-style bread, sliced about ½-inch thick

3 large garlic cloves, peeled, halved, slightly bruised with a cleaver

Extra virgin olive oil

Fine sea salt

Heat broiler to 500°F, raise rack to about 3 inches from heat. Place bread slices on large baking sheet. Broil until bread is toasted and golden on one side. Repeat with other side. Immediately rub one side of each slice with the cut side of half a garlic clove. Discard garlic. Then take a pastry brush and coat bread slices with olive oil on the garlic-infused side. Serves 6.

Author with Big Grandma and Teeny Grandma

Formula One

And suddenly you just know... .
It's time to start something new and trust the magic of new beginnings.

~ Meister Eckhart

My three-month-old brother Tim rarely cried, but my two-year-old brother Jeff lost no opportunity to squeeze Tim's hand until he sobbed. Consequently, I escaped the din when I could, as far as my five-year-old legs could carry me. Not far, for I usually took off up the sloping hill behind the barracks-like married-student housing where we lived.

There, at the top of the hill near my home, a nineteenth-century white farmhouse leaned to one side, perched on a shaky stone foundation. And a barn, too, red paint faded to the color of old bloodstains, filled with cows, their thick warm bodies offering me respite, soft noses nuzzling my shoulders for the occasional apple I stole from the kitchen.

One particular day, after an adventure in the meadow between the long barracks-like buildings, I brought home a glass jar with holes in the lid, made by hammering a nail through the thin metal. A horde of angry honey bees inside the jar threw themselves against the glass, stingers at the ready, ignoring the juicy dandelion flowers I'd picked for their dinner. Mom glanced at me and barked an order. Tim sat in his crib, crying, inconsolable, as Jeff hovered behind the bedroom door, smirking.

"Get that jar of baby food out of the cupboard and open it. Hurry up!"

I ran to the cupboard and climbed up the small wooden stool near the counter.

"This one?" I asked as I turned to Mom with the jar in my hand.

"Yes, yes!" she said, her impatience signaling another tense flare-up.

I smacked the jar with a table knife. A little button thingy popped up. Twisting the lid on the jar with my small hands, I pried it off awkwardly and ran to Mom with both the jar and Tim's sterling silver spoon. Teeny Grandma, Mom's mother, gave us all little spoons like that, bonuses from her job as a bookkeeper at Baranov's, a swanky jewelry store in San Diego.

Mom cooed at Tim and waved the spoon around, touching his lips. He opened his itty-bitty rosebud of a mouth and began swallowing whatever was in the jar. The lid still in my hand, I noticed a few globs of something white stuck on the inside of the lid. I licked furtively at the globs, cleaning the surface with my tongue

The taste seemed familiar to me, hitting me with memories of something I knew not what. If I'd known then what "ambrosial" meant, that's the word I might have used.

Mom put the rest of the pudding in the refrigerator, the lid on tight.

Later, as Tim and Jeff napped, I asked Mom why Gerber tapioca pudding, rich with the flavor of sweetened condensed milk, tasted so familiar.

She guessed that it probably was due to my being premature. The doctors encouraged her to make a type of formula supplemented with sweetened condensed milk. After I grew bigger and gained enough weight over my three-pounds-and-five-ounce birth weight, they switched me to evaporated milk formula.

I snuck over to the refrigerator and opened the door. With my fingers, I scooped out a few tablespoons of that sweetness. Putting my finger in my mouth, I sucked the pudding off my skin.

At that moment, I discovered the meaning of real pleasure.

Evaporated-Milk Baby Formula

13 ounces Pet evaporated milk

20 ounces water

2 tablespoons Karo syrup

Heat all ingredients together and pour 4 ounces into each of 6 bottles. Feed every 3-4 hours.

Marshmallow Casserole

*Ponder well on this point: the pleasant hours of our life are all connected by a
more or less tangible link, with some memory of the table.*

~ Charles Pierre Monselet

I climbed the steep stairs one step at a time, my short five-year-old legs
pausing on each. The porch light glowed above my head, sunlike, even though
it was late November, always dark as soon as Daddy came home from work at
five o'clock.

It was Thanksgiving, which meant nothing to me, just another day. But
eating at another family's house, now that was something new and different.

Daddy pointed at the doorbell, so I pushed it, a loud ring that I could hear,
followed by footsteps clunking across the floor behind it, a very dim sound for
me. A tall, smiling man opened the door and scooped me up.

"You must be Cindy! I'm Jim, and this is Donna, and that baby she's holding is also named Cindy. How about that?"

Jim set me down on a sofa, its rough tapestry-like upholstery scratching
my bare legs, the tulle petticoat under my dress riding up to my waist. The aroma of roasting turkey filled the room. And my nostrils. My stomach growled.

"Mom, I'm hungry!"

"Shh, we'll eat in a minute," Mom whispered as she headed to the tiny
kitchen to help Donna with the food, leaving baby Tim with Daddy.

Finally, after what seemed an eternity to me, Jim said, "Let's eat!"

We sat at the small yellow Formica table, the babies in highchairs, Jeff and
I each perched on a slippery stack of thick phone books.

Jim held out his right hand to me, his left to Donna. He closed his eyes,
and so did Donna. But I didn't. As he said grace, I saw Daddy rolling his eyes.
Prayers and Jesus had no place in our house.

Donna began dishing up the plates.

That's when I saw it.

The casserole. Its top dotted with ... marshmallows! Oh!

I loved marshmallows in hot chocolate. Especially when the hot milk melted the marshmallows slightly, when they were still recognizable as marshmallows, but with the delicious gooeyness only seconds away.

Donna plopped a huge spoonful of the casserole on a plate, along with sliced turkey, a bit of bread dressing, and a fist-size serving of green beans. Mom signaled to her that was quite enough. Donna handed me the plate.

I sniffed the casserole, its cinnamon smell promising even more gustatory delights. I liked cinnamon, too. So I filled my spoon, took a bite, and almost threw up.

Tears spurted from my eyes. No one noticed me, so busy were they talking or attending to the babies. No one saw me take my napkin and spit the orange mess into the pristine white starched cloth. Throughout the meal, I ate around the casserole, and when no one was looking, I added another bulging spoonful to the napkin. And another.

What an abomination! I didn't know the word then, but it certainly fit.

Donna nodded at me, approving my empty plate as everyone finished eating.

I held the now-soggy napkin in my left hand, waiting for everyone to leave the table. When Daddy came over to help me off the chair, I stuck the napkin as far under my plate as I could.

Later, snug in my twin bed, covered with heavy blankets and one of Big Grandma's tied quilts, I asked Daddy about the marshmallows.

"What was that orange stuff under the marshmallows?"

"Oh, those were sweet potatoes," he replied as he tucked the covers around me. And grinned.

"What are sweet potatoes?"

"As far as I know, they're a type of root vegetable, like a white potato. People in the South eat them a lot," he told me. I didn't know what he meant by the South, though.

"I hated them!" I said, sticking out my tongue.

"Yes, I know. That was quite the trick you pulled with that napkin."

"I never want to eat sweet potatoes again," I said.

"I don't blame you, I don't like 'em either. It'll be our little secret, OK?" He winked and kissed me on my cheek. "Good night."

I rolled over, smiling.

I never did eat sweet potatoes again for many years. That was one food discovery I tried to forget.

But I always wondered how such a distasteful dish went mainstream.

Come to find out, the Angelus Marshmallows Company hired Janet McKenzie Hill in 1917 to invent some new recipes for their product. Ms. Hill, who worked on the Boston Cooking School magazine, invented the hateful casserole. And savvy marketing did the rest.

One Thanksgiving, near the end of my radiation treatment for breast cancer, I sat in a booth in one of my favorite restaurants, the Old Ebbitt Bar and Grill on 15th St. NW, steps away from the White House in Washington D.C. One option on the set menu included Sweet Potato Gratin. I ordered it, thinking that I could use some vitamins at that moment, which sweet potatoes certainly provide. With a slight shiver of trepidation, I took a few bites of the steaming dish, rich with the surprising aroma of chiles, remembering my five-year-old self and the disappointment of that marshmallow-topped orange mess.

One bite of that gratin, though, and I tasted a world of difference, proving that food adventures never really end.

Author celebrating first snowfall!

Sweet Potatoes au Gratin in Creamy Chipotle Sauce

2 pounds small sweet potatoes, peeled, sliced ¼-inch thick

2 cups grated Gruyère cheese, divided

3 tablespoons unsalted butter

½ cup finely chopped yellow onion

1 teaspoon finely minced garlic

2 cups heavy cream

2–3 chipotle chiles in adobo sauce

1 teaspoon fine sea salt

1 teaspoon freshly ground black pepper

¼ teaspoon dried thyme leaves

Preheat oven to 375°F. Blanch sweet potatoes in salted water until slightly tender. Drain immediately and layer in a greased baking dish, with half the cheese between each layer. While sweet potatoes cool, sauté onion in butter over medium heat until translucent. Add minced garlic and cook for 30 more seconds. Set aside. Blend chipotles with cream until smooth. Mix in onion/garlic mixture. Season sauce with salt, pepper, and thyme. Cover sweet potatoes with the chipotle cream sauce. Sprinkle with remaining cheese. Bake approximately 30 minutes or until sauce bubbles on sides of baking dish and top browns. Serves 6.

Bringing Home the Bacon

Thank God I arrived the day before yesterday, the first of the month, at this port of San Diego, truly a fine one, and not without reason called famous.

~ Junípero Serra

My grandparents' house in Ocean Beach—a suburb of San Diego, California—consisted of three tiny bedrooms and one bathroom. Ostensibly bedrooms. It was more like two bedrooms and a walk-in closet the size of a small prison cell.

Outside, under the looming avocado trees that my green-thumbed grandfather raised from seeds, sat a small guesthouse, where Daddy slept while in high school, tucked away from his four older sisters. Until a family of skunks invaded the crawl space, and someone—probably my grandfather whose temper could compete with a flamethrower when provoked—tried to evict them. Skunks being skunks, they fought back with their smelly, potent weapon. A rank odor still permeated the walls and floor twenty years later.

So when we visited, somehow the six of us bedded down in the main house, all in all probably 1,000 square feet in size. As did my grandparents.

I preferred the front bedroom, as my grandmother called it. A large four-poster bed filled most of the space, and gauzy white curtains framed the windows. Nothing better in the world than lying in that soft bed in the early morning, watching the ocean breeze ruffling those curtains and feeling cool salty air spreading itself over me like an extra blanket.

The kitchen?

Small, like a galley kitchen, it nonetheless boasted a breakfast nook off to one side, where my grandparents ate when not inundated with family. Large clean windows overlooked the poinsettia tree overhanging the alley—a tree, not a houseplant in a pot. An avocado tree loomed behind the house, its cool shade bathing the staircase leading to ground level. A gas stove, built-in vegetable storage bins, and a pantry with wooden shelves reaching all the way to the ceiling rounded out the work area. A big wooden cutting board and lots of sharp knives rested on the small counter next to the stove. A large refrigerator hummed next to the back door. Big Grandma kept slab bacon on the top shelf of the refrigerator, close to the frosty freezer compartment.

That slab of bacon fascinated me because the only bacon I knew came thinly sliced and cellophane-wrapped.

And that slab bacon is what my grandfather caught me and my cousin Joan, both of us eight years old, frying one summer morning. We'd woken early and in the dimness of dawn, we'd sliced the bacon quite unevenly. Giggling over the tiny forks meant for frying bacon, shoving each other to the side when it was time to turn the bacon, our laughter brought him to the kitchen. Our long reddish curls testified to our grandmother's Scots heritage, as did our blue eyes, also like hers. And those curls swung quite close to the hissing gas burner that we'd managed to light without an explosion.

"What are you doing?" he bellowed, his white sleeveless undershirt revealing his hairy chest. I later learned these were called "wife-beaters," but he never raised a hand to his wife nor his five children. However, he could dole out a tongue-lashing with the best of them.

"We're frying bacon, can't you see?" Joan quipped.

Oh dear, talking back, cruisin' for a bruisin'.

"Don't you talk to me like that!"

He grabbed her and marched her off to a corner in the living room.

That left me in charge of the blackening bacon. I pushed the hot grease-filled skillet away from the burner and turned off the heat. The one plate I found in the cupboard, blue plastic, would have to do. I lifted each piece of bacon out one by one as my grandfather stomped back into the kitchen.

"Kids!" he mumbled as he made coffee in a dented aluminum percolator.

"Want some bacon, Bobo?" I asked. That's what we called him, a name bestowed on him by one of my older cousins who couldn't say "grandpa" several years before.

"Yes, of course."

He grabbed the plate, poured himself a cup of coffee, and motioned for me to come out the back door to the stairs. We sat on the top step and munched on bacon and licked our greasy fingers, talked about snow and Washington State where I lived when I wasn't visiting. An only child, he'd lived there, too, when his father homesteaded near Wenatchee, until his mother's breast cancer forced them to make the long journey back to her home and family in Avoca, in Wisconsin.

Many years after he died, while going through boxes of old papers, I found a school picture of him. Sitting off to the side all by himself, the rest of his classmates huddling together for the photo. He was probably about eight or nine years old in the picture. His mother died when he was eight. Making him an outsider, at least in his mind.

The same age as I was when we ate bacon together.

Joan stood by the screen, whispering, "I'm sorry, Bobo. I'm sorry."

"Come on out here, we've got a few extra pieces," he motioned to the empty step next to him. She sat, and he wrapped his arms around both of us.

"Do you know what 'bringing home the bacon' means?" He leaned back against the wall of the porch. We shook our heads.

"Well, a long time ago, in England, married people won a slab of bacon called a 'flitch,' if they proved they didn't argue for a year. So the husband could say he brought home the bacon!" He smiled, laughing. "Who knows? My father used to say it was rubbish. But it's a good story."

That was how Big Grandma found us, giggling some more, snuggled up against him.

I always wondered about the bacon story he told. That led to wondering about other food and stories surrounding them, too.

Food history. Or food fakelore?

Bobo and Big Grandma

Bacon Jam

½ pound thick-slice bacon, cut into 1-inch pieces

1 medium yellow onion, finely chopped

1 large shallot, finely minced

2 garlic cloves, peeled and mashed

¼ cup dark brown sugar

2 tablespoons real maple syrup

3 tablespoons apple cider vinegar

1 teaspoon mild chili powder

Over medium heat, fry bacon pieces until crisp in a heavy skillet. Set aside to cool on paper towels. Measure fat remaining in pan. There should be at least 3 tablespoons. Reserve any extra bacon grease in a small bowl and refrigerate. Add chopped onions and shallots to the skillet. Cook over medium-low heat until onions caramelize–this could take a while. Be careful not to let the onions burn, so stir often. Add garlic, sugar, maple syrup, vinegar, chili powder, and reserved bacon pieces. Turn heat to simmer, let cook for about 10 minutes. Mixture will thicken like jam. Serve warm or cold with cheese and crackers. Great on burgers, too. Makes approximately 1½ cups.

Spaghetti Mi Amore

Taste memories tend to be the strongest of associative memories that you can make.

~ Hadley Bergstrom

Spaghetti meant only one thing to me as a child.

A can of Campbell's tomato soup, another of cream of mushroom soup, stirred into a pan where grayish hamburger backstroked in grease along with half-cooked chunks of celery and onions, each piece the size of large red kidney beans. Mushy noodles floating underneath like white worms swimming in blood. That was it.

Quick. Oh yes. Easy. Oh yes. Delicious? Um, no.

Spaghetti meant something tasteless, characterless.

Not until I babysat for a family whom I'll call the Barolinis did I find food that spoke to my soul. That night set me on the path I trod, seeking the peace and tranquility of the archetypal family kitchen bursting with flavor and the love of food.

When Mrs. Barolini called me to ask me to babysit, she mentioned that I would be eating with her kids that night. Would spaghetti be OK? I wanted to say "No," but polite girls needing money in those days did not often say "No" to babysitting jobs.

I wasn't expecting to be swept off my feet that night, that's for sure. But I did at least experience an epiphany.

When I walked into the Barolinis' house, shrugging off my scratchy wool coat, a huge bowl of red sauce sat on the kitchen table. Meatballs as big as Daddy's handballs rested on top of mounds of glistening, pale yellow spaghetti. Slabs of olive oil-and-garlic slathered bread stacked on another plate. Impatiently, the Barolini kids waved at me to hurry up and sit down. No formal greetings necessary when hunger loomed. That food smelled like nothing I'd ever smelled before. Saliva pooled under my tongue, but I didn't want to be seen drooling like my baby sister Paula.

I needed no more prompting. As Mrs. Barolini scribbled the phone number where they could be reached in case of emergency, I sat down in a chair, grabbing the serving spoon and dishing up my plate in a flash. My charges were half done eating by that time because Mrs. Barolini dished up their plates as soon as she heard Mr. Barolini and me walking through the door.

I ate like a wolf with a fresh kill, gulping the food on my plate in gasping, almost orgiastic bites, wadding up balls of bread and stuffing them into my mouth. Olive oil and garlic and sauce made from real tomatoes and rich red wine ran down my chin, spotting my white blouse with tiny red and gold dots. For a moment, a strange, almost electrical, feeling buzzed through me.

It was sheer simple happiness.

Since happiness at my family's dinner table was as rare as a day without air, that was a new sensation for me. And I wanted it more than anything, again and again.

I gobbled another three or four meatballs and licked my fingers clean before I washed the dishes that night. What a delicacy that spaghetti seemed to me, a kid whose diet depended on the continuing production of the Campbell Soup Company's repertoire of soup-based sauces. No offense to Campbell's, but it thrilled me to learn there was more to eating than a can of soup.

When Mrs. Barolini walked through the door at 11 p.m., her eyelids sagging, I begged her for her recipe. She said, "Of course, I'll write it up for you."

So she did.

Due to that eureka moment, that epiphany, cooking became my passion. My natal family served as my guinea pigs, Mom's kitchen my laboratory. Until I left for college.

Whenever I returned home for Thanksgivings or spring breaks during my college years, Jeff and Tim stood at the top of the stairs, leaning over the deck railing in the back of our house, waiting for me to get within earshot. Then they'd beg me to make Sweet and Sour Pork or Mrs. Barolini's spaghetti.

Mrs. Barolini's recipe hung on the wall of the many kitchens in my life, from Honduras to Burkina Faso and beyond.

It still does.

Mrs. Barolini's Italian Spaghetti, Ragù

3 tablespoons extra virgin olive oil

1 pound lean ground beef

1 medium onion, diced

½ green pepper, diced

1 garlic clove, minced, or to taste

3 (8-ounce) cans tomato sauce

1 cup California Burgundy wine (or California claret or Chianti)

1 teaspoon mixed Italian seasoning (basil, oregano, marjoram), or to taste

½ teaspoon fine sea salt

1 teaspoon granulated sugar

½ pound (2 cups broken) spaghetti, cooked al dente

1 cup grated Parmesan

Heat oil in a heavy pot over medium-high heat. Add hamburger, sauté until well-browned. Stir in onion and green pepper. Cook until onion is transparent. Add garlic, cook for 30 seconds more. Mix in tomato sauce, wine, seasonings, and sugar. Cover, reduce heat, simmer gently for one hour, stirring occasionally. Remove from heat, stir in ½ cup of the cheese. Pour sauce over cooked spaghetti, sprinkle with remaining cheese. Serve with lots of garlic bread. Serves 6.

Tuna Noodle Casserole

I had a mom that wasn't a good cook, so I would eat my grandma's food.
It was amazing because it brings back a time almost in Technicolor.

~ Debi Mazar

Aunt Ellen pulled the hissing, foaming casserole out of the oven. The air in the kitchen smelled suspiciously like fish.

I hated fish for a number of reasons.

But in San Diego, especially Ocean Beach, fish seemed to be everywhere. After all, one of my earliest memories was of fishing on a large boat with Daddy and Bobo, my grandfather. That day, a man caught a stingray and hacked it to death right in front of me, the scuffed wooden deck running red with the creature's blood, the air rent with my screams as my grandfather hugged me close, turning my face away from the horrible sight.

"What's that, Aunt Ellen?" I asked, scrunching up my fourteen-year-old face and sticking out my tongue, a silent "Yuck," which my aunt did not see.

"Tuna noodle casserole," she mumbled as the hot pad slipped in her hand. "TNC."

She grabbed the wobbling pan in the nick of time, keeping it from crashing to the floor. To my way of thinking, crashing would have been a good thing.

Although TNC reached its nadir in the 1950s, the first documented recipe seems to have been "Noodles and Tuna Fish en Casserole," published in 1930 in *Sunset Magazine*, contributed by "Mrs. W. F. S." from Kennewick, Washington. Campbell's introduced its banner Cream of Mushroom soup in 1934, blessing housewives with a quick and easy way to avoid making white sauce from scratch. None other than M.F.K. Fisher, my favorite food writer, sang that soup's praises in her version of tuna casserole in *How to Cook a Wolf*. She said it well: "… condensed mushroom soup, while far from perfection, is a very present help in time of culinary trouble." A lesson I confess I would also appreciate much later when, strapped for time and money, as I reached for a can of cream of chicken soup or cream of celery.

The standard TNC recipe called for cans of cream of mushroom soup, gloppy, sticky, and just plain terrible, served to countless numbers of children. Most of whom hated it.

I also loathed Tuna Noodle Casserole, a classic dish at *my* house, Mom's version thick with large squares of semi-cooked onion and soggy worm-like noodles. The noodles glistened, too, white like maggots. Mom always chopped onion too coarsely for my taste. By the time meals ended in my house, I usually had collected several tablespoons of semi-raw onion, all of it hidden under the rim of my plate. This quirk of mine became a family joke, because there were a few times when I wasn't fast enough to hide the evidence in a used napkin. Guilty as charged.

"Now go wash your hands, and then sit at the table," Aunt Ellen commanded in her firm and stern nurse's voice.

Knowing she meant business, I ran to the bathroom and thrust my hands under the faucet, rubbing my fingers over the smooth bar of Ivory soap. I dried them on one of the threadbare towels, all the while gazing around the small room, noticing its light lime-green wall tiles, so different from the stark white ones in my widowed grandmother's bathroom, whom I was visiting for a month that summer.

I sat at the table in the dining room, where Aunt Ellen kept dozens of family pictures. My eyes moved over the faces, then stopped on one. I cringed as I looked at the face of the cousin with thick, almost girlish lips. Instantly I remembered when I was five, and he was fifteen. It happened during one of my grandparents' visits to Pullman. They'd brought him along. He caught babysitting duty while the adults left the barracks-like apartment where we lived, to go who knew where. On that hot July day, he tried to molest me on my parents' bed, his hand down my underpants. I whimpered, "That's not nice!" when a car drove up. Mom had forgotten some small item. I never saw anybody move so fast in my life, before or since.

I'd prayed he wouldn't be visiting Aunt Ellen while I was there.

Aunt Ellen set the casserole down on the table. I perked up at the sight of it.

"Are those potato chips on top?"

Mom never bought potato chips.

"Yes, honey, they are," she said as she dug into the gooey percolating mass with a large metal spoon.

"Hold up your plate, that's a girl."

She dolloped a serving the size of a Frisbee onto my plate. I was sure I wouldn't be able to eat that much.

"Thank you," I said as I took a small bite of the casserole. And I knew then that I would empty the plate in the span of a few minutes. Maybe, just maybe, I would beg for another helping, I thought, as I gobbled down everything.

I did.

That memorable moment stuck with me, although I never cooked tuna-noodle casserole in my many kitchens as an adult. Ever. Tuna rose in price, one reason for my reluctance to repeat history. Another was that I gravitated to cooking food from so many other culinary cultures, with an almost infinite number of choices available every day. Why make something like tuna casserole when so many other options clamored for attention?

Years later, I visited Aunt Ellen toward the end of her life. I called and asked her if she could make that casserole again for me. Surprised, she said, "Honey, I don't remember that!"

However, when I walked through the door of her house, the aroma of that casserole greeted me first. As delicious as I remembered.

Sadly, it was the last supper I ever ate with her, as it turned out.

Memory soothes many hungers. But not all.

Aunt Ellen's Tuna Noodle Casserole, Modified

Kosher salt and freshly ground black pepper

¼ cup unsalted butter, plus more for the baking dish

8 ounces small Portabella mushrooms, sliced

1 medium onion, finely chopped

¼ cup all-purpose flour

2 cups whole milk

1 bay leaf

1 cup unsalted chicken broth

¼ teaspoon dried thyme leaves

8 ounces rotini, cooked

1 (5-ounce) can tuna, drained and flaked

2 tablespoons chopped fresh flat-leaf parsley

2 cups grated sharp white Cheddar

1½ cups crushed potato chips, original flavor

Preheat oven to 375° F. Grease a 2-quart casserole with butter. Set aside. In a frying pan, cook mushrooms until browned—do not turn until well-browned on the first side, and then turn for a second. Add onions and sauté until golden brown. Stir in flour. Cook until flour taste is gone. Pour in milk, bay leaf, and broth. Heat until thickened. Remove bay leaf. Sprinkle with salt and pepper to taste. Stir in thyme, cooked pasta, tuna, parsley, and 1 cup cheese. Scrape mixture into casserole and smooth top. Sprinkle with remaining cup of cheese. Top with crushed potato chips. Bake 20 minutes, until bubbling. Serve after casserole rests for several minutes. Serves 6.

Old-Fashioned Tuna Noodle Casserole (TNC)

2 cups cooked noodles

1 (5-ounce) can tuna

1 (10-ounce) can cream of mushroom soup, seasoned with one of the following: Worcestershire sauce, curry powder, dry sherry

Buttered corn flakes or cracker crumbs

Preheat oven to 450°F. Grease a casserole dish. Layer noodles, tuna, noodles, etc. End with noodles. Top with soup. Spread cornflakes or cracker crumbs over the top. Bake about 20 minutes or until topping browns. Serves 6.

Author (center, on floor) and Daddy's extended family

Barf on Maggots

Here, for instance, is what a woman in Mexico told me she always gave her children for a fever: twelve little crabs stewed in water.

~ M.F.K. Fisher

Children can be cruel.

In naming a dish by the unappetizing moniker of "barf on maggots," my siblings and I insulted not only Mom but also legions of mothers of many, if not most, poor people in America. At least in certain parts of the country. The South. The Midwest. The West.

Anywhere a mother—and it was usually a mother—needed to practice economy in the kitchen, as lady cookbook authors such as Lydia Maria Child of the nineteenth century put it. Child's *The Frugal American Housewife: Dedicated to Those Who Are Not Ashamed of Economy*, published in 1832, initiated a trend toward economy in American cooking, a backlash against the perceived pretentiousness of European cuisine, mostly French-influenced. A republican style of eating, democratic and equalitarian. A stomach filler and hunger killer.

Mom made this dish with ground beef and a can of cream of mushroom soup. She served it over plain white rice, not biscuits as Big Grandma did. Once I started cooking dinner most days after Mom returned to school, I dubbed it "Barf on Maggots," not exactly a ringing endorsement of her cooking.

Little did I know what I was eating.

But Paul Bunyan did.

Legend has it that a logging camp cookee—or cook's assistant—made it one day with coarse cornmeal, there being no flour at hand. The men grumbled and noted the mouthfeel resembled sawdust. Hence the name "Sawmill Gravy." It was a dish that graced many a plate during the Great Depression. Usually, cooks included sausage in their concoctions.

Once I left home for good, this simple dish never again appeared on my dining table. Or on any plate of mine. It wasn't that I disliked the taste, or even the texture, gummy as it could be if allowed to cook too long. When that happened, the gravy thickened and clumped, reminding the cook to add more milk to thin things out. No, the reason I left it behind was clear: as I've said, there were so many other dishes to cook in this life. The spirit of culinary discovery never possessed Mom.

But that spirit guided me to many things, not least of which was food.

Yes, it *was* cruel to name the dish with such an unappetizing name. Truth be told, it *did* look like barf.

Sawmill Gravy

1 pound mild sausage, or 1 pound lean ground beef, crumbled

½ cup coarsely chopped button mushrooms, optional

2 tablespoons vegetable oil

2½ tablespoons all-purpose flour

1 cup whole milk, plus 2 tablespoons

½ teaspoon freshly ground black pepper

Fine sea salt, to taste

Fry meat over medium-high heat in heavy cast-iron skillet until well browned. Remove meat, leave drippings. Add oil if needed. Stir flour into drippings until all lumps disappear. Add milk slowly, stirring constantly until smooth and thickened. Stir in meat and black pepper. Salt to taste. Serve over fresh hot biscuits. Or rice. Or potatoes. Or toasted bread.

Soup Beans

You don't need a silver fork to eat good food.
~ Paul Prudhomme

Before I even scraped the snow off my feet and opened the back door, the aroma drew me in, like a cartoon character smelling something good to eat, something to chase, floating on air.

Soup beans!

In the old South, especially Virginia, ham was a life-saving food. It stayed "good" over the often harsh winters. For me, the aroma of a pot of ham and pinto beans—usually called soup beans—chased away my dread of dinner.

A ritual surrounded the cooking of soup beans.

Daddy would bring his rusty hacksaw in from the garage, using a fiercer-looking blade than usual to saw through the bone jutting out from the tapered end of the ham. His mother taught him how to do that, drawing on her experience living and cooking on her family's ranch in Globe, Arizona.

We usually ate soup beans after Easter.

Placing the Easter ham on the sturdy pig-shaped cutting board, Daddy started sawing. The grinding noise softened as he reached the pinkish jelly-like marrow. Then it started again. Sometimes he just snapped the bone if there wasn't much left to saw through. He'd hand the smaller portion of the ham to Mom, who wrapped it in foil and stuck it in the small freezer at the top of the refrigerator. Sometimes Daddy used an ice pick to pry the frozen ham out of the freezer, frost-free freezers not being terribly affordable at the time. Westinghouse advertised one for $395.50 in 1951. Translated into 2021 dollars, the price was equivalent to $3,779.52. The average annual income in 1951 came to $2,799.16.

Easter came and went, but not so the snow and cold wind of an eastern Washington State spring.

Because I loved soup beans so much and the well-buttered cornbread steeped in thick, gooey honey that went with them, I never stopped cooking them. Instead of Mom's plain recipe—beans, ham, salt, black pepper—I began adding a few other ingredients to the pot.

Onion. Garlic. Dried thyme. Hot sauce.

Nothing fancy, a few flavor enhancers, that's all.

Soup beans came to symbolize much more than a decent supper when Daddy died. Every time I cooked soup beans after his death, I'd remember him holding that saw, its jagged teeth clogged with flesh and bone.

Hams sold in the average modern American grocery store taste nothing like the hams braising in the pots of my childhood. Puny ham hocks taste something like those of the past. But the brine-infused, plastic-wrapped hams jumbled together like children's wooden blocks in meat department bins do nothing to bring back childhood memories.

Taste memory is a powerful thing.

Losing it takes away a sense of continuity with the past.

Soup Beans from My Childhood

1 pound dried pinto beans

½ yellow onion, finely chopped

3 garlic cloves, peeled and minced

½ teaspoon dried thyme leaves

2 teaspoons Louisiana-style hot sauce

The end of a large smoked ham

Soak beans overnight or bring to a boil in pot of water, boil for 2 minutes, turn off burner, then leave on burner for an hour. Drain and return beans to pot. Add the remaining ingredients. Pour in water to cover by 1 inch. Bring to a boil, then lower heat to low. Simmer for 3-4 hours, or until beans are soupy and ham is falling apart. Serve with cornbread. And lots of butter and honey. Serves 6.

Tacos and Tabasco

The wind would blow, the sand would settle, and in some as-yet unforeseen manner time would bring about a change which could only be terrifying, since it would not be a continuation of the present.

~ Paul Bowles

Whenever I spy a bottle of Tabasco on a restaurant table or when I'm cruising the condiment aisle at my local grocery store, I remember when it started.

My love affair with the fiery hotness of chile peppers, that is.

Like a scar or a mark on the wall, the where and the how of something that happened in the past often sticks in the mind, setting details firmly into memory.

It was May 10, 1962. Seattle. The day I saw John Glenn.

More than that brief glimpse of space hero Colonel Glenn, more than his million-dollar smile as he walked down the stairs of some anonymous building, more than me and Daddy hanging over the railing, more than the gawking at the first American shot into the eternity of outer space, I remember the taco. But, even more than the taco, I remember the scorching fire of Tabasco on my lips, the kiss of promise.

There's an island in southern coastal Louisiana where Tabasco peppers grow. Since 1868, when Edmund McIlhenny harvested his first commercial crop of peppers, the McIlhenny family carried on the tradition. "Tabasco" meant "a place where the soil is humid" or "place of the coral or oyster shell." It may well be that the peppers used for Tabasco sauce originated in the state of Tabasco in Mexico, near the isthmus.

I didn't know this when I trudged behind my parents and siblings, searching for food at the fair, all of us very hungry. It was after two in the afternoon when we discovered the food court. Except for one little place nestled way in the back of a gymnasium-like space, everything seemed to be shut down.

Pedro's Tacos still dished up its wares, alone among the empty bleachers, providing its patrons with ample places to sit and eat.

Mom and Daddy grew up in San Diego, right across the border from Mexico. They always talked about tamales sold by Mexican ladies draped in rebozos, ornate shawls, squatting on small three-legged stools in front of large metal buckets filled with steaming hot tamales. But I never heard Mom and Daddy mention tacos. Maybe they did, and I just didn't hear them.

Daddy ordered ground beef tacos for all of us, two each, plus some potato chips. The man behind the counter said he didn't have any more drinks, as he'd sold them all.

"But there's a drinking fountain at the top of the bleachers, a bit of a climb from where we are," he said, as I started dousing my taco with Tabasco sauce. The bright red label caught my eye. Besides that, I thought the taco needed more flavor, fledgling cook as I was at the time.

Daddy nearly shouted at me when he saw what I was doing.

"No, no, you need to stop now. It's going to be too hot!"

I just laughed.

Then I took a bite. My eyes teared up. I huffed and gulped for breath, sure that steam would pour out of my throat. Or at least my ears, like Yosemite Sam in the Saturday cartoons I loved so much.

I dropped the taco on the bleacher seat next to me and turned, running as fast as I could up the rows of seats until I found the water fountain. The cold water put the fire out for mere seconds. Back I went to the taco. And back again to the water fountain, this time with the second taco in my hand, no Tabasco soaking it.

Daddy climbed up the bleachers. He sat next to me on the floor, where I'd parked myself by the water fountain.

"Next time, you'll listen to me, won't you!" He laughed. "Hot, wasn't it?"

"Yes, but you know, I kinda liked it," I retorted.

Back at home, I begged Mom to buy a bottle of Tabasco sauce. Since then, I've had a bottle of Tabasco in nearly every kitchen I've ever cooked in.

Memories of space hero Colonel John Glenn faded, but not the ones surrounding Tabasco and chiles. Not until years later did it dawn on me that a larger story hid behind that iconic bottle, a history of conquest, enslavement, greed, and culinary migration.

Your Own Tabasco Sauce

1 pound fresh tabasco chile peppers, stemmed and washed

2 cups high-quality distilled white vinegar

2 tablespoons fine sea salt

Put all ingredients into a stainless-steel pot, bring to a boil. Once mixture boils, reduce heat to simmer, cook another 5 minutes. Remove mixture from heat, cool completely at room temperature. Once cooled, purée mixture in a blender. Meanwhile, clean a wide-mouth, quart-size glass canning jar. Pour in puréed chile mixture. Seal tightly, refrigerate for two weeks. After two weeks have passed, strain sauce through a fine-mesh sieve over a stainless or glass bowl. Pour sauce into a glass jar or bottle, seal tightly once again, and refrigerate. Store sauce, refrigerated, for up to a year. Freezing not recommended. Makes approximately 2½ cups.

Vegetable Beef Soup

The smells were supernacular.
~ M.F.K. Fisher

Soup is a dish common in nearly all culinary cultures. But, as I've said many times, in my childhood home in Pullman, Campbell's took pride of place. The endless options included:

Tomato Soup

Chicken Noodle Soup

Chicken with Rice Soup

Bean with Bacon Soup

Manhattan Clam Chowder

New England-Style Clam Chowder

Vegetable Beef Soup

Cream of Celery

I seemed satisfied with this fare, until one day when I came home from first or second grade, I cannot remember which. Suffice it to say that saliva filled my mouth as I tore off my red rubber boots and tracked dirty snow all over the kitchen floor. Daddy stood at the stove, the aroma of fried beef hung in the air. Something fragrant bubbled in the big aluminum pot in front of him.

"What's that, Daddy?" I asked.

"Vegetable beef soup," he said as he dumped a cup of frozen corn into the pot.

Compared to Daddy's vegetable beef soup, Campbell's version could only be called an obscenity. The primary reason for this discrepancy—in this case, a rose could not be called a rose, nor could the soup from a can hold a candle to the real thing—was eugenol, a compound found in cloves. The secret ingredient in Daddy's soup, a large pinch of ground cloves, turned out to be a trick practiced by savvy cooks since the Middle Ages. He learned that tidbit of culinary genius from a family friend, Bill O'Neill.

All I knew at the time was this: When I realized that I'd be eating that soup for dinner, I almost walked on air up to my second-floor bedroom. Somehow the snow outside and the quarter-inch icy lace pattern on the inside of my bedroom window disappeared. Snuggled under four heavy blankets, and one of Big Grandma's tied quilts, I thought I'd discovered Paradise.

Or close to it.

When I took my first bite of the soup, if I'd known the word at the time, "nectarous" described it well.

Canned soups, though, meant Paradise to other people. John T. Dorrance, a chemist working for Campbell's, came up with the idea for condensed soups in 1897. Condensing soup meant it could be sold in smaller cans, for a lower price. A boon for many. Especially women who were tired of cooking from scratch every single day.

I still preferred Daddy's soup.

Daddy's Vegetable Beef Soup

¼ cup extra virgin olive oil

2 pounds beef chuck roast, cut into 1½-inch squares

½ medium yellow onion, finely chopped

½ bell pepper, green or red, finely chopped

3 garlic cloves, peeled, finely minced

2 (15-ounce) cans tomato sauce, unsalted

4 cups (1 quart) beef stock, unsalted

2 tablespoons Worcestershire sauce

1 cup rutabaga, peeled, cut into ½-inch dice

3 medium russet potatoes, peeled, and cut into 1-inch chunks

½ package frozen mixed vegetables or fresh equivalents (green beans, corn, lima beans, carrots)

¼ cup flat-leaf parsley, minced

1 tablespoon Louisiana-style hot sauce

1 teaspoon dried thyme leaves or 4–5 sprigs fresh

¼–½ teaspoon ground cloves, or to taste

½ cup pearl barley

1 teaspoon granulated sugar

Freshly ground black pepper, to taste

Fine sea salt, to taste

Brown meat in the oil in large Dutch oven over medium-high heat. Add onion and green/red pepper. Sauté until onion is translucent, then add garlic, cook another 30 seconds. Toss in all remaining ingredients, simmer on low heat until meat is fork tender. Soup is better the next day. Serve with bread, salad, and fruit. Serves 6 hearty eaters.

Author on the left, with sister Paula and Jeff

Eggnog Salad

I love Jell-O. I love the way it comes in rainbow colours,
wiggles and jiggles and looks like brains.
~ Megan McDonald

Mrs. Gibb held up the box of lime-flavored Jell-O like a priest holding up the host at Mass. She chirped, "Girls, today we're going to make Jell-O!"

I rolled my eyes at that and smirked, my head turned away so Mrs. Gibb didn't see me. Or I hoped she didn't. Her lazy eye wandered off to one side, so I could never be sure exactly where she was looking. Yet, given my own eye issues, I was hardly one to belittle a person with vision problems.

Like most of my friends in my high school Home Ec class, I'd been cooking family meals for several years by the time Mrs. Gibb announced her Jell-O lesson. I found the whole Jell-O-making exercise an insulting, annoying endeavor, to say the least. Jell-O held no great mystery for me, although the "melts in your mouth" jingle was true, even if that tune originally meant M&M candies.

In my house, when Jell-O appeared on the table, it arrived naked as a newborn baby, devoid of adornment. But at Big Grandma's Baptist church in San Diego, ladies brought complex Jell-O salads to church suppers, glorious with rainbow hues, all red, green, yellow, and orange. All loaded with chopped walnuts, canned fruit cocktail, chunks of crunchy celery, or dotted with tufts of whipped cream.

Jell-O first appeared on grocery shelves in 1897, thanks to the efforts of cough-syrup magnate Pearl Bixby Wait and his wife May, of LeRoy, New York. The inventors capitalized on the Victorian love of fancy jelly molds, concocted from an arduous process based on collagen from boiled-down animal bones and connective tissue. Because of the complexity of this process, until Jell-O appeared on grocery shelves, only royalty and other wealthy people could enjoy aspics and jelly molds with any frequency.

The Christmas that Daddy made his first eggnog salad, I swooned over both the texture—creamy—and the flavor—eggnoggy. I watched as he sprinkled plain gelatin powder over cold water, puzzled as to why it was colorless and sugarless, unlike Jell-O. It never occurred to me that gelatin could be anything other than the gleaming red, green, or yellow sugary crystals pouring out of the familiar little wax-paper pouches in their squarish cardboard boxes.

If Mrs. Gibb had spoken a bit more about the history behind Jell-O, I might not have rolled my eyes that day. If she'd invited us to choose a decorative mold like our Victorian grandmothers used, maybe I wouldn't have been so dismissive.

Why did Daddy's eggnog salad delight me so much? Elegance and mysterious and delicious, all that indeed. Very romantic and alluring.

Maybe there was a little Victorian in me after all.

But in my innocence and ignorance, I never realized what it took for some people to enjoy such things as aspics made from scratch by a legion of cooks, aspics served on highly polished silver platters by dozens of liveried servants.

No wonder Jell-O found its way into the average American kitchen.

Daddy's Eggnog Holiday Salad with Peach Halves

3 envelopes unflavored gelatin

¾ cup cold water

4 cups (1 quart) eggnog, divided

¼ cup granulated sugar

¼ teaspoon freshly grated nutmeg

1 cup heavy whipping cream, whipped

1 (29-ounce) can peach halves, drained

½ cup heavy whipping cream, whipped

Mint leaves, for garnish

Sprinkle gelatin over the cold water in a saucepan. Leave for 1 minute, then stir in 1 cup eggnog, sugar, and nutmeg. Over medium-low heat, warm until gelatin and sugar dissolve. Stir from time to time. Pour in remaining eggnog, stir gently. Place saucepan in the refrigerator until mixture thickens, more or less an hour. Whip the 1 cup of cream, fold into cooled eggnog mixture. Spray a ring mold with cooking oil spray, pour in eggnog mixture, chill until firm, or at least four hours. Unmold onto a decorative serving dish with enough room around the edges to place the peach halves, pitted side up, evenly spaced around the eggnog mold. Place or pipe dollops of the ½ cup of whipped cream inside each peach half. Garnish platter with mint leaves. Serves 8–10.

Broccoli and Milk

Never eat broccoli when there are cameras around.
~ Michael Stipe

Along with liver, broccoli hiked early on to the top of my list of most-hated foods. Mom studied at the culinary school of "boil-it-until-it's-mush." Meat. Fruit. Vegetables. Nothing escaped her pot of boiling water.

Especially not broccoli.

The smell of broccoli stewing away on Mom's stove sent me scurrying to my second-floor bedroom, putting a towel under the door to keep the stink out, braving the winter cold in that near icebox of a place.

Because my parents grew up during the Great Depression, their food philosophy followed the "eat it or wear it" version. Or, in other words, "you eat everything on your plate, you hear?" Or else. No one wanted to know what "or else" entailed. Turning my nose up at broccoli and refusing to eat it simply would never happen. Not at that table, not in that house.

What to do?

I devised a sneaky plan for eating this horror. Everyone drank milk at dinner at the time, skim milk because of Mom's fear of getting fat. Two spears of olive-green broccoli, not just the flowery parts, but the woody stems, too. Unpeeled. That's what faced me. Limp as wilted tulips, the spears lay on the plate, unadorned. Not even a wedge of fresh lemon at hand. No hollandaise sauce in sight.

I cut each spear in half.

Moving my glass of milk close to the left side of my plate, I'd grasp the glass in my left hand and grip a spear half with a fork in my right. I tossed the broccoli to the back of my mouth and chugged enough milk to force the broccoli down my throat. Amazingly, I never choked. I avoided chewing the broccoli and eliminated the taste and smell of it, all at the same time.

The thing about broccoli, though, is that it's good for human bodies.

Like, really, really good. Nutritionists love broccoli, which evolved from wild mustard. As the British like to say, it ticks all the boxes: rich in fiber, swimming in vitamins, and a powerhouse of minerals. The Romans grew it, and a variation is still popular in Italian cuisine, Calabrese broccoli.

No matter. As a child, I still wouldn't have crossed the road to eat it even if I'd been starving. If I'd had a choice.

On a more positive note, swallowing boiled-to-death broccoli taught me an important lesson about tolerance, not of the food itself, but also how to eat food that I deemed unappetizing, to please other people, a trait very important for my future.

Ironically, my little brother Tim craved broccoli. And anything cruciferous, including Brussels sprouts, which Mom never touched. Tim could cook quite well, and one of his favorite go-to recipes was a casserole based on that 1950s classic, ubiquitous Campbell's Cream of Mushroom soup.

Ironically, despite the presence of two ingredients I detested—broccoli and cream of mushroom soup—I never spit bites of this dish into a clean napkin or used the old milk trick.

Tim's Broccoli Casserole

1 (10.75-ounce) can condensed cream of mushroom soup

1 cup Duke's mayonnaise

1 large egg, beaten

¼ cup yellow onions, finely chopped

3 (10-ounce) packages frozen chopped broccoli

8 ounces shredded sharp Cheddar cheese

Fine sea salt and freshly ground black pepper, to taste

¼ teaspoon paprika

2 cups breadcrumbs, sautéed in 4 tablespoons unsalted butter

Preheat oven to 350°F. Grease a 9x13 inch baking dish. Beat soup, mayonnaise, egg, and onions in a medium-size mixing bowl. Place frozen broccoli into a large mixing bowl and break it up into smaller pieces. Add soup-mayonnaise mixture, mix well. Stir in cheese until evenly incorporated. Season with salt, pepper, and paprika–take care not to add to much salt as the soup is quite salty in and of itself. Spread mixture into prepared baking dish. Smooth top of casserole. Sprinkle with breadcrumbs. Bake for 45 minutes to 1 hour. Serves 6–8.

The family (author in striped shorts)

First Cake

Cooking is one failure after another, and that's how you finally learn.
~ Julia Child

As the old saying goes, "It takes the cake."

None of us likes to recall our culinary disasters, and each of us—no matter how good a cook we may be—must claim at least one major culinary disaster to our credit.

Julia Child had her broken omelet.

Grant Achatz had his charred lobster thermidor ramekins.

Cat Cora had her burned chicken.

With me, it was a cake.

Every time I make a cake, I am reminded of my first "from-scratch" cake, in the days when "cake" meant cake mixes like Jiffy or Duncan Hines, big sellers for very good reasons. The summer I turned ten years old, I decided one scorching day to bake a white cake with a gooey chocolate frosting as a surprise for Daddy. He often reminisced about the "from-scratch" cakes Big Grandma made. Mom never made a cake from scratch. I also had no experience doing such a thing.

Carefully, I read the recipe in one of Mom's few cookbooks, *The Modern Encyclopedia of Cooking*, by Meta Givens. My first cookbook, the "Red Plaid" *Better Homes & Gardens Junior Cook Book*, only called for boxed cake mixes in its recipes. But I loved Big Grandma's cooking and her gentle ways. That's why I opted to go for it and bake a cake, like one of hers. I told Daddy what I was going to do before he left for work that morning.

Nostalgia, indeed.

Baking powder, sour milk, flour, salt. I measured and sifted it all dutifully into a bowl. Tablespoons, teaspoons, cups, all new to me. Butter whipped with sugar, eggs beaten in one by one, milk scalded briefly in a small saucepan. Oven preheated to 375°F. Even neophyte cooks like me could easily follow the well-written directions.

I poured the batter into the greased, floured, and papered cake pans, for the first time ever. Excited, ready to eat the fruits of my labor as soon as they emerged from the oven, I set the timer. And sat at the kitchen table, like a proud mother waiting for her child to wake from his nap.

After about ten minutes, the smell of something baking wafted from the oven.

I always have had a sharp sense of smell. So even in my culinary inexperience, I knew something wasn't right with my cake. The air in the kitchen smelled funny, like one of my baby sister Paula's sour diapers or something equally distasteful. Nauseating, as a matter of fact.

My heart started beating faster. I knew I must have done something wrong. But what was it?

Mom walked into the kitchen, sniffing, and noticed the same odor. After another ten minutes, she opened the oven to look at the cake. It wasn't rising at all. The sour smell became even more pronounced as the minutes ticked by. Anxiety rose even higher in me as I realized that I'd made a mistake. A big one.

"What on earth did you put in that cake?" Mom asked.

We consulted the cookbook and went through the list of ingredients. I showed her how much of each I'd put into the batter. When we got to the baking powder, the light bulb in my brain turned on because it said, right there in black and white, "3 teaspoons baking powder." And a bunch of stuff with perplexing scientific names, like "3¼ tsp. tartrate or phosphate type."

I put three *tablespoons* of baking soda into the cake! No wonder it smelled like somebody's armpit, or worse, and wasn't rising!

Mom explained what I did wrong, smirking a little but realizing, I suspect, that we all make mistakes, especially when we do something for the first time.

Just then Daddy came home for lunch.

"What is that awful smell?" he yelped, tossing his raincoat on the boot box.

"It's Cindy's cake," Mom told him, laughing. Jeff and Tim stood behind her, giggling.

The atmosphere in the kitchen suddenly reminded me of how the air felt moments before a thunderstorm, thick, heavy, and crackling with unseen and foreboding energy.

I moved back, leaning against the edge of the kitchen countertop. Daddy grabbed one of the two cake pans and waved it under my nose.

"What is this? What?"

His face reddened, and I smelled the odor of the cigarette he'd tossed aside before he walked through the squeaky backdoor, the hinges needing a hefty dose of grease or something. He slammed a pan down on the counter and, with his hands, yanked out the still-hot pancake–thick "cake." Then, with his other hand gripping me by the neck, began shoving wads of "cake" into my mouth, forcing me to swallow it. Crying and swallowing don't usually work well at the same time. Neither does screaming. After a minute, he stopped, tossing the "cake" on the floor.

"Clean it up, you stupid idiot."

I never, ever repeated that mistake. And made double sure that I read recipes thoroughly before starting any baking or cooking.

Maybe Daddy made a mistake at work. Maybe he'd had a bad day.

Maybe.

That was only time he ever laid a cruel hand on me.

White Cake with Chocolate Frosting

Makes one two-or-three-layer cake

    3 cups cake flour

    1 tablespoon baking powder

    1 teaspoon fine sea salt

    1/3 cup soft unsalted butter

    1/3 cup shortening

    1¾ cups granulated sugar

    ½ teaspoon almond extract

    2 teaspoons vanilla extract

    4 egg whites, unbeaten

    1 1/3 cups whole milk

Grease two 9-inch layer pans for thick layers or three 9-inch pans for medium layers. Line bottoms with waxed paper and grease paper, then flour pans. Preheat oven to 375°F 10 minutes before baking. Sift flour, measure, resift 3 times with baking powder and salt. Cream butter and shortening with mixer until smooth and shiny, add sugar gradually, creaming thoroughly. Stir in flavorings. Add egg whites in 2 portions, beat vigorously with mixer after each addition until fluffy. Add flour and milk alternately in 3 or 4 portions, beginning and ending with flour, beating gently until smooth after each addition. Turn into prepared pans. Bake two layers for 23 minutes or three layers for about 20 minutes, or until cake tests done with a skewer inserted into the center that comes out dry.

Chocolate Frosting

2/3 cup unsalted butter

2 teaspoons pure vanilla extract

Pinch fine sea salt

¾ cup unsweetened cocoa

2¾ cups confectioner's sugar

1/3–½ cup whole milk

Cream butter in a mixing bowl with electric mixer until fluffy. Add vanilla and salt. Mix confectioner's sugar with cocoa in a small bowl. Stir cocoa/sugar mixture into butter. Add milk until frosting is easily spreadable. Frost cake as desired. Makes 2 cups or so.

Sweet and Sour Pork

The way you cut your meat reflects the way you live.
~ Confucius

Until I turned fifteen, the only Chinese food I'd ever eaten came from the kitchen of one of Daddy's graduate students, John Woo. John served luscious sweet and sour pork, as well as crisp, plump egg rolls at the plant pathology department's Christmas parties, held in the wood-paneled basement of his rental house. He joked with me that he would fix chocolate-covered ants someday, just for me. I suspected he loved to hear the other kids and me squeal in disgust at the mere idea of eating ants. I also suspected that he played Santa Claus at those parties.

One Christmas, discouraged at seeing all the other kids with their "books" of Life Savers of every color and flavor and staring at the set of jacks in my hand, I asked Santa why he couldn't bring me Life Savers instead the following year.

"Well, you need to talk with your parents," Santa replied, hinting that perhaps Santa didn't have all that much say in what he carried around in his pack. When I asked Mom about it, she shrugged. "You don't need all that candy. You'll get fat. And besides, it's not good for your teeth. We can't afford to go to the dentist if you get cavities."

When John left for a job somewhere else, Chinese food also disappeared. John's food was the most exotic food I'd tasted in my short time on the planet, aside from my few brushes with Italian-style pasta and fire-hot tacos.

I drew the line at chocolate-covered ants, but sweet and sour pork became a weekly dish after I discovered the Time-Life Foods of the World cookbook series. Although Paula hated it, I began cooking sweet and sour pork often for my family after Mom started in graduate school. Those books—twenty-seven of them—opened up a whole new world of cooking for me. Unfortunately, I could not afford them at the time, although now they sell for mere peanuts on the internet. But from the books I checked out from my local public library, I copied many recipes into spiral notebooks.

Including a recipe for Sweet and Sour Pork from *The Cooking of China*, by Emily Hahn.

Over the years, I tinkered with that recipe as I learned more about Chinese cuisine. Or at least Chinese cuisine in America. Canned pineapple, all I could buy in those days, added a most exotic touch to the dish. John Woo's version focused on the sauce, reddish in color, brightened with chopped green bell pepper and sliced carrots, seasoned with ketchup and Worcestershire sauce, both with origins in ancient Chinese cuisine.

Based on a popular sweet-sour Cantonese dish, the Americanized version of Sweet and Sour Pork was created by people far from their home in China. Building the transcontinental railroad, living in canvas tents, shoveling hundreds of pounds of rock every day, suffering either extreme heat or extreme cold, they hewed out a cuisine much different from what they were used to. As Peter Liebhold stated in an interview for *The Guardian*, "All workers on the railroad were 'other'."

My Sweet and Sour Pork, in Memory of John Woo*

2 pounds boneless pork, from pork butt, cut into 1-inch cubes

½ cup cornstarch

1 teaspoon fine sea salt

Peanut oil for deep frying, preferably peanut oil that tastes like peanuts

2 tablespoons peanut oil, from deep frying

½ medium yellow onion, cut into 1-inch squares

1 large green bell pepper, seeded, cut into 1-inch squares

2 medium carrots, peeled, cut into ¼-inch slices

Fresh ginger, peeled, cut into ¼-inch slices

2 teaspoons peeled, chopped garlic

1 cup chicken stock, unsalted, preferably homemade

5 tablespoons brown sugar

5 tablespoons red wine vinegar

2 teaspoons low-salt soy sauce

2 tablespoons cornstarch, dissolved in ¼ cup cold water

Red pepper flakes, to taste (optional)

Fresh pineapple, peeled and cut into 1-inch cubes (use canned if fresh is not available, but there will be a slight metallic taste to the fruit)

1/3 cup chopped salted cashews for garnish

Preheat oven to 170°F. Mix pork with cornstarch and salt in a large bowl. Coat meat evenly. Heat about 4 cups of oil in a large heavy pot. When oil sizzles the end of a wooden spoon, put in as many pork cubes as possible without crowding, cook until golden brown. Drain browned meat on paper-towel lined baking sheet, keep warm in oven. Repeat until all pork is cooked. **For Sauce:** use 1–2 tablespoons of oil used to fry pork. Add onion, green pepper, carrots, and ginger. Sauté until green pepper is wrinkled and onion almost translucent. Add garlic, cook for 30 seconds. Pour in chicken stock, along with brown sugar, vinegar, and soy sauce. Boil until sugar dissolves, then stir in cornstarch/water mixture. Stir to incorporate, continue stirring gently as sauce thickens. Add pepper flakes if using. Add pork cubes, mix to coat meat with sauce. Serve immediately over white rice, topped with chopped cashews. Serves 6.

*Adapted and embellished from *The Cooking of China*, by Emily Hahn. (Time-Life, 1968)

Plant Pathology Department Christmas with Santa (author on left in white blouse)

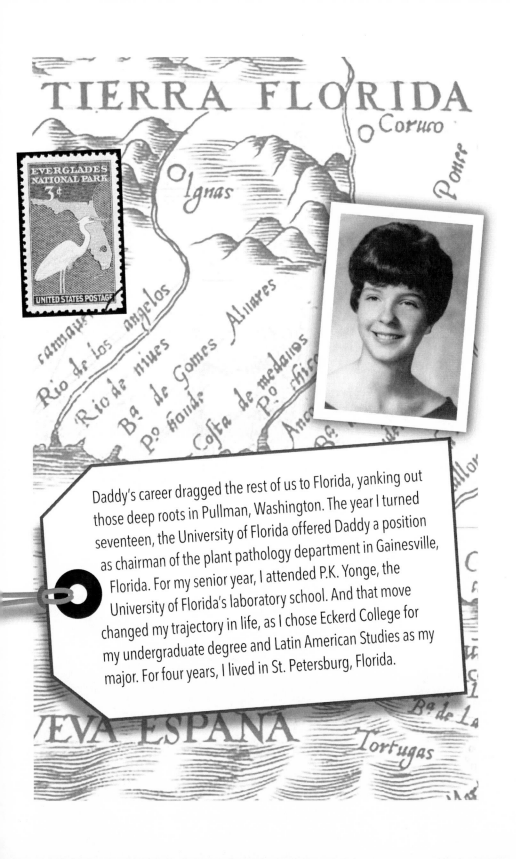

TIERRA FLORIDA

Daddy's career dragged the rest of us to Florida, yanking out those deep roots in Pullman, Washington. The year I turned seventeen, the University of Florida offered Daddy a position as chairman of the plant pathology department in Gainesville, Florida. For my senior year, I attended P.K. Yonge, the University of Florida's laboratory school. And that move changed my trajectory in life, as I chose Eckerd College for my undergraduate degree and Latin American Studies as my major. For four years, I lived in St. Petersburg, Florida.

Stone crabs

Stone Crabs

You're from Florida. There's got to be more holes to hell
in Florida than in any other state.

~ T. Kingfisher

The news landed hard, like John Wayne's massive fist punching my gut.

"I got the job in Florida," Daddy said as we all sat at the kitchen table at the end of June.

All I could think of was that I would be a senior in a brand-new high school. I jumped up from the table and ran upstairs to my bedroom, trying not to sob too loudly.

All summer long, we packed.

One day, I came home from the town swimming pool and found my Beatles collection—paperbacks, magazines, photographs, and dolls—stuffed into the rusted old oil can in the alley, the one used to burn trash, flames spitting cinders into the air. Daddy burned most of the collection. Crying, I salvaged what I could from the last cardboard box lying in the scorched dirt next to the can. A couple of magazines and four small dolls, replicas of the Fab Four.

The move devastated me. I pretended to be undaunted by it all. But I'd lived in Washington State for fourteen years, for most of my conscious life. I'd never had to make new friends. My best friend and I met in kindergarten.

The day of departure arrived.

As Daddy drove away in the unreliable blue Ford station wagon he and Mom bought for the trip, my childhood faded away fast, lost in the rearview mirror. True to form, the car broke down in Denver, Colorado. Mechanics took three days to fix it, something to do with the radiator. My parents somehow managed to scrape up enough money for the delay, but with much grumbling and flaring of tempers.

Meanwhile, we holed up in one room in a cheap Mom-and-Pop motel around the corner from the garage. Across the street, a movie theater featured a series of James Bond films starring Sean Connery. We sat through all of them.

Goldfinger, From Russia with Love, Thunderball, You Only Live Twice. The scenes of Europe captivated me in a way that words on the pages of books never did.

Florida, on the other hand, was another story. Another world. Almost another time in history.

For Florida was the South. As in Deep South. At least north Florida was. Something I knew little about. From the beginning, my new hometown of Gainesville proved to be a challenge. On many levels, not the least of which was going to a recently desegregated school. "White" and "Colored" signs still marked a deep divide.

It was a completely different world from the one I'd ever known.

Solace came in the form of food, of course. Especially seafood. A special kind of seafood.

Stone crabs.

I first ate stone crab claws in Cedar Key, Florida, a small fishing town on the Gulf of Mexico. One of the three or four oceanside restaurants served skate-board-sized platters of these succulent claws, selling for thirty cents a pound wholesale a few years earlier. The only packaging on these claws was the stony shell, which shattered all over the place as I wrestled with the critters and gouged out the sweet flesh in the leg portion of the claw.

Sitting at a plastic-covered table overlooking the gentle waves of the Gulf, watching brown pelicans flying low over the rippling tides, I cracked claws with nutcrackers and dipped the meat in melted butter. Scraping the tender white melliferous flesh off the claw with my front teeth, not unlike eating tender arti-choke leaves, I noticed the sun setting to the west as seagulls screeched, diving in swarms to snatch food tossed at them by the restaurant's cooks. Heavy-bel-lied, big-billed pelicans scooped up fish innards and heads discarded out the backdoor of the restaurant, their loose jaw pouches swinging like an old cat's fat stomach as she lurches after a snake in the woods.

Melted butter became the one dipping sauce I ever wanted for those crabs, but cooks often paired other sauces with these unique crustaceans, whose habi-tat ranges all the way from the North Atlantic coast to Belize. And not just the Gulf of Mexico.

Change comes hard sometimes. A strange town. A new school. Class-mates who'd been together for a decade or more.

A recipe for "Otherness."

Mustard Dipping Sauce

½ cup mayonnaise, preferably Duke's

2 teaspoons dry mustard

1 teaspoon Worcestershire sauce

Lemon juice

Fine sea salt, to taste

Mix all ingredients until well-blended. Serve chilled with chilled stone crab claws. Makes approximately ½ cup.

Honey Mustard Sauce

½ cup honey

½ cup Dijon-style mustard

½ cup cider vinegar

¼ cup Worcestershire sauce

2 teaspoons Tabasco sauce

1 teaspoon fine sea salt

1 tablespoon chopped parsley

Mix all ingredients except for parsley. Bring to a boil, cook for 3 minutes. Cool. Stir in parsley, refrigerate sauce. Serve with chilled stone crab claws. Makes approximately 1½ cups.

Spoon Bread

*Many of America's historical cornbreads were staple breads
for people who didn't have many other options.*

~ Jeremy Jackson

Mrs. Barnett set the casserole down on the trivet in the center of the table. I caught a whiff of the steam pouring out of the jiggling, jelly-like center.

"Please hold up your plates, girls," she asked. None of us needed another invitation. Julia and Ann, the twins, Catherine, the reserved older sister, and I obeyed instantly.

The fluffy, white mixture on my plate resembled a picture of a soufflé I'd once seen in a magazine, maybe *Better Homes & Gardens*. Taking my fork, but waiting for Mrs. Barnett to take the first bite, I sniffed at the fried chicken and the bright green peas rolling around on my plate. A quick glance assured me that it was safe to start eating, the hostess having raised her fork.

My first bite seared itself into my memory. Soft, silky smooth, creamy, the flavor so new to me I couldn't help but burst out with a question.

"What is this? It's wonderful!" I exclaimed.

Mrs. Barnett smiled.

"It's spoon bread, an old and popular Southern dish," she told me.

Never mind that the Barnetts came to the University of Florida from Wisconsin, where if people thought about spoon bread at all, they probably figured it was for babies or toddlers. Dr. Barnett taught statistics.

I was sitting at the Barnetts' table because, for some reason, Mrs. Barnett took me under her wing, the new kid at a school where everybody had known each other since kindergarten. She sensed my loneliness. I met her twin daughters Julia and Ann, a year younger than me, in my French class. Her other daughter Catherine was a freshman at Eckerd College in St. Petersburg. Catherine had dated the boy on whom I had a crush. Her face bore deep scars of ravaging teenage acne, marring her natural beauty.

Committed Unitarian Universalists, the Barnetts became my family-away-from-my family. Dinner hours were calm, filled with discussions about politics and social justice action. I tagged along with them to St. Petersburg, to help register Black voters during one of the most turbulent elections in American history. We slept on the wooden floor of an old Quaker meeting house and ate sandwiches packed by determined women like Mrs. Barnett. A lot of singing went on, too, with guitars twanging "Kumbaya" and "Blowin' in the Wind," late into the long, dark nights.

I lay in my sleeping bag, the creaky ceiling fan above whooshing hot air, thinking of the Freedom Riders of a few years before. I felt a certain sense of kinship with them, thankful they'd paved the way, making it possible for those nights under that fan in St. Petersburg.

By taking me into their community, the Barnetts raised my awareness of the larger world on so many levels.

Soft-Center Spoon Bread

2 tablespoons unsalted butter

2 cups water

1¼ teaspoons fine sea salt

½ teaspoon freshly ground black pepper

1 cup fine white cornmeal

1 cup whole milk

4 large eggs, separated

¼ cup freshly grated Parmesan cheese (optional)

¼ cup grated Swiss cheese (optional)

Preheat oven to 350°F. Drop 2 tablespoons of butter in a 2-quart soufflé dish, or other similar pan, and melt in oven while mixing batter. Heat water, salt, and pepper to a boil in saucepan over medium-high heat. When water starts boiling, add cornmeal slowly, whisking constantly. Lower heat to medium-low, cook 1–2 minutes, continuing to whisk or stir with a wooden spoon, until cornmeal forms a mass and almost comes together into a ball. Keep stirring for a few seconds to dry the mass a bit. Remove pot from heat. Stir in remaining butter and the milk. Add cheeses if using. Beat in egg yolks. Using a mixer, whip egg whites in a clean bowl until stiff but not dry. Stir ¼ of the egg whites into batter to lighten mixture, then fold remaining egg whites into batter. Pour batter into hot buttered dish. Bake on center rack for 50-55 minutes, or until puffed and lightly browned. Spoonbread is done when center is still soft, but crusty along the edges. Serve immediately. Like a soufflé, spoonbread will deflate quickly. That said, it is good left over, too. Serves 6.

Cedar Key, Florida

Catfish

"It's Florida," Annalie said. She hefted her purse up and down as if she were working out with weights. "Even Mickey Mouse probably carries a piece."

~ Brian Freeman

Welaka sat on the banks of the St. John's River, in that spot a wide, tea-hued stream, with cypress knees poking from the shallows. Omnipresent Spanish moss hung low on the pines and other trees, curtaining intense light in the summer and filtering weak light in the winter. The town itself consisted mostly of fish camps—weather-beaten cabins painted white with dark green trim, rusted wall air-conditioners tilting like picture frames askew after a wild party.

Florida is a flat, swamp-thick place, where nothing natural rises much higher than a palm tree or a centuries-old live oak festooned with Spanish moss. Nevertheless, Native Americans found much sustenance in the estuaries and springs dotting the landscape: alligator, water birds, and many species of fish.

Including catfish.

Every stereotype of backwoods north Florida loomed in front of me as I walked up the wobbly wooden steps to the door of Sunset Landing, a fish shack cozied up to the banks of the river. An old hound lying on the splintered porch. Outside, tables hugging the edges of the dock, their wooden tops covered with plastic, red-checked tablecloths. A young man spitting tobacco on the porch. Pickup trucks idling in the parking lot, rifles resting on gun racks. Mosquitoes dive bombing bare legs and the sound of hands slapping.

But inside, I sniffed the aroma of authentic food cooking.

Catfish, cornbread, hushpuppies, shrimp in plastic baskets, catfish fingerlings, and deep-fried dill pickles. Waitresses crisscrossed the minute dining room with round cork-lined trays loaded down with amber bottles of Budweiser beer.

Mom darted as fast as she could through the crowded restaurant to grab the only remaining empty table, the one closest to windows overlooking the river. With my back to the window, I couldn't see the sputtering motorboats or the cormorants swooping low to seize fish with their sharp beaks and snakelike necks.

Daddy took his beer and gulped half of it at one go, as usual. The rest of us sipped Cokes or ice water. Then our waitress plopped a large platter heaped with fried catfish in front of Daddy, a smaller one of shrimp in front of me. Hushpuppies rolled off my platter like large marbles as I grabbed at the food, my hunger larger than I realized.

I sat there, watching my family eating, "stuffing their faces," as the saying goes. They ate catfish, and I ate shrimp. They laughed and talked and poked each other in the ribs from time to time. They ignored me. I might as well have been outside with the mosquitoes and the hound.

Welaka Fried Catfish

4-6 catfish fillets, or fingerlings, about 1-2 pounds

1 cup whole buttermilk

Fine sea salt, to taste

¾ cup fine white cornmeal

½ cup all-purpose flour

1 teaspoon garlic, mashed into a paste

1 teaspoon freshly ground black pepper, or to taste

½-1 tablespoon Cajun seasoning, or to taste

Peanut oil for frying

Soak catfish in buttermilk for about 15 minutes. Meanwhile, mix dry ingredients on rimmed baking sheet with mashed garlic. Preheat oven to 200°F, place another baking sheet topped with a baking rack in the oven. Begin heating peanut oil in a large deep cast-iron skillet. When oil begins bubbling, dredge fillets in dry-ingredient mixture. Drop a few fillets in hot oil and cook until golden brown on one side, flip, and cook other side. Place cooked fillets on rack in oven. Repeat. Serve with coleslaw, French fries, and tartar sauce. Or hushpuppies, if preferred. Serves 4.

Bulgogi (Korean Barbecued Beef)

August in Florida is God's way of reminding us who's in charge.
~ Blaize Clement

An August afternoon in Florida reminded me of a winter storm in Pullman, driven by an Arctic blast. Only in reverse.

Walking out the back door of the house, barefoot, dressed in the shortest shorts I could muster, I gasped at the thick, suffocating, oppressive humidity. At the foot of the stairs, Daddy had primed the big black charcoal grill. The lighter-fluid-soaked charcoal briquettes caught fire, sending smoke signals to the squirrels and the birds perched in the long-leaf pines. Rain would soon be coming, as it did almost every summer afternoon, cooling the air and ground.

Sweat beads dotted Daddy's forehead, the balding patches on the top of his head turning as pink as the meat marinating in the glass baking dish sitting on the grill's metal shelf. Finally, he speared the meat with a BBQ fork and plopped it onto the glowing rack. It was then that my nose caught a hint of an unusual aroma.

Garlic. Soy sauce. Ginger. Asian flavors.

"What's that, Daddy?" I asked as I raced down the steps.

"*Bulgogi*," he replied, shoving the meat to the hottest part of the fire.

"OK, so what's that?" I asked again.

"Korean barbecue," he grinned.

"Where did you learn about that?"

"I saw a recipe in a magazine."

He cursed as the flames licked at his thumb. He didn't tell me that *bulgogi* originated during Korea's Goguryeo era, which held sway from 37 B.C. to 668 A.D. It likely began as *maekjeok,* a kebob-like skewered meat dish. *Maekjeok* evolved into *neobiani,* a dish preferred by Korean royalty, defined by marinated beef, sliced thin and grilled.

After charring the meat about five minutes per side, Daddy speared it again and set it on a platter.

"Take this upstairs, will you please? Thanks." He closed the top of the grill and handed me a platter nearly overflowing with reddish juices. As I carefully carried the meat up the back steps to the kitchen. I was glad the platter was a bit indented, like a shallow bowl. Otherwise, the drippings would have spilled all over me.

When Daddy came upstairs, he took a sharp knife and cut the meat into thin strips, on the diagonal. Mom made garlic bread the usual way, a grocery store loaf of cottony French bread. She dipped the bread into the bloody-looking juices on the platter while the rest of us piled the meat on top of plain white rice.

Garlic had come a long way in America by then. And in my house, at my table, too.

Bulgogi

2 pounds beef top sirloin (or London Broil), scored on both sides

6 garlic cloves, finely minced

2 green onions (or scallions), thinly sliced

4 tablespoons low-salt soy sauce

3 tablespoons white sugar

1 tablespoon toasted sesame oil

1 tablespoon rice wine

1 tablespoon sesame seeds

1 teaspoon minced fresh ginger

1 teaspoon freshly ground black pepper, or to taste

More sliced scallions for garnish

Place all ingredients in a large resealable plastic bag. Lay bag in a pan, refrigerate. Marinate for at least 2-3 hours or longer. Flip bag from time to time. Before cooking, prepare a hot fire on the grill. Remove meat from bag. Discard remaining marinade. Grill for 3-6 minutes per side, depending upon thickness of meat. Place cooked meat on a cutting board, slice on the diagonal. Sprinkle with extra sliced scallions. Serve with white rice, pineapple, and a spicy cucumber salad such as *Oi Muchim*. Or maybe kimchi. Serves 4-6.

Sukiyaki

Sukiyaki is all about the sauce, a mixture of soy sauce, mirin, sake, and sugar.
~ Matthew Amster-Burton

Never mind that the rules stated explicitly that there was to be "No cooking in dorm rooms." When I opened the windows, to mask the aroma of the food, the smell of the Gulf of Mexico mingled with the odor of scallions and soy sauce, mirin, and crushed ginger root.

I'd never eaten a bite of Japanese food before I met Meiko and Ryoji, exchange students spending a year at my university.

Meiko's dorm room became an improvised kitchen. She set the electric skillet on the linoleum floor and plugged it into an extension cord. Then, gesturing to Ryoji like a surgeon preparing to operate, she held out her hand for a wicked-looking cleaver. I fingered my neck as she laid the sharp cleaver on the wooden cutting board she'd balanced across the arms of a wooden desk chair.

With rapid motions, Meiko transformed the thick ribeye steak into paper-thin slices. She explained that it was one of the *nabemono*-style, or Japanese hot pot, dishes often served in winter.

"The idea for *sukiyaki* came from the Meiji, and there are two kinds of *sukiyaki*," Meiko intoned as she sliced green onions on the diagonal and separated them into neat piles, green versus white. "*Kanto* and *Kansai*, the two styles, that is." She planned to cook the *sukiyaki* in the Kanto style, meaning everything would cook in the sauce, or *warishita*. As for Kansai style, the thinly sliced beef cooks first, then the sauce added, vegetables last.

While Meiko busied herself with the *sukiyaki*, Ryoji fired up the rice cooker and prepared the rice. The rest of us—four Americans—stood around watching, eager to try this new dish, cooked by two homesick people missing their families and their country. Ryoji brought out several ornate silk cushions and arranged them on the floor around the skillet. We knelt on these as he handed us blue-and-white porcelain bowls and pairs of ivory-handled chopsticks.

A scoop of rice first. Then came the struggle to fish out pieces of meat,

Napa cabbage, and mung-bean noodles from the pot using chopsticks. Silence broken by tiny, murmured cries of appreciation filled the air. The look on my friends' faces as they savored the taste of their homeland. That look and that longing would become familiar to me.

The face of exile.

Sukiyaki

2 tablespoons sake

¼ cup mirin

1 tablespoon brown sugar

¼ cup soy sauce

1 tablespoon vegetable oil

2 cups dashi stock

12 ounces thinly sliced fatty beef

½ block firm tofu, sliced into ½-inch thick slices

5 dried shiitake mushrooms, rehydrated, sliced into ½-inch segments

1 package enoki mushrooms, ends trimmed and rinsed

2 cups Napa cabbage, cut into 2-inch pieces

2 cups arugula or leafy endive, crushed

2 scallions, sliced on the diagonal, white and green parts separated

1 bundle dried mung bean vermicelli noodles, or shirataki noodles, soaked in cold water and drained

2 cups steamed white rice

Mix sake, mirin, brown sugar, soy sauce, oil, and dashi together. Set aside. Prepare vegetables. Heat skillet or wide pot. Pour in sauce. Arrange meat and vegetables in skillet, cook until meat is no longer pink. Do this step batch by batch. Allow everyone to take what they want. Serve with white rice in deep serving bowls. Enjoy the camaraderie of cooking together. Serves 3-4.

Mutton and Mint Jelly

*A writer need not devour a whole sheep in order to know
what mutton tastes like, but he must at least eat a chop.*

~ William Somerset Maugham

In the early years of the twentieth century, mutton appeared on American tables. A lot.

Hard as it is to believe, mutton cost more than lamb. First-class passengers on the Titanic dined on mutton, while second-class passengers made do with spring lamb. Then came World War II. Service members ate a lot of mutton, usually canned, making SPAM look like a delicacy fit for royalty in comparison. Forced to eat mutton in place of scarce beef and pork during the war, Americans tuned up their noses after the war ended.

Mom never cooked mutton or lamb. Her mother, Teeny Grandma, often prepared lamb chops. But I wouldn't know, since I only went to her house once to eat. She did not serve sheep in any form that day.

Memories of my first bite of mutton still haunt me.

At 4 p.m. on the day I discovered mutton, my stomach growled. Loudly. The campus dining hall didn't open until 5 p.m. Dizzy with hunger, I popped a precious quarter into a Coke machine, drank the sugary liquid as fast as I could, and gobbled the rest of a Snickers bar leftover from my bag of Halloween candy. It was a good thing I did. Later that night I discovered an enormous cockroach hiding in my roommate's trash can in our dorm room. Not for the first time, either.

At 4:50 p.m., I couldn't stand it any longer. I headed for the dining hall. Sand burrs clung to the leather straps on my sandals as I crossed the wide-open, barren space separating my dorm from the center of campus. In late April, the Florida sun radiated heat as well as light. It bore down fiercely on my head. Beads of sweat tickled my nose and drenched my forehead.

Around the dining hall, a few tattered palm trees and some strange vegetation, maybe a coontie cyad or two, struggled for life on what used to be a landfill jutting into Boca Ciega Bay.

I climbed the metal steps to the door of the dining hall and stood waiting with a few other hungry stragglers. The doors finally opened. We all
shuffled inside. I picked up a brown plastic tray and tossed some silverware on
it, plus a couple of white paper napkins. A worker punched my meal ticket.
The clatter from the kitchen clanged louder as I edged my way to the front of
the serving line.

There it was, my dinner.

Slabs of thinly sliced, rather gray meat, a big container of something
green and Jell-O-like nestling near it.

I motioned to the work-study student behind the counter that I wanted
the meat, so he tonged two slices of meat. With a nod of his head, he asked me
if I wanted the green stuff, and I nodded "Yes." Then further down the line,
another work-study student piled on mashed potatoes, green peas, and a piece
of Wonder bread painted with butter-flavored margarine.

I looked around for my friends, most of whom ate at 6 p.m. Not seeing
anyone I knew, I sat at a table by myself and started in on the meat. Taking my
fork, I cut a few bite-size pieces, then speared one, dipping it first in the green
Jell-O and shoving it into my mouth with the speed of a starving dog wolfing
down a can of Alpo.

Just as fast I spit it out.

The gamey taste of the mutton, the lanolin-rich fat sticking to the roof
of my mouth, and the odious combination with what turned out to be mint
jelly, well, it made me want to drop everything and run to the restroom on the
other side of the dining hall. Instead, I grabbed the plate and stalked over to the
serving line.

"What is this?" I asked, trying not to be too angry.

"Mutton," the boy replied, serving another person as he spoke.

"Well, why wasn't it labeled? I can't eat this stuff. I want some chicken
instead."

"No, you can't have anything else," he retorted.

The campus meal plan didn't allow for seconds. Or substitutions.
Apparently.

Dejected, I went back to my seat and ate the mashed potatoes, peas, and
bread.

I slept hungry that night. As do many people around the world.

Mint Jelly

1½ cups fresh mint leaves, rinsed and packed

3¼ cups water

2–3 drops green food coloring

½ teaspoon freshly squeezed lemon juice

1 box pectin (1¾ ounces), like Sure-Jell

4 cups granulated sugar

Boil mint leaves in the water in a medium saucepan. Drain, but save 3 cups of this mint-flavored water. Return mint water to pan. Add food coloring and lemon juice, then stir in pectin to dissolve. When mixture boils, add sugar, stirring constantly. When stirring doesn't stop the boiling, cook for another minute. Remove from heat, pour into four sterilized jelly jars. Store in refrigerator. Makes 4 half pints.

Marina at Cedar Key

The Fish Shack

While living in Florida I realized that I could never stay there, because it's so damn hot. There's only like three months when you don't feel like you're on the cusp of hell.

~ Jennifer L. Armentrout

One summer I worked as a line cook in a fish shack in Cedar Key.

Brown pelicans swooped down into the gentle surf behind the fish shack, intent on being the first to scarf up the day's shrimp peelings. I swung the three-gallon red bucket of fishy offal with my right hand, soaking my bare tanned legs as the bucket clipped the edge of the weathered porch. In midair, three pelicans caught the flying guts of mullet and the crunchy peels of over twenty pounds of raw shrimp, heads included. I sank into the faded pink lawn chair bolted to the restaurant wall, painted a sea-foam green best suited to a hospital room.

More pelicans circled above me, vulture-like in their yearning for blood and guts. The surf surged against the pilings below the splintered wooden porch where I sat. The sweltering midsummer sunshine squeezed sweat from my every pore, my Marlins ball cap catching it a bit before the saltiness trickled into my eyes. The porch swayed a bit in the gusting wind. I eyed a half dozen thunderheads banked on the horizon, looking for all the world like sails of English ships of the line come to battle the Spanish.

Lost in my reverie, dreaming of a coolness not possible in a Florida seafood shack, I didn't hear her opening the squeaky screen door behind me.

"Hey, you, you need to get back in here. We got a sixer sitting down right now." Lee held the door open with her foot and took a drag off her cigarette, its bright red tip flickering. Her fuchsia flip-flops caught on the door frame as she backed into the restaurant, flicking the cigarette over the side of the porch. Then, in a maneuver any fighter pilot would envy, a pelican plummeted toward it, but whirled up fast when it sensed the hot putrid odor of tobacco, not the stink of fish guts.

Under my breath, I whispered, "Yeah, bitch." Only ten minutes to go until closing. "Damn," I grabbed the bucket and slammed it against the wall.

"Sorry, fellas, no more," I said as I rinsed out the bits and pieces of fish and shrimp. When I yanked the door open, its squealing hinges brought still more pelicans gliding in the air near the porch. Pavlovian, I thought.

I glanced at the order tickets clipped to the wire above the window dividing the kitchen from the dining room, flapping like laundry hung on a clothesline. Three shrimp, one broiled flounder, and two scallop. Double fries all around.

"You take the shrimp, I'll do the rest," Lee barked at me, her gravelly voice whipping over me, her blond ponytail swinging with every movement of her skinny ass.

I dredged the shrimp in the Old Bay-seasoned flour/cornmeal breading, let them rest a moment on the prep tray, and then carefully lowered them into the fry basket. They puffed up a bit with the breading and turned golden in the time it took me to count to fifteen. I felt Lee's breath on my cheek as I pulled the wire basket from the effervescent grease.

"Hurry up. Get that plate under the heat lamp." She grabbed the other fry basket, filled it with French fries, and plunged it into the sputtering oil. Drops of boiling oil splattered across my left arm.

"Ouch," I yelled, "You burned me."

She smirked, turning to plate the flounder and the scallops.

I pulled out the rest of the shrimp, while she fussed over the fries. Candy, the waitress, drummed her fingers on the counter.

"That sixer, they're gettin' cranky, ladies," she whispered.

I stared over her shoulder at the six corpulent men lounging at the one full table. Why didn't Candy tell them we weren't serving? That's the rule: fifteen minutes before closing, no service. Sorry.

Lee didn't say anything, tossed the decorative kale on the plates, and shoved them across to Candy, who balanced three steaming plates per arm and made her way across the dining room.

A man's drunken voice carried across the dining room into the kitchen, slurring. "Hey, you, girly, I want some more of that there tartar sauce, ya hear?"

Candy rolled her eyes as she marched into the kitchen and opened the walk-in refrigerator. "I'm gonna piss in their next beer!" she hissed.

Twenty minutes passed. We cleaned up the kitchen, watching the clock.

"If they don't leave in five minutes, I'm gonna go out there and give them the check and stand there till they pay. Then I'm gonna go to the door and hold it open for 'em." Lee muttered.

Lee waited those five minutes. They paid. And stood up.

But Mr. Tartar Sauce grabbed Lee and kissed her right on her big red lip-sticked mouth. She smacked him in the left eye with her fist. He howled, swung wildly, his fist hitting something soft. Lee went down, her fingers clutching the greasy beige carpet.

Candy screamed. I called the cops.

Lee spent the night in jail. For assault. Mr. Tartar Sauce, it seemed, was a Big Man in Pasco County.

That's the thing about the restaurant business. The customer is always right.

I guess.

Cedar Key Fried Shrimp

2 pounds shelled and deveined shrimp, butterflied, rinsed, and kept wet

½ cup all-purpose flour

½ cup fine ground white cornmeal

2 teaspoons Cajun seasoning or Old Bay

Oil for frying

Tartar sauce and cocktail sauce for serving

Heat oil to 375°F. Mix flour and cornmeal with seasoning. Dredge shrimp in dry ingredients, making sure to coat all sides. Fry until golden brown. Serve with tartar sauce and cocktail sauce. Serves 4.

Black Beans and Rice

I'll serve something black. Bean soup, licorice, coffee.
~ Stephanie Kallos

I'd just turned twenty-one.

To celebrate, several friends treated me to a fancy celebratory dinner at the Columbia Restaurant in Ybor City, Florida. Jean drove us there in *her* twenty-first birthday gift—a brand new Mercedes the color of ripe plums, from her wealthy parents who later died in a murder-suicide. Her father shot her mother and then killed himself.

Jean pulled up to the restaurant entrance and handed her keys to the valet, speaking to him in Southern-accented Spanish. I started up a short flight of terracotta-tiled steps into the building.

It was as if I'd walked into the house of a Spanish grandee in post-Islamic Spain. Lush green gardens surrounded a central courtyard, fountains spurting crystalline blue water, azulejo tiles covering desert-sand-yellow plastered walls. I had a feeling, only in reverse, the one I get when I leave a dark theater after a particularly riveting film, where I've melted into the screen and become one with that fantasy world.

A waiter, spiffy in a crisp black tuxedo, approached us with four menus, handing one, with the prices on it, to my friend Bret. We women made do with a simple listing of the offerings.

Picadillo.

The waiter hovering at my elbow, I ordered the *picadillo*, hurrying, trying to seem grown-up when I was anything but. The dish came pungent with chopped olives and capers, red oil tinging the rice on my plate, henna-like. Because I was old enough to order a drink, Bret and Jean insisted that I did so. A lime daiquiri. I thought. After that, everything blurred.

The alcohol drew me into a dreamy haze. I lost the sharpness of the moment. Memory flees and hides when it's least desirable, especially when I struggled to recapture the moment. I vaguely remembered black beans, white rice, and a chopped lettuce salad with pineapple.

Black beans. A marvel to me. I wanted to cook those beans at home in my kitchen. After combining several recipes gleaned from different sources, I declared my attempts a success.

And so did my family.

From then on, black beans and rice appeared regularly on our table. Daddy took to them so much so that he asked me for my recipe, which called for vinegar to be added at the end of cooking.

After that magical night, with the barest of taste memories to guide me, I recreated a dish using one of the few natural foods humans eat that are black.

Bean soup, licorice, coffee.

Frijoles Negros (Black Beans)

2 cups dried black beans, soaked and drained

6 cups water

1 medium ripe tomato, cut into wedges

½ medium yellow onion, cut into wedges

½ green bell pepper, cut into thick slices

1 bay leaf

1 garlic clove, peeled

½ cup extra virgin olive oil

½ medium yellow onion, finely chopped

½ green bell pepper, finely chopped

4 garlic cloves, peeled and minced

1 teaspoon oregano

2 teaspoons ground cumin

1 tablespoon fine sea salt

½ teaspoon freshly ground black pepper

2 tablespoons red wine vinegar

2 tablespoons Louisiana hot sauce, or other similar hot sauce

White rice, cooked

Chopped fresh cilantro and yellow onions for garnish

Put beans in a heavy pot, cover with water by 1½ inches. Add tomato, onion, green pepper, bay leaf, and garlic. Bring to a boil, lower heat, cook until beans are tender, about an hour or so. Meanwhile, make *sofrito* in a heavy skillet: sauté onion and green pepper in olive oil until onion is translucent. Stir in minced garlic cloves, cook for 30 seconds longer. Add oregano, cumin, salt, black pepper, vinegar, and hot sauce. Let mixture bubble for about 30 seconds, then scrape *sofrito* into beans. Simmer beans for another hour to meld flavors. Serve with white rice, garnished with chopped onion and cilantro. Serves 4-6.

College graduation, author with Mom and Daddy

Chapel Dinners, Crossing Borders

As we live a life of ease
Every one of us has all we need
Sky of blue and sea of green
In our yellow submarine
~ The Beatles

"Hey, man, what are you guys cooking? Smells good." Naked from the waist up, the barefoot, long-haired kid poked his head into the chapel kitchen.

"Hey yourself, you can't come in here. No shoes, no shirt, no service." Lori snapped at him as she mixed lamb *kefta* with her hands. Bret unloaded more of the brown paper grocery bags. Tomatoes, zucchini, and a two-pound bag of white rice spilled across the counter. I've never liked the taste of lamb or mutton, even after several years in Morocco. So, although Lori originally made these with ground lamb, not an easy commodity to find even in today's grocery stores, beef tastes better to me. Lori shared a lot of other recipes, but this was the only one we ever cooked together. After one trip back to the Middle East, she brought me an elaborate faux-silver ankle bracelet and a blue silk shawl from the bazaar in Damascus. I treasured both for many years until they disappeared during one of my many moves.

At that moment, Reverend Carlson walked up to the shirtless kid.

"You can't be in here without a shirt and shoes. Read the sign!"

Flashing the peace sign, à la Winston Churchill and Woodstock, the kid bounded off, humming "Yellow Submarine."

I handed Reverend Carlson our permit to use the kitchen.

Drawer by drawer, he checked the condition of the kitchen, which he and his wife had donated in honor of his dead father. Turning to leave, he said, "I expect this place to be even cleaner than it is now when you're done!"

Bret, standing behind the Reverend, rolled his eyes at me. I smiled and said, "Sure, Reverend Carlson. We'll do that. This is our fourth time using the kitchen."

"OK, then I'll see you tomorrow, with the key," he said and walked out into the bright sunshine of St. Petersburg, Florida.

Every month some of my friends and I cooked in the kitchen in Eckerd College's chapel, dishing up menus such as the lamb *kefta* from Syria on that night's menu. Lori's experience as the daughter of an ARAMCO oil executive guided us that night, as we sat on her ornate rugs, pretending to be in Damascus. Or if the chapel kitchen wasn't available, we went in for a pseudo-Japanese scene, sitting around an electric frying pan filled with ingredients for sukiyaki, with the help of Meiko and Ryoji. Usually, twelve of us ate together. Each person chipped in $2.00 to cover food costs.

On the mornings of the dinners, always a Saturday, Bret drove me to the grocery store in his 1956 black Lincoln Premiere, nicknamed "Mariah." We carried our haul back to the chapel's tiny kitchen. Around 1 p.m., people started piling in, grabbing a knife or a pot, pitching in to help with the cooking. Since we all lived on campus and ate in the common dining hall, our communal dinners became the highlight of the month. Even lamb, not my favorite meat on the planet, sounded good after weeks of institutional gray beef with library paste gravy.

This cooking started when a bunch of students from Dr. Frank Figueroa's Spanish class decided to make rice and beans and were looking for a place to cook. When I asked Dr. Brundage, my mentor, for help, he said, "Try the chapel kitchen. Carlson's a bit fussy about it, but I'll let him know you'll take care of it right."

Dr. Brundage, best described as a well-meaning but crusty blueblood from New England, taught history, primarily Latin American history, emphasizing Mesoamerica, which meant mostly the Aztecs. But he also studied the Inca, eventually writing several books about both cultural groups.

Ever since I found *National Geographic* magazine about the cannibalistic Aztecs stuck between the saggy sofa cushions at my childhood friend Sarah's house, I wanted to know more about them. Call me a looky-loo, and that'd be right. I hate blood and gore, but pictures of the Aztecs summoned me like Sirens beckoning Odysseus. I couldn't *not* look.

For my initial January winter term at Eckerd, I signed up for my first course with Brundage. In it, he introduced me to the Olmecs, a mysterious group of ancient, indigenous people who left little evidence of themselves in the archaeological record other than their enormous carved stone heads with grimacing jaguar-like smiles. These gigantic heads sprawled like a bunch of broken bowling balls in the jungles near Veracruz, Mexico, left there when the Olmecs suddenly disappeared forever.

The Olmecs weren't the Aztecs, but a close substitute. At the end of that January, I turned in a paper detailing the multitude of scholarly theories about Olmec culture. A week later, Brundage told me that he'd submitted it for the annual history prize. I didn't win. "Too many footnotes" the judges wrote in red across the front. No matter. Flattery will get you everywhere, and when Brundage asked me if I'd be interested in being his student, it felt like a marriage proposal. I said "yes."

An uneasy relationship ensued over the next four years. Brundage was seeking a substitute for his brilliant artist daughter, who lit out one hot Florida summer afternoon when the air turns languid, and thunderheads gather like Beefeaters changing the guard in front of Buckingham Palace. And I was searching for a way to know the world and be at ease in it.

But first, I needed to learn Spanish if I were to major in Latin American Studies.

From the day that I walked into Dr. Frank Figueroa's beginning Spanish class to a cheery *"Buenos días, como estás?"* I was hooked on the Spanish language. Despite my hearing issues, I progressed quite well overall, chiefly because the sounds fit into the range I could hear.

Dr. Figueroa, born in Puerto Rico, came at life with a sensitivity in his Latino soul that was sometimes hard to watch. He grew up on New York's lower West Side and wanted to leave behind all the stereotypes generated by "West Side Story." If he thought a student mimicked his English in jest, he swore in a cacophony of street Spanish and kicked the student out of the room.

But Dr. Frank could teach Spanish. Yes. Both in the classroom and out. I met several Cubans and other Spanish-speaking students through the raucous after-class parties that he loved and threw on every whim possible.

"Que plato cocinaremos este fin de semana, chica?" Raúl would ask and the plotting started. What would we cook for our next dinner?

My second year at Eckerd College, Austin College in Sherman, Texas, offered a Winter Term experience focusing on the history of Mexico. I wanted to go, badly. But, of course, the issue of money reared its ugly head. I begged Mom for permission to go, to pay for it all. After selling my soul by promising to iron, clean, and cook on my school breaks for the next year, I walked into

Eckerd's admissions office and signed up.

I was on my way to Mexico City.

The journey began.

Lori's Syrian Kefta (Kibbe) (made with beef)

2 pounds lean ground beef

1½ cups bulgur wheat (cracked wheat), soaked in hot water for 15 minutes, excess water squeezed out

1 large yellow onion, finely chopped

Fine sea salt and freshly ground black pepper, to taste

¼ cup pine nuts, crushed and chopped

2 teaspoons ground cinnamon

2 teaspoons dried mint

Olive oil for baking sheet

Sauce for Kefta:

Plain whole-milk yogurt mixed with 2 garlic cloves peeled and minced, diced cucumber, salt, chopped fresh mint

Preheat oven to 375° F. Mix all ingredients except the sauce. Using about 1/3 cup of meat, form into elongated, thick cigar-shaped lozenges. Place on greased baking sheet. Bake 25–30 minutes, or until meat is lightly browned. Serve with yogurt sauce, pita bread, and various Middle Eastern-style salads. Serves 4.

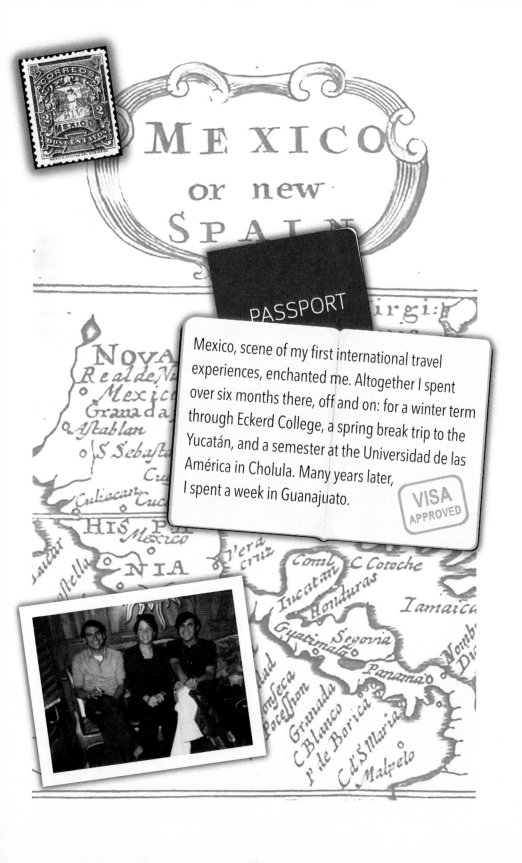

MEXICO or new SPAIN

Mexico, scene of my first international travel experiences, enchanted me. Altogether I spent over six months there, off and on: for a winter term through Eckerd College, a spring break trip to the Yucatán, and a semester at the Universidad de las América in Cholula. Many years later, I spent a week in Guanajuato.

VISA APPROVED

Skull, Day of the Dead

Tacos de Pollo

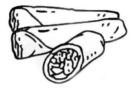

Then we invariably have frijoles (brown beans stewed), hot tortillas—and this being in the country, pulque is the universal beverage.

~ Fanny Calderón de la Barca

The traffic hurtled by at 7,382 feet above sea level. And I stood on a corner of Insurgentes Sur in Mexico City, tapping my fingers against my purse, cursing the long stoplight.

I watched dozens of men hanging onto ladders suspended from the backs of swaying buses. The air filled with sooty diesel smoke spewing from exhaust pipes. Tinkling mariachi music faded away amidst the incessant roar of engines and horns. After several minutes, the light finally changed. I darted across the street, my friend Sherry a few steps behind me.

"Whew," she panted, "can you believe this? I can hardly breathe."

We, two nineteen-year-olds, headed straight for the little restaurant we'd noticed earlier when the van brought our study group to the Hotel Colonia that afternoon.

In all its chaos, Mexico City bewitched me, for it embodied the themes of Octavio Paz's *The Labyrinth of Solitude*.

Tiny green and red Christmas lights twinkled under the eaves, and dozens of laughing people sat at tables covered with white tablecloths, eating off large oval platters filled with meat, tortillas, beans, rice, and vegetables. Antonio Aguilar's voice crooned over the loudspeaker. A waiter dressed in black pants and a long-sleeved white shirt motioned for us to sit at one of the tables.

"*Gracias,*" we murmured as he bowed and handed us two laminated menus, sticky with old grease. "Thanks."

I opted for chicken *flautas* after sneaking a look at another diner's plate overflowing with fried corn tortillas stuffed with shredded chicken, drenched in thick cream, garnished with flowery radishes and lime wedges. *Flautas* meant "chicken tacos," just a fancy way of saying it.

That dish seared something forever in my mind, thanks to the crunchiness of the *flautas*, paired with the creaminess of the guacamole and the *crema*, seasoned with a squirt of fresh lime, fired with the hot bite of green salsa. Whenever I encounter any of these tastes or textures, when I smell tortillas frying or hear Antonio Aguilar's voice, memories of that night leap into my consciousness. They transport me—figuratively anyway—back to that moment, to the darkness of the velvet-black sky and cacophony of that vibrant city, the clatter of plates, and the Babel-like chatter of fellow diners.

Oh yes, those daiquiris packed a terrific wallop at 7,382 feet above sea level.

We staggered across Insurgentes Sur, dodging busses, taxis, motorcycles. And I fell, fully clothed, into my bed at the hotel, nearly asleep as I plumped up the pillow. For a moment, I lay there, watching the gauzy white curtains fluttering in the cool breeze of the night, thinking for some reason of my grandmother's house in San Diego. I wasn't homesick for home, but I was for her.

Strange. But not surprising.

Flautas

2 dozen corn tortillas

Vegetable oil, for frying

Toothpicks

2 pounds boneless, skinless chicken breasts or thighs, cooked and shredded

Shredded lettuce

Diced tomatoes

Sliced avocado

Radish slices

Red onion slices

Crema or sour cream

Mexican farmer cheese, crumbled

Refried beans

Preheat oven to 200°F. Heat oil in heavy skillet until oil ripples across bottom of skillet, almost smoking. Dip each tortilla into hot oil, cook for about 10 seconds on each side. Remove oil from heat. Transfer each tortilla to a paper-towel-lined baking sheet. When all tortillas have been softened, take two tortillas, overlap them so that one covers about half of another. Repeat. Lay cooked chicken in center of the tortillas, the long way. Then roll up each pair of tortillas the long way, like a jelly roll, fasten shut with a few toothpicks. Add enough oil to skillet to depth of about ½ inch. Heat oil over medium-high heat. Place each *flauta* into oil, frying until bottoms of tortillas crisp up. Carefully remove toothpicks, flip *flautas* over to crisp other side. Keep warm in oven on baking sheet with rack inside baking sheet. Repeat until all *flautas* are cooked. Serve three *flautas* on each of four serving plates, garnished with lettuce, tomatoes, avocado, radishes, and red onion. Drizzle some *crema* over them, top with crumbled cheese. Serve sided with refried beans. Serves 4.

Going to the Yucatán (author third from left, front row)

Coconut Ice Cream

Forget art. Put your trust in ice cream.

~ Charles Baxter

In 1526, Spanish conquistador Francisco de Montejo began his campaign of conquest of the Yucatec Maya. It was not easy, nothing like Hernán Cortés's conquest of the Aztecs in 1519. Not until 1697 did the Spanish subdue the peninsula, thanks to Mayan resistance in the Petén Basin, part of modern-day Guatemala.

Reading about the Yucatán while sitting in an air-conditioned college library on Florida's Gulf Coast was one thing. But quite another to trudge through tall grass and clamber up steps of the Uxmal and Labna pyramids in blistering April heat.

After hours of bumping over pot-holed roads, red dust creeping its way into my nostrils with every turn of the bus's wheels, I looked forward to a double dip of coconut ice cream.

But not any coconut ice cream.

Once the unairconditioned bus disgorged us—wilted like freshly picked passion flowers—I headed to the grandfatherly man with the cart that bore a resemblance to a kid's lemonade stand. He parked every day at the corner a few houses down from the missionaries' compound. I'd discovered him while walking alone, escaping the constant chatter of other students from my university on spring break with me in Mérida. Our chaperone, Dr. Figueroa, kept a hawk-like watch over us, but we devised ways to slip out from under his gaze.

The day before we were to board a Pan Am flight back to Tampa, one of the guys in our group came down with strep throat. This turn of events was serious stuff for the missionaries, a husband-and-wife team who'd been working in the area for twenty-five years. No one knew where he'd picked up the germs. Perhaps it happened when we stayed a few nights at the missionaries' beach camp, in Progreso, north of Mérida on highway 261. The small, thatched huts where we slept on hammocks, packed together like anchovies in a tin can. That might well have been the source.

But the source didn't really matter.

The missionary's wife barked at us to line up in the courtyard. She set up a small table with a huge green bottle of purple-brown iodine and a pile of gauze squares. Gripping each of us by the neck, she ordered us to open our mouths. She then swabbed our throats vigorously with a square of iodine-doused gauze held in place by surgical forceps. Dr. Figueroa, never one to pass up a comic moment, took advantage of it to film us as we were being dosed. But, of course, he refused to be filmed when *he* got the treatment, too. The sick guy crept off to his hammock in the isolation room, the rest of us cursing him.

I darted to the girls' dormitory and grabbed my purse. There was only one place I wanted to be then, to soothe my throat, other than back safe and sound in my room at the university.

The ice cream man.

"*Buenas tardes, Señorita*," he said. "*¿Helado de coco*, no?" I replied in my poor Spanish, the equivalent of "Yes, coconut ice cream." With a delayed "*Por favor.*" Please.

He plunged his hand into the freezer compartment of the cart, white mist pouring out like a genie released from a bottle. Pristine white ice cream appeared then, studded with flecks of raw coconut, unsullied by dark miniscule vanilla seeds or chunks of fruit like the other flavors in the freezer.

One lick and my whole body chilled immediately, like walking face-first into a blizzard, snow falling at a slant.

He looked at me, his smile revealing a few gaps where teeth should have been.

"*¿Hasta mañana, no?*"

Tomorrow. I nodded and turned around on the narrow sidewalk.

But I left the next day.

I missed him. I missed the market ladies clad in their white smocks edged with embroidery in every color of a painter's palette. I missed the starveling dogs sniffing hesitantly at my skirt hem as I passed. I missed the white stucco walls and the cool courtyard of the missionaries' house.

And I missed that coconut ice cream most of all.

Coconut Ice Cream

6 egg yolks

¾ cup granulated sugar

1 cup sweetened shredded coconut, packed

½ cup whole milk

1½ cups heavy cream

1 cup light coconut milk, canned

1 (14-ounce) can coconut cream

In a large bowl, whisk together egg yolks and sugar until light and fluffy. Set aside. Add coconut to medium heavy saucepan, set over medium-high heat. Stir until coconut appears toasted, about 7 minutes. Do not allow it to burn. Add milk, heavy cream, coconut milk, and coconut cream. Bring to a simmer. Scald mixture without it coming to a boil. Before that point, remove from heat. Slowly pour hot coconut milk mixture into yolk mixture, starting with a small amount at first, whisking constantly. Then add more, still whisking, until all eggs are combined. Return mixture to pan. Over medium-low heat, stir slowly until custard thickens, about 5 minutes. Do not allow to boil. Pour custard into a clean bowl, place over an ice bath to cool, stirring occasionally. Refrigerate custard until cold, at least 1 hour. Transfer custard to an ice cream maker, freeze according to the manufacturer's instructions. Makes 1 quart.

Author at Cholula pyramid

Patio restaurant

Mole Poblano

*A traveller on foot in this country seems to be considered as a sort of wild man
or out-of-the way being, who is stared at, pitied, suspected,
and shunned by everybody that meets him.*

~ Karl Philipp Moritz

The city of Puebla sprawls across a high plateau, surrounded by volcanic mountains scrunched together in a neo-volcanic axis, as geologists call it. Tongue-twisting names lure travelers, like Sirens, not so different from those tempting Odysseus:

Popocatépetl.

Iztaccihuatl.

Citlaltépetl.

Matlalcueyetl.

I woke in the morning in my minuscule apartment in Puebla to the sight of those legendary peaks. Their snow-capped summits greeted me daily as I boarded a diesel-fumes-spewing, gear-grinding bus to the campus of the Universidad de las Américas in nearby Cholula.

But Puebla was known for something more than the frosty white tips of Popocatepetl and Iztaccihuatl.

One of Spain's planned colonial cities, Puebla boasted a long history of superb cooking, thanks in part to Spanish nuns who established convents in the city. Known for their sweet confections, these nuns also drew inspiration from Arab culture. After all, Arabs ruled Spain for nearly 800 years. Nuns also turned to cookbooks, such as *Los Cuarto Libros del Arte de la Confitería* (The Four Books on the Art of Confectionary) by Miguel de Baeza (1592), and Francisco Martínez Montiño's 1611 *Arte de Cocina, Pastelería, Vizcochería y Conservería* (Art of Cooking, Pastry, Savory Pastry and Preserves).

According to legend, nuns at El Convento Santa Rosa dreamed up *Mole Poblano* for a visiting archbishop. However, the dish shows signs of Persian origins, with some New World ingredients—such as chocolate—included in the mix.

Before I ate *Mole Poblano* for the first time in a rundown hole-in-the-wall eatery near the *zócalo*—or the main square—I knew nothing of this story.

My friends Pablo and Celina insisted that I try the legendary *Mole Poblano*. I gave in, though I preferred *Flautas de Pollo*. When the waiter ceremoniously set my plate on the table in front of me, I sighed. The dark brown-red sauce reminded me of the color of something unmentionable in polite company. But I said nothing. Toasted sesame seeds sprinkled over the top of the dish helped, as did the sight of sliced turkey nestled under the blanket of sauce. I cut a small bite and put it in my mouth.

Love at first bite.

A dish perfect for someone far from home, a stranger in a strange land.

Quick Mole Poblano

4 Roma tomatoes

1 yellow onion, cut into thick slices

2 garlic cloves, peeled and mashed

5 tortilla chips

4 cups unsalted cups chicken stock

1 (8.25-ounce) jar Doña Maria Mole

½ tablet Ibarra Mexican chocolate

¼ teaspoon ground cinnamon

Fine sea salt, to taste

¼ teaspoon ground anise seed

2 pounds poached chicken breasts, sliced in half the long way

1 tablespoon toasted sesame seeds to garnish

Cook tomatoes, onion, and garlic in water until onion is tender. Drain, transfer to a blender along with tortilla chips. Set aside. Add 2 cups chicken stock to saucepan, stir in jar of mole sauce, mix in until dissolved. Stir in tomato mixture, chocolate, cinnamon, salt, and anise. Pour in more chicken stock to reach the consistency of gravy.

Return chicken pieces to sauce to warm through, then place a piece of chicken on each serving plate. Top with a few spoonfuls of sauce, sprinkle with toasted sesame seeds. Serves 4.

Top: Iglesia de Nuestra Senora de los Remedios, backed by Popocatépetl volcano
Bottom: Cathedral of Puebla

The Chinese Dinner Flop

I have no house only a shadow.
But whenever you are in need of a shadow, my shadow is yours.

~ Malcolm Lowry

The hands on the clock inched toward 9 p.m.

And that's when I knew they weren't coming.

How I came to that small space—six feet wide and eight feet in length—would require more words than I could fit into a 500-page book. Suffice it to say that I needed a place to live while I attended classes for a semester at La Universidad de las Américas in Cholula, Mexico. Since the apartment I settled into came without a single stick of furniture, not even in the kitchen, the only fixtures a cement sink and a gas hook-up for a stove, I sought out Puebla's central market on a rainy September afternoon. There I bought a two-burner gas cooker, among other paraphernalia such as a few examples of the ubiquitous blue enameled cookware resting on every street vendor's stovetop. Cheap, durable, and practical.

Next came a small rustic table made of unfinished pine for my countertop and a metal hutch painted white, to store the few blue plastic dishes I hauled back in two string bags to the apartment. A dull knife and a few bowls, and I was ready to take my place at the stove.

Except I failed to understand how hard it would be to feed myself despite my culinary skills. After all, I'd been cooking daily since Mom shanghaied me to cook family dinners nearly every night as she worked toward her Ph.D. Throw in the fact that I obviously could not afford a refrigerator and would need to shop every day for food. Time simply didn't allow for that with my class schedule and bus trips to Cholula from Puebla and back.

Most days I freeloaded meals at Pablo's family's table.

But as the weeks went by, and Pablo talked about his friends, I wanted to meet them.

That meant throwing a dinner party. Which meant cooking something

Chinese, to celebrate Pablo's mixed heritage. At the beginning of the twentieth century, his grandfather, father to Pablo's diminutive mother, emigrated to Mexico from Canton, to work on the railroads in the early 1900s. He was in good company, as Mexico experienced a wave of Chinese immigration from the 1870s until the 1930s.

But Pablo's mother never cooked Chinese food, so she couldn't teach me.

Instead, I turned to Emily Hahn's *The Cooking of China*, one of the Time-Life Foods of the World cookbooks. The recipe booklet fit nicely into my suitcase when I left Florida for my semester abroad in Mexico. I'd also packed Hsiang-Ju Lin's more sophisticated tome, *Chinese Gastronomy*.

The menu?

White Rice

Sweet and Sour Pork

Crab Egg Foo Yung

Simple and manageable with my limited *batterie de cuisine*.

The day of the dinner, I flagged down the diesel-belching bus that passed by my apartment every morning. The driver leered at me, as usual, but I moved, as usual, to the middle of the bus, took the window seat, and parked my string bags on the seat next to me, to fend off would-be Casanovas.

At the market, I filled my string bags with fatty pork, pineapple the color of sunflowers, bright green scallions, woody ginger, plump green bell peppers, brown jumbo eggs, and white rice. The only item left on my shopping list was four blue crabs. The vendor wrapped them up, warning me—as had Pablo's mother—that the crabs needed to be cleaned well.

To make a long story short, I didn't do what they told me to do. I'd never dealt with any kind of crabs with shells, just stone crabs and bulk crab meat. It showed.

The carpet-covered cement floor of the tiny apartment served as the "table." I set the "table" for eight, seven guests and me. I borrowed large white plates from Pablo's mother, glasses, and forks, too. Except for the final dish—the crabs—at 8:30 p.m., everything was ready. Even though I could only cook on my small two-burner gas "stove," a hot-plate-like contraption surfaced with blue enamel just like my pots, I planned to cook the crabs at the last minute, the stir-fry method perfect for the timing.

I opened the "apron" of one crab with one of my dull paring knives. And gagged. It smelled like the hole in an outhouse. All the crabs, the same thing.

The rank odor permeated the whole apartment. Nothing else could happen, other than to throw them in the garbage can outside the wall surrounding the apartment building.

At 9 p.m., my eyes red from crying over the crabs and the no-show phantom guests, Pablo and Martin and I sat cross-legged on the floor and ate.

In my heart, I knew why I'd been shunned. To Pablo's friends, I was a loose American girl, living on her own, doing heaven only knew what in that apartment, without a chaperone.

An outsider yet again.

Crab Egg Foo Yung

Sauce:

> ¾ cup unsalted chicken stock
>
> 1 tablespoon low-salt soy sauce
>
> ½ teaspoon fine sea salt
>
> 1 tablespoon cornstarch mixed into 2 tablespoons cold chicken stock

Heat stock, soy sauce, salt. When mixture begins to bubble, stir in cornstarch mixture. When thickened, set aside and keep warm.

> 4 eggs, beaten in a small bowl
>
> ½ pound cooked crab meat
>
> 4-5 shiitake mushrooms, cut into julienne, about ½ cup
>
> ½ cup fresh bean sprouts, rinsed, drained, remove green hulls
>
> 4 tablespoons vegetable oil
>
> Sliced green onions for garnish

Add crab, mushrooms, and beans sprouts to eggs. Heat 1 tablespoon of oil in skillet, heat on high. Spoon about 1/3 cup of egg mixture into pan. Cook until golden brown, about 1 minute. Flip pancake and repeat on other side. When browned, place pancake on a warm plate, repeat process for remaining batter. Serve pancakes with sauce. Top with sliced green onions. Serves 4.

〜〜〜〜〜〜〜

Sopa de Fideos

Soup is the song of the hearth ... and the home.
~ Louis P. De Gouy

Like many Mexican *amas de casa* (housewives), Señora Pérez, or *Mamá*, cooked *sopa de fideos* nearly every day. It filled stomachs and decreased the demand for the more expensive main courses that follow. As a sign of elevated social status, *Mamá* employed a diminutive Indian woman, who helped her with all the household chores. I never learned her name, knowing her simply as "*la criada*."

La criada set the soup plate down in front of me, her hand shaking a little. A dash of soup spilled onto the white cotton tablecloth. Clutching her mouth with her free hand, *la criada's* eyes darted to the end of the table where Señor Pérez sat, king-like, a monarch on his throne, master of all he surveyed, his toad-like mouth chewing the smoky noodles in the *sopa*.

He was too busy spooning soup into his mouth to notice.

She slunk away, through the door into the steamy kitchen.

At the quiet insistence of their mother, motioning with her hands as she stood in the doorway, watching us all, Pablo, Francisco, Celina, and Pechugo quickly made the sign of the cross, then grabbed their spoons. No one talked. Guttural sounds of slurping filled the room, not unlike the muted humming of a small motor.

I took my first bite of the tomato-flecked broth, edging my spoon around the little nest of noodles resting in the center of the bowl. If I'd known about wine-tasting at the time, this is what I would say: Garlic and lime and black pepper and essence of tomato meld together in perfect harmony for a cold October day in central Mexico. Definitely worth the trouble to seek out and buy.

A plate of fresh corn tortillas, wrapped in a pristine white cotton towel, appeared at my elbow. I hadn't heard *la criada* tiptoeing behind me as she laid the plate down, nodding encouragingly as I glanced up, seeing her dark eyes were red-rimmed and shiny with tears. Had Señora Pérez lashed her with angry whispers about her clumsiness? Was it the sooty air in the kitchen?

I would never know.

I remember those moments. That dish. That taste.

But those eyes. Most of all, those eyes.

Sopa de Fideos (Celina's Mamá's Pasta and Tomato Soup)

3–4 tablespoons peanut oil

4 ounces fine vermicelli, preferably the kind formed into nest-like shapes (*nidos*)

¾ pound ripe plum tomatoes or 1 (16-ounce) can diced tomatoes

2 cloves fresh garlic, peeled and finely chopped

¼ medium yellow onion, finely chopped

6 cups unsalted chicken broth plus 1 cup water or 4 chicken bouillon cubes and 7 cups of water

Juice of two limes

¼ cup fresh flat-leaf parsley, chopped (or cilantro, if preferred)

Fine sea salt, to taste (careful with this if using bouillon cubes)

Heat oil in a large pot until smoking. Add vermicelli without breaking them up. Fry until a deep golden brown, careful to keep them from burning. Stir constantly. Drain off all but 2 tablespoons of oil and keep vermicelli in the pot. Remove pan from heat for a moment. Put tomatoes, onion, and garlic in a blender, blend until completely smooth. Add tomato mixture to vermicelli, continue cooking over high heat, stirring and scraping the bottom of the pan, until mixture is almost dry. Add stock and water (or bouillon cubes and water). Stir in ½ the parsley. Bring soup to a boil. Lower heat, simmer soup until pasta is soft, about 20 minutes. Add lime juice to pot, stir, ladle soup into individual serving bowls. Sprinkle with more parsley. Serve with fresh, warm corn tortillas, but flour tortillas are fine, too. Serves 4.

Day of the Dead

Must I go like the flowers that perish?
Will nothing remain of my name?
Nothing of my fame here on earth.
At least my flowers, at least my song!
Earth is the region of the fleeting moment.

~ Ancient Aztec poem

Aside from christenings and Christmas, the Day of the Dead, celebrated on November 2, is one of the biggest feast days in Mexican popular culture, with deep roots in Aztec practices. According to an anonymous Spanish chronicler writing in 1553, "They used to celebrate the feast of the dead, because they offered in their honor to the devil many turkeys, corn, blankets, clothing, food and other things. Every household celebrated a great feast. They incensed the images they had of their dead parents, kinsmen and priests." The ancient Aztec belief that death was simply another part of the cycle of life permeates to this day with its overtones of Spanish medieval Catholic customs.

Food formed the centerpiece of these feast days, as I learned from Pablo's family on November 2. My classes at La Universidad de las Américas in nearby Cholula wouldn't start again for three days. So I experienced a very eye-opening cultural experience that day.

Everyone in Pablo's family packed up various mole sauces, tortillas, pozole, candied squash, *pan de muertos* made into human shapes, tamales, and fresh fruit, and picnicked on top of family graves after scrubbing off lichen, stains, bird droppings, and weeding around the graves. They placed fresh flowers, marigolds mostly, and burning candles on the graves, watched old friends attending the graves of their loved ones, shared reminisces, and told stories about the dead. To miss this annual ritual was simply unheard of. Pablo and I couldn't dream of doing anything else, going anywhere else until late afternoon, not until we'd visited the cemetery. There, his four grandparents lay in eternal repose under thick slabs of cement, their fading photographs attached to the headstones a testimony to the relative shortness and impermanence of earthly life.

For days before the feast, Pablo's mother and her maid cooked the picnic foods. His brothers bought sugar skulls decorated with the names of each family member, both living and dead.

And mine as well.

Seeing "Cindy" written in squiggles of orange and blue frosting on a sugar skull scared me, coming as I did from the "*norteamericano*" way of viewing death as something to be strenuously avoided. Yet, watching the gaiety and the contentment in remembering the dearly departed, chatting with Pablo's aunts and uncles and cousins gathered in the cemetery, all that modified my perspective on death a little. Instead of mourning and weeping and gnashing of teeth, I saw joy and love. A true manifestation of the Catholic belief in the "communion of saints."

That November day, the sun glowed like the star it is. But the chill air, around sixty degrees, promised the gray, drizzly days of late November. I pulled my rebozo tighter around me to keep out the wind as I helped Pablo's mother by setting put the dishes along the edge of the graves of her parents. Her Chinese father's features didn't seem out of place among the photographs of the mestizo visages of the other graves. He'd come to Mexico from Canton to work on the railroads at the end of the nineteenth century.

Pablo's father's parents looked very "*indio*," but I said nothing, remembering how one time early in my stay I'd mentioned how Indian his father looked, meaning it as a compliment in my ignorance. I immediately regretted saying anything because of Pablo's indignant reaction. Despite the *indigenista* movement of the 1930s and later, aided by the muralists Diego Rivera and Juan O'Gorman, no one wanted to appear *indio*, the butt of jokes for their poor Spanish and clumsy ways.

After the families finished scrubbing the graves clean and strewing bright orange marigolds around them, Tio Jorge broke out bottles of pulque and tequila and passed them around to the men. I wondered how he dared lift a bottle of any alcohol to his lips, especially after too much booze in his gut caused a car accident in which his wife, Pablo's aunt, lost her left eye.

To be honest, I loathed the taste of those maguey-based beverages with their long pedigrees in Mesoamerica. Pulque, or *octli* in the Nahuatl language, comes from the fermentation of the maguey plant, a member of the agave family and long a sacred plant in Mexico. I didn't even like beer then, much less pulque. Its fruity flavor resembled nothing I'd ever tasted before. Women didn't drink, or at least they didn't in public, so I passed the bottles onward when they came my way.

But I noticed that Pablo's sister Celina took a swig from time to time. Later that night, I found out why: she was pregnant. Unmarried, with no hopes of ever being married. "*Espero un niño*," she told me tearfully. "I am with child."

She faced a life filled with shunning.

Pork Chile Verde

2½ pounds boneless pork butt or shoulder, cut into 1½-inch pieces

Fine sea salt and freshly ground black pepper, to taste

2 cups flour

¼ cup peanut oil

1 large yellow onion, cut into 1-inch chunks

3 poblano chiles, seeded, cut into 1-inch chunks

3-4 jalapeño peppers, seeded, finely chopped

3 garlic cloves, peeled, finely minced

1½ pounds tomatillos, roasted in a 450°F oven for about 30 minutes, then puréed in blender after peeling off the papery skin

2 teaspoons dried Mexican oregano

2 teaspoons ground cumin

1 large bunch cilantro leaves, chopped (1 cup or so), plus extra for garnish

3 cups unsalted chicken stock

Grated Jack cheese

Flour tortillas

Season pork with salt and pepper. Dredge pork in flour, shake off excess. Heat oil in a large, heavy-bottomed pot over medium-high heat. Brown pork well, until all sides are crusty. Cook meat in batches if necessary. Remove pork to a plate covered with a paper towel. Add onion, poblanos, and jalapeños to the pot, cooking and stirring over medium heat for approximately 20 minutes until poblanos show signs of softening. Add garlic, cook about 2 minutes, stirring constantly. Add pork and tomatillos to onion-chile mixture. Stir in oregano, cumin, and cilantro. Pour in chicken stock, bring mixture to a boil. Reduce heat to low and cook, covered, for 2 hours. Pork should be fork tender. Add salt and pepper to taste if needed. Serve in bowls garnished with more cilantro and grated Jack cheese. Best with flour tortillas. Serves 4-6.

Day of the Dead Altar

Shrimp Cocktail

*I and my companions suffer from a disease of the heart
which can be cured only with gold.*

~ Hernán Cortés

During a vacation break from La Universidad de las Américas in Cholula,
I decided to take a trip to Veracruz. The mysterious Olmec culture originated
there. And the topic still fascinated me. The little I'd heard about the food of the
place intrigued me, too. I asked my friend Pablo to go with me to explore this
other part of Veracruz's history, the place where Hernán Cortés landed on April
22, 1519 on his way to conquering central Mexico.

A soot-pumping bus carried us through Orizaba, grim and grey, formerly an Aztec garrison, now a thriving industrial city.

Gently modified over time by Spanish-Moorish cooking styles, Veracruz's cuisine incorporated African and Amerindian influences from the Caribbean islands, particularly Cuba. The *Jarachos*, or *Veracruzanos*, certainly knew
how to wield a wooden spoon, no doubt about it.

Walking along the decaying waist-high sea wall made of *coquina*, rough
shell-filled cement, I noticed that the material resembled that found in all Span-
ish-era forts in the Americas, including Veracruz's own Fortaleza de San Juan
de Ulua.

Not until that first bite of food in a small hole-in-the-wall restaurant did
the mix of cultures become apparent to me. The restaurant seemed ordinary
enough, hidden in an arch-covered promenade overlooking the *zócalo*, or main
square, painted bright neon blue, walls decorated with frayed Coca Cola posters
dotted with fly corpses. Small shrines dedicated to the Virgin of Guadalupe
hugged the far corners of the dining room, candles burning, sending smoke
into the face of the Virgins, who didn't seem to mind, their benign smiles blessing all who looked upon them.

But I ignored the Virgins.

Instead, I gaped at a huge red snapper, *Huachinango a la Veracruzana*, slapped down in front of my neighbors at the next table, sizzling in a tomato sauce laced with cinnamon and capers and green olives, another of the culinary joys of Veracruz. With roots in Arab cooking brought to Mexico by the Spanish, *Huachinango* is no doubt Veracruz's most famous dish.

But another famous dish beckoned as well.

Absolute simplicity itself, this delight was none other than the famous *coctel de camarones*, or shrimp cocktail, of Veracruz.

I'd been told the best way by far to savor a shrimp cocktail meant seeking out one of those little open-air "cafés" dotting the wide sandy beach *paseo*, boardwalk, as ocean breezes blew softly through white tarps serving as shields from the relentless tropical sun. Pulling out rickety metal chairs at one of the four or five wooden tables squeezed together under the tarp, I learned quickly to watch out for splinters on the underside of the table. Since most women probably wouldn't be wearing nylon or silk stockings, it would only be skin that tore if one forgot. Plastic-covered menus usually hung from one of four poles holding up the "ceiling." Or there'd be a menu written in white chalk on a blackboard propped up on the sidewalk.

I stared at the *copa* or sundae-like dish set in front of the customer at the table next to me, filled to the brim with glistening pink shrimp nearly the size of large éclairs. Specks of cilantro clung to the shrimp and thin slices of fresh lime coiled over the edges of the dish. Avocado chunks and smidgens of hot green chile added a delightful crunchy texture.

When the cook asked me what I wanted, I didn't hesitate: shrimp cocktail. The cook smiled, signaling that I'd made a splendid choice. He set to work. First came the *copa* itself, dug out of a sizeable ice-filled cooler, like one of those portable ice cream wagons, the kind with gaudy pictures painted on the outside and lined with gunmetal-colored steel inside, like I used to see at county fairs in the States.

Steaming in the hot, humid air, the frozen glass *copa*, set on the metal countertop, filled rapidly as the cook threw in chunks of avocado, small cubes of green hot pepper and white onion, plus nuggets of scarlet-red tomato. But the largest rosy shrimp I've seen this side of Italy, where they're called prawns, those really caught my attention. With a deft flick of his wrist, the cook feathered everything with finely chopped, emerald-green cilantro. Then came a drizzle of lime juice and a sprinkling of dried oregano and crushed salt. Finally, the crowning touch, a brief anointing with dark green olive oil, just a few teaspoons.

But it was not yet ready.

A tiny lacey doily on the saucer gave the masterpiece a slight hint of elegance as the cook lowered the *copa* onto the center of the plate. A thin long-handled fork wrapped in a rough paper napkin, reminiscent of French forks used for picking out snail flesh from their shells, sat on the saucer, flanked by two thin rounds of crusty French-style bread.

As the cook placed the *copa* in front of me, I recalled legends of the Aztec chief Moctezuma and his daily 300-dish meals. I gazed at my one-dish meal, a true masterpiece, hating to deface it. Words evaporated in the presence of such beauty. The pink of the shrimp and the pale green of the avocado gleamed through the cut glass of the cup. Like stained glass, or the jewels and gold the Spanish searched for so hard.

They looked in the wrong places.

The riches of Mexico lay elsewhere.

Coctel de Camarones (Mexican Shrimp Cocktail)

12 large shrimp, shelled, deveined, cooked

1 Hass avocado, peeled and coarsely chopped

1 jalapeno chile, seeded and finely chopped

1 large tomato, seeded and coarsely chopped

2 tablespoons yellow onion, finely chopped

2 tablespoons carrot, peeled and grated

2 tablespoons fresh cilantro, coarsely chopped

1/3 cup fresh lime juice

1 garlic clove, peeled and finely minced

Fine sea salt, to taste

Freshly ground black pepper

Pinch dried oregano

2 tablespoons vegetable or olive oil

Cilantro for garnish

Lime wedges for garnish

Layer shrimp and remaining ingredients, except for lime juice, in tall sundae glasses or water goblets. Mix lime juice with salt, pepper, and garlic. Pour over ingredients in the goblets. Drizzle olive oil over top of ingredients. Garnish each *copa* with a sprinkle of chopped cilantro and lime wedges. Serve on saucers lined with ornate paper doilies. Pass slices of crusty French bread. Sunshine optional. Serves 2.

Centro histórico de Puebla

Tacos Árabes

Tacos are like what the voices of a hundred angels singing Bob Dylan while sitting on rainbows and playing banjos would taste like if that sound were edible.
~ Isabel Quintero

Red and yellow leaves swirled at my feet as iridescent grey pigeons flashed their colors in the weak fall sunlight, dipping and bobbing across the sidewalk, seeking crumbs. A sudden gust of wind made me shiver in my thin faux suede coat. Out of the sun, the shade under the porticos felt as cold as a walk-in refrigerator. Blue and green and yellow buses belched acrid smoke, dirtying not only the air, but also causing ring-around-the-collar. At the end of any given day, I found signs of soot on my blouse collars and the cuffs of long sleeves when I changed clothes.

A chorus of beggars' voices joined the cacophony of buses. Chiclet sellers fought with flower vendors for attention from the people huddled at tables set outside the restaurant.

Not just any restaurant. La Oriental.

Opened in 1933 by Yerbagues Tabe Mena y Galeana, a Lebanese immigrant, one of many who left the Middle East and settled throughout Latin America. La Oriental began by selling shawarma, a Lebanese "taco" formed with lamb inside traditional wheat-based pita breads. The cooks changed the ingredients from lamb to pork, as it was cheaper and the locals preferred it. Lime juice and chipotle salsa, along with cilantro, onions, and guajillo chiles, added signature touches to the recipe.

But one thing never changed.

The revolving vertical spit, a cooking method with origins in the Middle East, remained a tradition. Slices of raw marinated pork threaded onto a long spear-like pole, snapped into place with a metal top, spiraled around and around like a circus merry-go-round, nudging up against flames billowing from a blistering hot fire, cooking the meat from the outside in. *Tacos al pastor*, another name for the pillow-soft flour tortilla wrapped around tender slivers of pork cut off the spiral, one of Puebla's signature dishes.

And something more.

The source of a resilient and virulent case of Montezuma's revenge that I simply couldn't shake.

I attributed it to the pork *tacos árabes* I loved to eat in the *centro* at La Oriental. Unfortunately, the *al pastor* method of cooking the meat on that revolving spit turned out to be a hotbed for nasty proliferating bacteria.

Cooking *al pastor* demands a certain balance between the amount of meat threaded onto the spear and the rapidness with which it cooks. Anything less unleashes a steamrolling bacterial overgrowth.

Of course, I did not know any of that then. The same problem existed on Rue Huchette in Paris, near the Saint Michel metro stop, where many tourists arrive after red-eye flights and jarring train trips from Charles de Gaulle airport, their stomachs churning with hunger pangs.

But in Puebla, I always sat at a table under the portico, close to the door at La Oriental. Picking at the plastic tablecloth with one hand, I held up the other with two fingers splayed when the waiter came running, his greasy notepad opened, his fingers fumbling the pencil behind his ear.

"How many, *Señorita?*" he asked, his eyes dropping to check out my legs beneath the blue denim mini-skirt I wore. He backed off when Pablo put his hand on the chair next to me.

No matter if I ate elsewhere or at Pablo's house, Montezuma's Revenge plagued me. I grew weaker, lost weight I couldn't afford to lose. No doctors seemed to be able to help me.

In the end, I left Mexico two weeks early. Within a week, I'd shaken off the sickness.

I suspected later that the culprit lay with *Giardia lamblia*, from drinking unsafe water.

Chipotle Sauce for Tacos al Pastor

8 dried guajillo chiles, toasted, stemmed, seeded

2 cups hot water

2 tablespoons vegetable oil

½ medium yellow onion, peeled, thickly sliced

4 garlic cloves, peeled, lightly mashed with the side of a cleaver or chef's knife

1–2 canned chipotle chiles, plus 1 tablespoon *adobo* from the can

¼ cup chopped fresh cilantro

1 tablespoon fresh lime juice

1 tablespoon fresh orange or pineapple juice

Coarse sea salt, to taste

Be sure to wear rubber gloves when handling chiles! Tear chiles into rough pieces and place in a medium-size stainless steel or glass bowl. Add 2 cups hot water and let soak at least 2 hours or overnight. Drain, reserve soaking liquid. Heat oil in a small skillet over medium heat. Add onion and garlic. Sauté until golden, about 5 minutes for onion and 1 minute for garlic. Place onion and garlic in blender. Add drained chiles, 1 cup soaking liquid, chipotle chiles, *adobo*, cilantro, and citrus juices. Purée until smooth. Transfer to a bowl. Season to taste with coarse salt. Can be made 1 week ahead. Spoon sauce into a glass jar, cover, and refrigerate. Makes approximately 2 cups.

Weevily Beans

*Don't you know that in the Navy you must always
choose the lesser of two weevils?*

~ Patrick O'Brian

Like Jack in the story "Jack and the Beanstalk," I couldn't resist the mysterious beans. They wore many colors, a little like Joseph with his hue-drenched coat. Scheduled to fly out of Mexico City to Tampa the next day, I knew that Daddy would love those beans, so I bought a kilo, two pounds, more or less. I needed more weight in my suitcase like I needed a hole in the head. Ignoring the practicalities, I opened my string bag, and the pig-tailed girl in the market dropped in the plastic bag of beans.

Around the corner, I gawked once again at the vast display of fresh chiles, their shiny taut skins glimmering in the sunlight streaming through the openings in the open-air market's metal roof. The dried chiles beckoned as well, their pungent aromas of wood smoke and just-plowed earth filling my nostrils as I walked by.

Beans in Mexico aren't limited to pinto, black, or red.

Seven thousand years ago, or so the experts believe, beans (*ayocotl* in Nahuatl and *Phaseolus vulgaris* in modern scientific lexicon) cropped up in central Mexico. Whether there are 200–400 varieties or only fifty native versions and twenty improved varieties doesn't matter.

What mattered was that I wanted to share those colorful beans with Daddy.

Into my lumpy suitcase they went. I piled clothes around them, knowing that they were contraband. I debated adding a couple of Aztec warrior dolls to the suitcase, too. Adorned with real feathers and faux yellow leopard "skin" painstakingly pasted onto their plastic bodies, those dolls were works of art. I chose instead to carry the dolls in my carry-on bag. The rough and tumble of the airplane's baggage hold probably would not be good for them.

Imagine my surprise at U.S. Customs in Tampa when the Customs officials ignored the beans. But worse, they threatened to cut into my dolls. It dawned on me that they probably thought I'd not miss the opportunity to smuggle in some Mary Jane, given my age, my wild unruly red hair, and my faded blue jeans. After all, I *was* coming home after months of living in Mexico,

"No, no, no!" I said, as the guy with the blond crew cut and piercing blue eyes reached into his pocket for a jackknife or something sharp.

"My father and little brother are outside there," and I pointed to the window in the door where I saw Daddy's smiling face and waving hand.

The Customs officials glanced at each other, some unspoken signal crackling in the air between them.

"OK, Miss, you can go."

I burst through the hospital-green door and dropped my luggage to hug Daddy and my brother Tim.

"What was that all about?" Tim asked, as he picked up my carry-on bag.

"Them," I pointed. "Those guys wanted to cut open my dolls. I guess they thought I was smuggling in some marijuana."

Daddy laughed one of his honking belly laughs.

"Well, you know, you do rather look the part!"

Nobody talked much on the long drive back to Gainesville. But as soon as we walked in the backdoor of the house, I grabbed Daddy's arm.

"I've got something for you! You know how much you love beans? Well, I have a surprise for you." And I dug through my suitcase for those colorful beans.

"Here," I said, thrusting the bulging plastic bag at Daddy. "Maybe you can make chili or something."

"Beautiful," he said as he eyed the bag. Then he set the bag down in the sink. "I appreciate you bringing those back with you, I do, but we can't eat them."

"Why not?" I asked, perplexed. "The beans look fine to me."

"Here," he pointed. I picked up the bag and looked through the dusty plastic. "What do you see?"

"Little holes, I guess. But so what?"

"Honey, the beans are full of weevils," he patted me on my shoulder as he pointed. "See, there's a little guy making a run for it." That's when I saw the tiny insect. Then another, and yet another.

That did it. I grabbed the bag and stomped down the stairs to the garage, where I tossed the bag of beans into the garbage.

What I should have done was put the beans into the freezer, waited a few days, and sifted out the dead bodies.

Frijoles de Olla

3 tablespoons vegetable oil or lard

1 small yellow onion, peeled and finely chopped

3 garlic cloves, peeled and minced

2 cups pinto or small red beans, soaked

1 sprig fresh oregano or ¼ teaspoon dried leaves, crushed

Fine sea salt, to taste

Heat oil/lard in a heavy pot like a Dutch oven, fry onion until translucent. Add garlic, cook for 30 seconds. Dump in soaked beans, cover with water about 1-2 inches above beans. Stir in salt and oregano. Bring to a boil, then reduce heat to simmer. Cover, cook until beans are tender, about 1 hour or longer. Serve beans in a bowl like soup with hot corn tortillas. Or make refried beans. Serves 4-6.

Quetzalcoatl, Feathered Serpent

I'd given up on my Peace Corps application being accepted, sure that my poor hearing would keep me out. However, one March day, in Gainesville for spring break, I heard Mom yelling about some package that'd just arrived in the mail. That enormous brown padded envelope held the keys to my future, in more ways than one. It took some digging through all the paperwork, but I finally found out where I was headed: Paraguay. But first there would be three months of language and technical training in Ponce, Puerto Rico. Starting on July 11, the height of summer.

Cook Stove, Puerto Rico

Hello Don Q

Ask not what your country can do for you,
but instead ask what you can do for your country.
~ John F. Kennedy

The clasp of my suitcase caught on my beige skirt as I stumbled into another girl standing at the luggage carousel. Her long blonde hair whipped across her straight white teeth when she whirled around, reacting to the push.

Seeing me, she relaxed. "I thought you were some guy putting moves on me. I'm Betty," and she held out her hand. For a moment, I wondered why she introduced herself to me, instead of just nodding and grabbing her suitcase as it barreled off the conveyor belt.

"You're going to Ponce, too, Peace Corps training?" She banged her knee with the heavy suitcase, grimacing.

"Yes, I am," I said, noticing that her luggage bore the same sticker as mine, a stylized American flag with "Peace Corps" in small white letters.

"Paraguay?"

"Yes," I answered as another girl walked up to us.

"Pat," she offered, as she set her plaid suitcase down. It reminded me of the kilt Mom sewed for me when I turned eleven.

The PA system droned something which I can't hear. Pat and Betty grabbed their suitcases and headed down the long corridor, running. I followed. Our plane waited now at another gate. My breath ragged as a sprinting mutt's on a hot, rainless Florida day, I arrived just as the gate opened for boarding.

The plane looked more like one of those vans for carting around residents of a nursing home than an airplane. I preferred the football field–size airplanes that flew between Miami and San Juan.

We crossed the tarmac and hiked up the stairs of the Prinair plane.

Ask not what your country can do for you, but instead ask what you can do for your country.

One seat on either side of a narrow aisle, twenty seats in total. The plane was smaller than I thought. One stewardess. It was an easy hop-skip-and-jump to Ponce on the other side of the island, twenty-five minutes tops. Piece of cake.

I settled into my seat, behind Betty. She was the talkative one. Pat said little. She stood at least six feet tall and self-conscious about it, she told me later. Up we went as the plane took off, darkness falling with the speed of a theater curtain at the end of a play. I stared at the blue vinyl covering the back of Betty's seat, resting my head on the windowpane as we gained altitude.

The clouds fluffed and then thinned, illuminated by the plane's lights as we passed over the Cordillera Central. Checking my cheap Timex, I settled back in my seat. Fifteen minutes to go until we arrived in Ponce. Betty sat up in her seat and turned toward me, saying "Hey, you know … ."

And then it happened.

At first, I didn't see the stewardess's frantic waving at me to fasten my seat belt. The small plane's engines roared in my ears, sounding like a much larger aircraft. It dipped like a bobbing apple at a Halloween party as Betty's head smacked against the luggage rack above. I grabbed my seat belt, panting, sweat running cold from my armpits. The lights in the plane went dark. I fumbled with the seat buckle, which finally met its mate and snapped shut.

The bottom fell out.

The plane dropped another dozen feet in a free fall. Pat broke her silence, shrieking, "We're crashing, we're crashing!"

I gripped the armrests, silent screams of "I'm going to die!" swirling through my head. My life did not pass in front of my eyes.

Not for the first time, I asked myself what I was doing there, on a doll-size plane hurtling through the inky black night sky over the Cordillera Central of Puerto Rico. Specks of light, isolated from each other and not in great swaths as I'd seen on other flights, other places, told me that if the plane crashed, we'd be in the middle of nowhere. If we survived.

After what seemed to be an eternity, the plane steadied. The pilot's soothing voice boomed over the intercom. Speaking like a father to his frightened children, he assured us that all was well, nothing dangerous to worry about, and we'd be landing in Ponce in five minutes.

"Our rendezvous in Samarra will have to wait," I whispered to Death. "See you later."

The plane fought the lightning and the thunder, gliding into the airport, just barely missing the power lines and smokestacks of the Don Q rum distillery, the aroma of caramelizing sugar cane hanging in the air like wet sheets on a sunny day.

I'd given anything for a swig of their product at the moment.

The pilot stepped out of the cockpit and opened the door for us. Like a bunch of puppies eager to escape their crates, we scrambled out. With my feet on *terra firma* once again, fighting an urge to kiss the ground, my heart shifted from my throat back into my chest. My hands still twitched as I pushed my red hair away from my face. My "come-to-Jesus" moment past, lugging my suitcase behind Betty and Pat, I asked myself, "What are you doing, chasing some pie-in-the-sky fantasy of saving the world?"

Ask not what your country can do for you,
but instead ask what you can do for your country.

Don Q Rum Piña Colada Recipe

1¾ ounces Don Q Gold Rum

1 1/3 ounces pineapple juice

1 ounce Coco Lopez Cream of Coconut

Dash Angostura bitters

One maraschino cherry

Blend everything but the cherry with half a cup of crushed ice. Serve in a tulip glass. Garnish with cherry. Umbrella optional. Serves 1 (adapted from Don Q website).

Rice and Red Beans

The Peace Corps is a sort of Howard Johnson's on the main drag into maturity.
~ Paul Theroux

No one waited for us at the arrival gate in Ponce, three young American women dazed by a bumpy flight, catapulted into another world. No one was there to tell us what to do. No one to tell us where to go for the night. We pooled our money and flagged down a cab in front of the airport. The cab driver seemed to know that we were seeking the Peace Corps training center. Through narrow, steep streets we drove, the driver leaving his lights off except at intersections, erroneously believing that keeping them on ran down the taxi's battery. He left us, and our suitcases, in front of the training center and sped off with a short burst of his horn.

Housed in a dilapidated former convent, the Peace Corps training center bore a great resemblance to my vision of a Spanish-style house. Small classrooms and offices with creaky wooden floors on the second floor overlooked a court-yard the size of a basketball court, all surrounded by red adobe walls punctured with arches and trellises.

We pounded on the worn wooden doors, sure we'd have to sleep on the street. To our surprise, a little window in the door popped open.

"So sorry, I was just on my way to the airport," a man said.

He opened the door, and we all three sighed with relief.

"I'm Raúl Cárdenas, and if you give me a minute, I'll take you to your *pensión*."

The *pensión* didn't look like much in the dark of night. Truth be told, it looked seedy, like a place on the wrong side of the tracks in some no-name Southern town.

Raúl knocked on the metal gate of the house, surrounded by a wall topped with shards of broken glass, glittering rainbows in the beams of the wrought-iron colonial-era streetlamps lining the sidewalk.

Despite the late hour, the woman who answered the door was the lady of the house, a widow we later learned, down on her luck, who rented rooms for Peace Corps volunteers. She led us through a narrow hallway jammed with heavy wooden Spanish-style furniture, up a winding staircase to the top floor, and pushed open a creaky wooden door. I suspected that the room, small, over-crowded with three cots, might at one point have been a maid's room.

At that moment, all I could think of was sleep. I don't remember if I even changed my clothes.

The next morning, I woke to sounds of a parrot chattering outside the open window. The bird balanced itself on the branches of a red-flowering jac-aranda tree. Everywhere I looked, crepe-papery bougainvillea cascaded over walls, purple, pink, white. The sounds of boats rang through the balmy air.

The adventure began with breakfast, flaky rolls smothered with *dulce de leche*, thick black coffee, freshly squeezed orange juice, and hard-cooked eggs. But it was dinner the night of that first day that stayed with me: red beans slath-ered over a pile of white rice, with spicy fried chicken on the side.

Red Beans

2 cups dried small red beans, soaked

6 cups water

1 medium ripe tomato, cut into wedges

½ medium yellow onion, cut into wedges

½ green bell pepper, cut into thick slices

1 bay leaf

1 garlic clove, peeled

3 tablespoons lard or vegetable oil

4 tablespoons *sofrito* (see page 136)

Fine sea salt, to taste

Chopped cilantro for garnish

Put beans in a heavy pot and cover with water by 1½ inches. Add tomato, onion, green pepper, bay leaf, and garlic. Bring to a boil, lower heat, cover, cook until beans are tender, about an hour or so. Heat *sofrito* in lard in heavy skillet until bubbly, then scrape it into the beans. Simmer until thick, but still slightly soupy. Serve over white rice, garnished with chopped cilantro. Serves 4-6.

Guaraní language class (Author in white pants)

Sofrito

*American imperialism is often traced to the takeover of
Cuba, Puerto Rico, and Hawaii in 1898.*

~ Noam Chomsky

Señora González stood a few feet away from me as I hovered, watching her cook *sofrito*.

The lard in the skillet sputtered into the air, spitting and hissing as she dumped in the *sofrito*, a seasoning mixture of chopped yellow onion, mashed garlic, ribbons of green pepper, fuzzy *culantro*, and feathery cilantro. She laughed at my timidity, her curly reddish-brown hair shaking as she expertly stirred the sputtering *sofrito*. After several minutes, she pronounced it done and added about a cup to the big pot of red beans simmering on the gas stovetop.

Chipped enamel testified that this was no brand-new stove but rather a workhorse that fed Mrs. González's brood of six children and a husband three times a day, seven days a week. The distance between their house and the Peace Corps training center in central Ponce prevented me from getting back in time for lunch, but I ate breakfast in the kitchen. To make things easy for her, I told Mrs. González that I only needed two hard-boiled eggs for breakfast, and that's what I ate most days for the three months that I roomed with her family.

My room, and I am stretching the truth by calling it that, was a former chicken coop in the backyard. I soon learned not to keep any food in there. Ants the size of small beetles crawled everywhere if I did.

Ants were not the only pests in the place.

I dreaded taking showers in the single bathroom in the house, for cockroaches lived in the drains, scurrying out in hordes once the hot water started flowing. Their sharp carapaces scraped against my ankles as I hurried to finish scrubbing my sweaty skin. A Florida girl, I thought I knew cockroaches, but those large palmetto bugs repulsed me.

Dozens of chickens lived in a hard-packed dirt enclosure near my shack, too. Most mornings roosters bellowed a cacophony. Sounding like a troop of

Harley-Davidsons, they cock-a-doodle-doo'd madly as the sun rose over the acres of plantain groves surrounding the barrio, shining hotly even at dawn on the cinder block houses, painted every pastel color imaginable.

But the most disturbing pest turned out to be the fourteen-year-old son of the family, whom I caught one night peering at me through the slats of the flimsy shack. And *he* caught hell when I told the Señora.

Once in a while, Señora González proudly offered me tamale-like *pasteles* with a filling rich with pork and raisins and capers, stuffed inside *masa* made not from corn but rather from pounded roots such as malanga and yams. I never took to them for some reason, perhaps because of the soft texture of the *masa*. Dinner occasionally consisted of chicken with white rice enriched with fried onion and *sofrito*-spiced red beans, all of which I gobbled down quickly. Usually, though, Mrs. González presented me with a plate of rice and beans and some bread, occasionally some fruit, generally mango or pineapple.

More and more, I started eating dinner in town with other Peace Corps trainees, arriving at the house too late to eat with the family. When I did eat there, I often took my plate to the chicken coop and ate alone. The rhythm of the González household seemed to have been disrupted by my presence. Their plump nineteen-year-old daughter, "the Princess," scowled at me, especially when her handsome boyfriend showed up in the evenings, flirting with me in true *macho* style as I stepped out of the nightly taxi. The teenage sons ogled me with googly eyes at the dinner table.

From my time on that island, *sofrito* and red beans stayed with me, appearing often in meals cooked elsewhere.

Sofrito

3 large yellow onions, peeled and roughly chopped

3 large heads garlic, peeled and roughly chopped

1 pound *ají dulce* peppers, seeded and stemmed

½ pound sweet bell peppers, green, seeded and stemmed, roughly chopped

3 bunches *culantro* leaves, tips removed, roughly chopped

2 bunches chopped cilantro, roughly chopped

Whirl everything in a food processor or blender, adding a bit of water to get blending started. Stays fresh for about 2 weeks in refrigerator. Freeze in small canning jars for longer use. Use several tablespoons to spice up beans, meats, poultry, sauces, etc. Makes about 2 quarts.

The Fly in the Hamburger

There are a zillion variables to a hamburger.
~ Danny Meyer

Frilly palm leaves swayed above my head, but I wasn't looking at them.

Instead, the cracked sidewalk held my attention as I tagged along with the rest of my Peace Corps Guaraní language-training group. Jamie the guy—there were two Jamies in the group, one male and one female—stopped at a smudged glass door and pushed it open.

Inside, no one greeted us as we traipsed in, just the silence that descends when strangers enter a place, and locals check them out, looking for guns or knives or maybe a sneer or two.

We sat at two tables and grabbed the yellowed laminated menus, greasy, fingerprint-stained, dimmed by time. One thing, and one thing only, were we after: hamburgers. So we waited for the waiter to take our orders.

And we waited.

Then we waited some more.

Finally, Jamie the guy stood up and yelled, "Hey, we'd like to order, please!"

Nothing happened at first.

A pimply young man finally walked over to us, clutching a pad of paper and a pen in his hand.

Not saying a word, not looking at us, he pointed. When his finger reached me, I said I wanted the hamburger with the special sauce, one of the few options on the menu. I dared not ask him what was in the sauce for fear he would rebuff me.

Silence hung over the moment. I noticed other customers snickering, whispering. Some even grinned when they looked at us but looked away when we returned their stares.

The hamburgers arrived about thirty minutes later, cold, with soggy French fries.

I picked up my burger and aimed it at my mouth. Jamie the girl screamed, pointing at the burger in my mouth.

"Look, look, at the bun!" She laughed.

I flipped over the burger. I saw what she meant.

A large dead fly, the size of a dime, lay embedded in the bun.

I plucked it out, along with a sizeable section of the bun, and kept eating.

I glanced over at the waiter and noticed the smirk on his face.

Despite the heat, a shiver flashed through me, as the proverbial chill shot down my spine. At that moment, I recognized what so many people in the world live with every day.

Prejudice.

The Puerto Ricans in that café did not like Americans from the mainland, at least not the WASP type.

That's what we were.

I never went back to that café again. But I have never forgotten how that hamburger and the waiter and the other customers made me feel.

Special Burger Sauce

½ cup Duke's Mayonnaise

2 tablespoons BBQ sauce

2 tablespoons catsup

2 tablespoons Dijon mustard, preferably Maille

2 tablespoons sweet pickle relish or chopped dill pickles

1 tablespoon Worcestershire sauce

1 tablespoon grated yellow onion

2 garlic cloves, peeled, mashed with a few dashes of fine sea salt

Fine sea salt and freshly ground black pepper, to taste

Mix all ingredients together, chill until ready to serve. Makes about 1 cup.

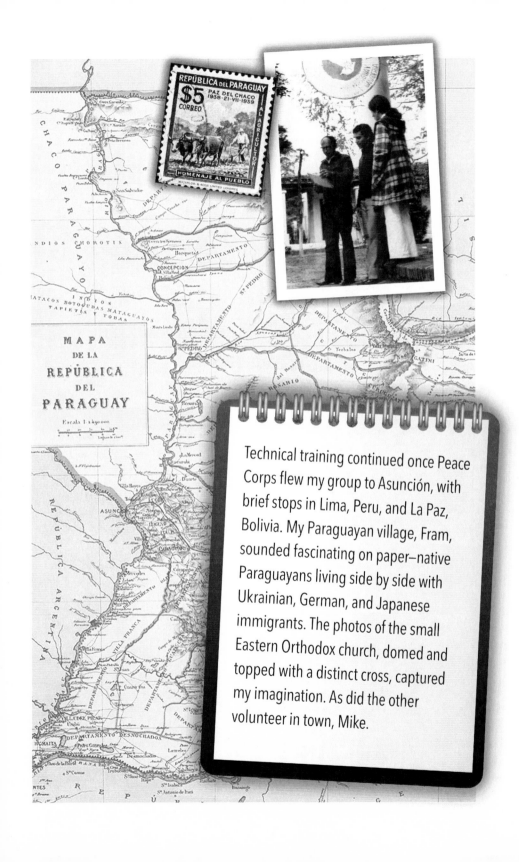

Technical training continued once Peace Corps flew my group to Asunción, with brief stops in Lima, Peru, and La Paz, Bolivia. My Paraguayan village, Fram, sounded fascinating on paper—native Paraguayans living side by side with Ukrainian, German, and Japanese immigrants. The photos of the small Eastern Orthodox church, domed and topped with a distinct cross, captured my imagination. As did the other volunteer in town, Mike.

Gaucho-Style Barbecue

The Cow

It is a gift, and you realize as soon as you cross the border into Paraguay, as I did, the first time in '82, that you are in a sort of a wonderland. Nothing is quite right: the buildings, they've got their own architecture, their own language; and everything is just a little bit off key.

~ John Gimlette

The Brahma cow stood still in the middle of the road, her long horns shrouded by the soft white mist of early morning rain. I saw her there, unmoving.

But Doc didn't. He was talking too much.

"Stop," I screamed.

Doc slammed on the brakes. Stopped talking. Too late.

The Land Rover slid slowly sideways into the cow. Hit her with a quiet thud, and the stunned animal tumbled into a deep ditch on the side of the road. She landed near the sagging wire of a dilapidated fence.

Doc didn't stop.

I gasped, the breath knocked out of me by the impact. As the Land Rover sped up, I twisted in my seat and looked back. The cow stood up and loped off with slow mincing steps toward a hole in the fence, waddling like a Chinese woman with bound "lotus blossom" feet. The cow's sad bellowing grew fainter by the second.

"Why didn't you stop to help that cow?" I asked.

Doc shook his head for a second, then said, "Well, if you hit something, or somebody, in places like this, you're supposed to keep going. That's what they told me." As an official U.S. Embassy dignitary, due to his position as the Peace Corps doctor, he had a point. In some cases, angry mobs pulled drivers from their cars and beat them to death, doling out instant justice to both guilty and the not guilty.

Naïve as I was, I knew that "they" meant the top brass sitting at desks in Washington, while we streaked along in the no-man's land dividing Paraguay from its much wealthier and more developed neighbor, Argentina. Across the

143

Rio Paraná, the bright electric lights blazed at night. Here, on the fringe of southern Paraguay, stars lit the night. Or maybe a full moon when there wasn't enough kerosene for the ubiquitous hurricane lanterns. Not a reality for the pencil pushers in D.C.

Even the road symbolized the chasm between civilization and this backwater.

"Highway" was a generous description of the main route south from Asuncion, the capital of Paraguay. Distinguished as "1" and paved, the two-lane road branched off at Carmen del Paraná, northeast, to Colonia Fram, my Peace Corps site.

The few things I knew about Colonia Fram came from a brief write-up in a tattered three-ring binder in the Peace Corps training office in Ponce. Ukrainian, German, and Japanese immigrants grew cotton there. A Russian Orthodox Church provided spiritual guidance and solace to many of these souls. The promise of cheap or even free land enticed whole families to settle on this Wild West-like frontier in southern Paraguay. There was another volunteer who'd been in the village for five months. The presence of another volunteer in the village was important to me. I knew I needed the support of a fellow American. That volunteer turned out to be Mike Bertelsen, my future husband. We'd met a few days after I arrived in Paraguay, at a big welcome party hosted by a few of the other volunteers who'd been in-country for a while.

Doc spun the steering wheel to the left. A crude, hand-lettered sign after an intersection read "Fram: 21.2 kms." About thirteen miles. On a muddy, red-dirt road. The Land Rover scuttled over bumps and potholes and ruts as deep as my grandmother's Dutch oven. Or deeper. Blinding rain burst from the gunmetal-gray sky, so torrential that the windshield wipers just moved water from one side of the slick glass to the other. It felt as if a dozen washerwomen sat above us, scrubbing their dirty laundry, emptying the dregs of their soapy buckets over us.

My stomach tightened as Colonia Fram appeared. The Land Rover dipped over a slight rise into the village, marginally big enough to be called a town. Doc drove straight to a small wooden building.

Three blond women stood on the rickety wooden porch of the local *pensión*, the leaky roof held up by three or four rough two-by-fours. All three of them could pass for New York City models, slender, eyes the color of a clear midsummer sky, testifying to their Ukrainian ancestry. The oldest one, Olga, held out her hand and hoisted me up out of the red mud threatening to suck me down into the earth.

My boots will never be the same, I thought.

"*Bienvenida!*" she exclaimed. Then the two Anitas stepped forward. I learned that one was Olga's daughter and the other a niece. Both looked to be about fourteen years old. Doc, meanwhile, lifted my hard-shell suitcase out of the back of the Land Rover and set it on the sopping wet wooden porch, the suitcase's French's-mustard-yellow providing the only color amid the grayness of the day. Then came the thud of my musty footlocker full of paperback books that every volunteer takes to their sites.

Doc hurried to leave. He'd be stuck there if he didn't. The authorities closed the muddy roads whenever rain softened the red clay so much so that deep furrows posed a danger to any future traffic. No one came in or went out until the ground dried up. Doña Olga assured me that could be days. She smiled, one front incisor missing.

I waved goodbye to my fellow Peace Corps volunteers as Doc pulled away.

I suddenly was alone in a village in southern Paraguay.

Walking through the *pensión's* main door, my knee-high leather boots tracking thick red mud, my nerves hummed like a tuning fork. My stomach growled, but as a stranger in a strange town, I hungered for something more than food.

It seemed like the first day at a new school. I didn't know anybody. The other volunteer in town, Mike, was not in Fram that day. Instead, he was twenty-five miles away in Encarnación, waiting for my arrival there, due to some crossed wires of communication.

The reality of my situation struck me. Any romantic ideas I entertained about being a Peace Corps volunteer vanished as the women led me to my temporary quarters, a room the size of a walk-in closet with a cot and a chair. The trunk of books and my small suitcase occupied one corner, the driest spot in the place. I smelled mildew, and wood smoke, too, coming through the cracks in the walls and the floor and even the door. They let in the rain as well.

What am I doing here!???

After fifteen minutes of niceties, I needed to find a bathroom. Bad. My stomach lurched. I opened the door, its hinges creaking like a suspenseful moment in a Stephen King film. One of the Anitas, the daughter, asked me what

145

was wrong. I stuttered, "*Baño, baño,*" and she wrinkled her forehead.

Oh dear Lord, what is the Spanish word for the can? The john?

I remembered, "*Servicio, por favor.*"

Anita pointed to the back of the yard. In my left hand, I clutched a fresh roll of toilet paper and started walking in the still-pouring rain. Briskly. Rain dripped off my hair and down my neck. There, up against the fence, I saw it.

A latrine.

I thrust open the flimsy wooden door, expecting to see a wooden seat elevated off the floor, a hole for my business, like latrines in old photos of rural America. Instead, I saw a hole in the floor. I pulled down my underwear under my skirt. Peace Corps warned female volunteers to never wear slacks or jeans in our villages. Only fast women did that. Excellent advice, for many reasons.

I squatted. There was so much rain that nothing stayed down in that hole, as the water table must have hovered right under the surface. I gagged and tried to relax. Rain poured onto my head and shoulders. I hurried, tossing the wadded paper into the hole, where it shriveled in the wetness.

Then I saw them.

Maggots. Thick, white, twitching. Boiling out of the muck that surged out of the hole.

What am I doing here!???

Tereré (Yerba Mate Tea)

1 tablespoon yerba mate

Hot water

1 *guampa* (cow horn drinking cup or tall heatproof mug)

1 *bombilla* (metal straw)

Place tea leaves in *guampa*, pour in hot water, let steep. Then put in *bombilla* and drink, adding water as needed. Usually, a group of people drink together, all from the same *bombilla*. Increase amount of tea as needed for more people, 1 tablespoon per person. Serves 1.

Manioc is *Chipa*

Cassava originated in Brazil and the tropical areas of the Americas.
~ Hector Rodríguez

"Chipa, chipa!"

The small Paraguayan girl, all of maybe eight-years-old, thrust an enormous flat basket draped with a smudged white cloth against the open window of the bus.

I smelled the warm cassava bread even before she flicked off the cloth with a flourish, much as a magician reveals the white rabbit cowering under his top hat. I pointed to the bread closest to me, and she held out her hand. Payment first, then food. I plunked one *guaraní* (about ten U.S. cents at that time) into her other hand, and she passed the bread to me after twisting it into a small paper napkin.

At that moment, the driver snorted, *"Jaha!* Let's go," and the bus slowly rambled down the rutted road, tiny tornadoes of red dust billowing behind us. I tore open the *chipa* as I settled back onto the wooden bench. I bit into the chewy, cheesy center first, the best part, just like I used to scrape out the frosting of an Oreo before eating the chocolate cookie part.

Cassava, the starchy tuberous root of a perennial tropical plant, didn't excite me much at first.

Stringy, bland, pale. Those words describe it well.

Cassava (*Manihot esculenta*)—known by myriad names but called *mandioca* or *mandió* in Paraguay—originated in central Brazil and/or Paraguay and spread worldwide. It provides energy, thanks to carbohydrates. In many regions of the world, that's not such a bad thing. Carbohydrate calories from *mandioca* ensure that other vital nutrients, such as protein, will not be diverted from calories necessary for tissue maintenance. Cassava might be either bitter or sweet. Both varieties contain varying levels of toxic cyanogenic glucosides, reduced by proper processing and cooking.

Peeled, cut into six-inch chunks, and boiled in salted water until tender enough so that a knife slips in easily, *mandioca* can still be quite fibrous. Tough, stringy cores must be removed. Generally, this is easy because as the chunks of mandioca cook, they split apart. Then the eater or cook can easily remove the core by hand.

After long days spent in Peace Corps training out in the Paraguayan countryside, I found my first bites of *mandioca* rather tasteless. The mild flavor, with little difference in degrees of blandness from the white potato, requires some sort of embellishment. That, I soon learned, came in a bottle plopped down on nearly every table. Pickled hot peppers, swimming in vinegar, livened things up considerably. And a big slab of grilled beef—*lomito*—didn't hurt either, provided that meat appeared in the local market at all.

The greatest pleasure of all with *mandioca* occurred when Doña Olga at my *pensión* fried it after boiling it. *Hêe*, "yes" in Guaraní. A crisp outer layer hid the tender insides, adding texture and mouthfeel.

Later, in the States—unless I bought it in a market geared strictly to people from Latin America or the Caribbean or Africa—*mandioca* tended to be old, with black lines running through the whiteness. So I constantly poked and prodded any *mandioca* for sale, hoping to find roots bearing wounds inflicted by some savvy shopper, who had broken off a tip of the waxed roots to peer into the whiteness, seeking those telltale black lines.

Years after leaving Paraguay, I still craved *mandioca*. With each bite, I remembered that little girl rubbing the red dust out of her eyes as she waited for the next bus to pull up along the side of the road, selling *chipa* to another traveler. I wondered what happened to her, like I often pondered Doña Olga's fate, a miracle worker in the kitchen, given local food shortages and lack of access to markets other than the village's.

I marveled at the power of food to forge connections, to rouse long-buried memories years after the fact.

Fried Yuca/Cassava/Manioc

2 pounds yuca, peeled, cut into 4-inch sections, boiled until tender

4 cups (1 quart) vegetable oil for frying

Coarse sea salt, to taste

Drain cassava. Heat oil in a heavy pot, Fry Daddy, or another fryer. Fry cassava pieces in batches until they begin to turn golden. Drain on paper towels. Serve with a favorite hot sauce. Serves 6.

Author with Daddy, before leaving for Paraguay

Doña Olga

Fram was founded on March 20, 1927 by Norwegian Pedro Cristophensen, along with Mateo Sanchez, a native of Carmen del Paraná. The old name of the place was Apereá. The residents of Fram are of Slavic origin (Poles, Russians and Ukrainians), German and Japanese.

~ Wikipedia

The sight of an old-fashioned iron stove.

The smell of wood smoke.

The aroma of beefsteak *milanesa*.

Or the crackling sound of empanadas, stuffed with ground beef and hard-cooked eggs, perfumed with a hint of cumin, frying in smoking-hot grease.

That's all it takes to reconstruct Doña Olga's magical touch in the kitchen, in my mind anyway.

Who was this cook, with the spirit of Tita in *Like Water for Chocolate?*

I met her the very first moment I stepped foot in the red mud of Fram.

At that moment, I entered Doña Olga's small-but-bountiful world and sampled her down-to-earth cooking.

That day she led me to a rickety thatched chair in front of a none-too-clean square table and bustled off down three short steps into the smoky kitchen. Soon a steaming cup of *yerba mate* tea, my first nourishment from Doña Olga's hands, warmed my cold, trembling fingers.

Pleased that I had taken to the warm tea, Doña Olga proudly placed in front of me three small turnover-like pastries on a small plate lined with a paper napkin and stepped back to observe my reaction. Tittering, she pushed a strand of blond hair out of her blue eyes and shoved a cork-stoppered wine bottle full of pickled hot peppers in vinegar towards me, indicating that I should douse the turnovers with a drop or two of that liquid fire. I did. My mouth closed around the first empanada I ever ate, the tender, flaky crust encasing a savory ground meat filling lightly scented with cumin, onions, a hint of garlic, black pepper, and warming hot pepper juice.

Day after day, amidst chickens cackling at my feet and stray starving dogs sniffing at my plates, I became an enthralled observer of the wizardry emanating from that dark sooty kitchen.

No doubt some of the chickens clucking at my feet eventually arrived at my table on a plate. Not often, though. Cooking a chicken was usually akin to killing the goose that laid the golden egg. In that household, indeed in the entire town, where no one never knew if there would be meat for sale, eggs lived up to their role as the perfect food. Many weeks often went by with no meat sold in the local market.

But when meat hung bloody in the early morning market, the endless fried eggs and rice gave way to celebration. Doña Olga highlighted her best creations: *bife a caballo*, beef steak done to perfection with a sunny-side-up egg perched on top. Or *milanesa*, beef steak flattened with a mallet and fried in breadcrumbs until golden brown in color.

Unfortunately, meat on the menu also meant *menudo*—tripe stew—with noisome whitish chunks of stomach flesh floating in broth, along with a few carrot and potato chunks. Over the years, I tried *menudo* again. The verdict was still "No thanks."

Knowing my intense dislike of tripe, Doña Olga made up for it by fabricating her version of *pain au chocolat*, thick cake-like chunks of sweet white bread, a speck of a chocolate bar buried in the center of the dough balls before baking. Like a child, I would break open the bread and eat the chocolate first. Bliss it was! Or the next day, she might turn her hand to a rustic version of *pissaladière*, spread with a tomato jam and an onion confit-like mixture, dotted with a half a black olive on each square piece. This "pizza" satisfied the longings of my pizza-deprived American soul. Sort of.

Insulated by the ignorance and arrogance of youth, it never occurred to me to ask Doña Olga for a single recipe. Yet, during that period of my life, her food saved me, nourished me, and gave me the strength to do the job I volunteered to do.

Alas, the only photos I took of Doña Olga were on a roll of film in a backpack that fell off my boyfriend Mike's motorcycle when we hit a rough spot in the road on the way to Encarnación. We never did find it.

All I have left are memories.

Bife a caballo

4 tablespoons extra virgin olive oil

2 1-inch-thick rib-eye steaks, trimmed of excess fat, sliced in half through the thickness, pounded to about ¼-inch thickness

1 tablespoon Worcestershire sauce

2 garlic cloves, minced

Fine sea salt and freshly ground black pepper, to taste

4 large eggs, cracked into individual serving dishes

Vegetable oil for frying eggs

Warm oven to 170°F, then turn off heat. Heat oil over medium-high heat. Rub both sides of each piece of steak with garlic, season with salt, pepper, and Worcestershire sauce. Cook steaks until well-browned, but still pink in the middle. Remove from stovetop, place on oven-proof serving plates. Keep steaks warm in heated oven. Meanwhile heat oil for eggs in a nonstick skillet. Add eggs one at a time and cook over-easy style. Season eggs with salt and pepper. Place each egg as it's cooked on top of one of the steaks in the oven. Serve with green salad and French fries. Serves 4.

Asunción, Paraguay

Three Stones and a Soup

*The kitchen, humble or rich, was a prime target of this decorous
insistence upon the duties of a good woman.*

~ M.F.K. Fisher

Dust, red as a circus clown's rouged cheeks, billowed behind the beige
Peugeot truck as it dodged wide potholes and deep ruts. In southern Paraguay's
dry season, dust was to be expected. And lots of it.

Fram, named for Fridtjof Nansen's Arctic exploration ship "Fram," meant
"Forward" in Norwegian. Never mind that no Norwegians lived within hun-
dreds of miles, save Mike, my fellow Peace Corps volunteer. Why the name
Fram? I never knew.

On my way to a cooking demonstration, miles into the countryside, I
mulled over the task at hand: cooking a soup using bland, mostly flavorless soybeans. Soybean cultivation began in Paraguay in 1921, introduced by Dr. Pedro
N. Ciancio, which he discussed in his book, *La soja y el problema alimentario
del Paraguay.* At the request of the Paraguayan government, Peace Corps urged
home economics volunteers to seek ways to broaden the use of these beans by
humans.

I'd asked the extension agent in the village multiple times if there'd be a
stove (*fogón*) for me to use at her site.

"¡*Como no*! Of course!" she'd assured me multiple times.

Consulting an American cookbook filled solely with soybean recipes, I'd
decided on one best suited to Paraguayan tastes: a soup seasoned with onions,
garlic, some herbs, salt, and black pepper. Not much else. I remembered the disastrous soufflé I'd attempted the previous week at the local church kitchen in a
cooking class for some teenage girls. I did not want to repeat that mistake. The
wood-fueled *fogón* burned the soufflé to cinders in a matter of minutes. A soup,
I knew, would be a safer bet on one of those stoves.

The driver pulled up to a whitewashed cinder block building about the
size of a garden shed. I jumped out and proceeded to unload from the back the

dented five-gallon aluminum pot I'd borrowed from Doña Olga at the *pensión* in Fram, fresh soybeans, and seasonings. Plus, a long wooden spoon for stirring, also courtesy of Doña Olga.

Inside the minute building, no stove, nothing for cooking, not even for boiling water for *tereré*, yerba mate tea.

My heart sank. Where was the *fogón*?

The agent bustled in, a plump woman about forty-five years old, missing a front tooth but otherwise impeccably dressed, her wide feet encased in high heels. In contrast, I wore a denim skirt, dusty leather sandals, and a prim white blouse, its Peter Pan collar now slightly pink with my sweat and red road dust.

"Um, where is the stove?" I asked. *¿Donde?*

"*Venga, venga*, come, come," she trilled, motioning with her hands, smiling.

I followed her outside, where at least twenty young girls and women stood waiting and giggling near a robust campfire. The agent pointed at the smoldering wood, around which three large and carefully placed stones formed a perfect triangular-shaped perimeter.

"There, there," she pointed. The *fogón*.

I blessed the gods and the Universe for all the prep work I'd done in my shack in Fram, particularly cutting up the onions and garlic. There was no place to do that on-site. I'd brought a dull kitchen knife, just in case.

I asked for volunteers to go to the well and fill the pot with water up to a certain level. That done, the agent and I balanced the heavy pot carefully on the three stones.

Looking at all the faces staring at me, the word *poseur* banged around in my head, a word well-loved by my high school French teacher, who spoke in a trembly Julia Child-like voice.

Who was I to deign to teach these girls and women something about cooking?

Somehow the time passed as each person shared their name and life story while we waited for the water to heat and the soybeans to soften. I'd brought paper cups that I'd found in a dusty shop in Encarnación while shopping with Kathy R., an older, more experienced volunteer. She'd suggested the cups as a way for everyone to have a taste without using the same spoon.

Polite smiles over the cup brims told me more than words could: soybean soup would not be gurgling away any time soon in Paraguayan kitchens, no matter how much garlic permeated the broth, how many chopped onions swam among the beans. Even though it closely resembled a popular Paraguayan soup, *Poroto Quesu*.

Instead, it would likely be a legendary dry soup gurgling over fires in those kitchens. *Sopa Paraguaya*, shrouded in myth and the mistiness of history, as so many iconic dishes are, that's what it would be, baked in the outdoor oven or another oven substitute. The recipe sprang from a tale told of a kitchen mistake.

Old wives and wags had it that a cook, or *machu* in Guaraní, added too much cornmeal to her boss's favorite soup, possibly *Vori Vori*. The hour for the midday meal drew closer, and she began to panic. One did not mess with Paraguayan President Don Carlos Antonio López's food. Thinking fast, the *machu* grabbed an iron pan, poured in the mixture, and thrust the pan into a *tatakua*, a native clay-and-adobe oven. Naturally, with so much cornmeal, the dish came out more like cornbread than soup. There was nothing to be done but to serve the mistake to Don Carlos, who loved it and christened it "*Sopa Paraguaya*."

That day, I learned more than the women who gathered to supposedly learn something from the foreigner.

What looks good on paper often ends up lost in translation.

Sopa Paraguaya

½ cup vegetable oil

4 medium white onions, finely chopped

Fine sea salt, to taste

Freshly ground black pepper, to taste

4 large eggs

2½ cups fine cornmeal

2 cups whole milk

12 ounces grated *queso fresco**

Preheat oven to 350°F. Grease a 2-quart terracotta or another baking dish. Heat oil in a heavy cast-iron skillet and sauté onions in oil until translucent. Season with sea salt and black pepper. Beat eggs in a large mixing bowl until foamy. Stir in cornmeal, then mix in onions and milk. Add cheese, blend in well. Scrape batter into prepared baking dish. Bake for 30–40 minutes or until surface is golden brown and a cake tester comes out clean. Cool and serve. *Use 8 ounces shredded mozzarella and 4 ounces grated Parmesan instead of *queso fresco* if necessary. Serves 6.

Exterior and interior of author's shack in Fram, Paraguay

Strawberries, Strudel, and Stroessner's Nazis

There was no reason for a revolution in Paraguay.
~ Alfredo Stroessner

The whipped cream tickled my nose as I scooped it off the top of the strawberries. And not just any strawberries. Lido Bar strawberries. *Fresas con Chantilly.*

Lido Bars nestle on narrow streets and wide avenues throughout the world, true.

This one straddled a corner in downtown Asunción, Paraguay. The last place I expected to find golf-ball-sized strawberries, tooth-stinging sweet. Much later, I learned that strawberries started as a cash crop in Paraguay in the 1920s, brought there by enterprising farmers in the region around Areguá.

A long, curved bar covered with worn Formica undulated snakelike from one side of the Lido to the other, red vinyl-covered stools propped close to each other. Fantastic when Mike snuggled against me, not so when it was some *macho* guy putting the moves on me.

Homesick Peace Corps volunteers bellied up to that bar whenever they converged on Asunción for their monthly mail call, hot showers, gathering with others nostalgic for Grandma's strawberry shortcake or strawberry glacé pie.

I dipped my spoon into the cream and took a long, slow bite, dragging out the experience for as long as possible. Touching home with my tongue. Dreaming of strawberry shortcake on a hot July afternoon, sitting on the porch back home, watching robins dipping their beaks in the water in the ugly cement birdbath, then fluffing their red chest feathers. Little *machos*.

Another treat with whipped cream, strudel, could be found in the Bavaria, a small German beer hall, where great wooden barrels filled with foamy beer reminded the owners and many of their customers of their homeland. Their Nazi homeland.

The German presence in Paraguay happened in two waves, the first with

Nueva Alemania in the 1880s, as Germans sought to create an Aryan colony. The second wave included Nazis fleeing their homeland after Germany lost the Second World War in 1945. Conveniently for them, Paraguay's president at the time or better said dictator, Alfredo Stroessner, was the son of a German immigrant from Bavaria who married into a wealthy Paraguayan family. He ruled with an iron fist, aided by a network of informers. His reach was long and pervasive.

Under Stroessner's rule, pedestrians needed to pay attention to what side of the street they walked on because military zones popped up everywhere in the capital. Rumor had it that if martial music filled the air, someone was being tortured in the building.

So naturally, German food and beer abounded in Asunción, a town with one stoplight. Relying on the advice of the Peace Corps doctor's wife, a true epicure, I sought out the Bavaria on a warm October afternoon, a perfect day for drinking beer.

The heavy wooden door stood open, allowing air to circulate from the cooler interior, a courtyard filled with flowering plants, mostly pink and red petunias, their faint perfume scenting the warm air. Off to one side, two fiftyish hefty blond women, chattering nonstop in German, rolled out paper-thin strudel dough. Plates of the cooked delicacy arrived with a cup or two of whipped cream burying the crispy strudel and soft pillowy apples bathed in sugar and cinnamon.

Back then, I was hungry all the time, so after the strudel, I usually asked for a menu and ordered a pint of beer, the head on it so stiff and strong that with one sip, I'd look like a female Santa Claus. Or at least my upper lip did.

Sometimes the owners would treat my fellow volunteers and me to pork knuckle (*Schweinshaxe*), a German specialty born in Bavaria's capital city, Munich. Rubbed with caraway seed, black pepper, and salt, the knuckles arrived at the table crispy and crunchy on the outside, thanks to the thick fat encasing the meat, but steaming and tender on the inside. Often the knuckles seemed larger than our heads, making for photo ops filled with the hilarity of youth.

Occasionally, a bunch of us headed to the Alemania, another mecca for substantial German food in Asunción. It was there that reality set in, from the first time the spiff tuxedoed maître d' clicked his heels and led us to our table. I always expected his right arm to shoot into the air with a "Heil Hitler" spewing from his lips. But that never happened.

There was every reason for revolution in Paraguay, given General Stroessner's iron-fist rule and sheltering of Nazis.

Strawberries with Whipped Cream

4 cups fresh strawberries, washed, hulled, sliced into thick slices, mixed with 2 tablespoons granulated sugar

2 cups heavy whipping cream, whipped into stiff peaks, flavored with 2 tablespoons of powdered sugar and ½ teaspoon pure vanilla extract

Place 1 cup of strawberries into each of four large dessert bowls. Top with ¼ of the whipped cream. Serves 4.

The Peace Corps guys at Kathy R.'s (Mike is second from right)

Carne Asada is Barbacoa

Beef eating is a bit like a national sport in Argentina.
~ Lauren Salkeld

I woke late the morning of the ferry crossing.

Still half-asleep, I nearly missed seeing the small wooden fishing boats and swooping seagulls as the boat steamed across the Paraná River between Encarnación on the Paraguayan side and Posadas on the Argentine side. Rolling green hills banked the river. Bands of crimson dirt roads crisscrossed those green hills. Ferries provided the sole way to pass from one country to the other, and they carried everything, from people to railroad cars. The Paraná served as a major highway in another way, stretching over 4,000 kilometers through Brazil, Paraguay, and Argentina, eventually emptying into the Atlantic, giving landlocked Paraguay a watery route to the broader world.

In contrast to sleepy, gritty Encarnación, Posadas was a large town, percolating with a lot more hustle and bustle than her sister city on the other side of the river. The cool air, thick with charcoal smoke and the aroma of beef grilling over subdued coals, woke up my appetite. The seagulls' cawing grew more strident as we closed in on land. Passengers tossed bread to them, which some of the birds caught in midair.

It must have been a major holiday, but I don't remember what the Argentines celebrated that day. But celebrating they were. My friend Kathy R. knew everyone worth knowing, even those not so much, and she had invited me to join her at the *finca* of a wealthy cattle baron. A sleek black car and uniformed driver met us when the ferry docked.

After driving miles into the Argentine countryside, the driver pulled into a field lined with red flowering flame trees. Smoke tumbled through the air, reaching toward the blue sky, the pattern of it reminding me of women's lacy mantillas worn at Mass.

Kathy and I walked toward the source of the smoke. A spit.

We edged closer to the spit where an enormous beef carcass, or part of one, slowly turned, over a pit of glowing embers, now skeletons of large trees. A man broke away from the crowd.

"Kathy, Kathy, *bienvenida*, welcome! This must be your friend," he said as he grasped my hand and barely touched his lips to my skin. "Come, come, we are going to feast now!"

Before we lined up for the meat, French fries, and salad, a priest took his place in front of the charred corpse. Intoning a blessing, he raised his arms to the cloudless sky and crossed himself, as did everyone else but me. I wasn't Catholic then.

As the last hand pulled away from the last chest, the crowd lunged toward the meat. The pitmasters cut off chunks of steaming flesh, plopping them onto wide white plates. Some pieces were larger than others. But even without a table and a chair, eaters could easily get by just using their forks, because the meat was so tender.

One of the women helpers placed a dollop of a greenish sauce on my plate. It glinted in the sunlight as I dipped my fork into it. Tentatively, I touched a bit to my tongue. A mixture of parsley, acid, and olive oil, I determined, with just a smidgen of hot pepper.

Kathy caught me taste-testing the sauce.

"That's *chimichurri*," she explained as she dipped a hunk of meat in her share of the sauce.

I took my fork, speared a hunk of meat, dipped it in the *chimichurri*. Then I put the whole chunk of meat in my mouth. Where it lodged in my throat, despite my having chewed most of it.

It was going nowhere. Not down, not up. Nowhere.

I realized that I was choking to death. Literally.

Hoping to wash down the meat, I tried swallowing some beer from the amber bottle I'd set down on a fence post. Nothing happened. The beer spurted out of my mouth. Bug-eyed, I grunted at Kathy, who stood staring at me like a deer in headlights, speechless, frozen in place. A quick-thinking young man saw me and bounded over, smacked me hard on my back. The chunk of partially chewed meat flew into the air and landed on the ground, where a hungry dog wolfed it down with a gulp or two.

Shaking, I sat in a chair the young man brought over to me.

I whispered to him, "You saved my life, you did. Thank you!"

"I know," he said, "no problem," and sauntered off to meet with his friends.

The rest of the day passed in a blur, more like a film with romantic pastoral scenery, edged by the red of the flame trees and a babbling creek reflecting the blue sky.

Back in Paraguay, I hailed a small taxi in front of Kathy's house, to the bus station, nothing more than an empty parking-lot-size field of red mud. There I caught a bus back to Fram, grateful to be breathing. Even the relentless blaring of tinny Paraguayan polka was music to my ears.

I was alive. Thanks to a stranger.

Chimichurri, a Take-Off on Italian Salsa Verde

1½ cups fresh flat-leaf parsley

½ cup fresh cilantro

1 teaspoon dried oregano

½ small red onion or small shallot

3 garlic cloves

3 tablespoons red wine vinegar

2 tablespoons fresh lemon juice

1 teaspoon fine sea salt

¼ teaspoon red pepper flakes, or to taste

¾ cup extra virgin olive oil

Mix in a blender, store in an airtight container. Sauce stays fresh for 5 days in refrigerator. Can be frozen for 1 month or so. Serve with grilled meats or fish. Also good stirred into plain cooked pasta, topped with grated Parmesan. Makes about 2 cups.

Doughnuts

The three top reasons why someone would need a Farm Journal *cookbook are: 1. they contain recipes that are tested over time and may go back over one hundred years; 2. they make wonderful gifts for people at Christmas and birthdays; 3.* Farm Journal *cookbooks are a form of this country's nostalgic past.*

~ Speedy Publishing

The miller poured the flour into a paper bag. He'd ground it to order, a mere two pounds, a favor to me, the *Norteamericana*. Usually, he told me, he ground many kilos at once, for the farmers and others who lived too far away for the smaller weekly orders like my landlady's. I inhaled the nutty aroma from the freshly ground wheat kernels, surprised that wheat smelled like anything. I was only used to the sterile white, basically dead bleached all-purpose flour sold in Safeways and Piggly-Wigglys back home in the United States.

In Fram, a cook's only option for flour depended upon the whims of the local miller.

I waved goodbye as I set out for my next ingredient, yeast.

That morning, I'd decided to try to make doughnuts.

Late the night before, I rummaged through the footlocker of paperbacks assigned to each Peace Corps volunteer and found a worn copy of Farm Journal's *Country Cookbook*. Leafing through it, homesickness creeping through me, I stopped at the recipe for glazed doughnuts.

"I could make that," I told myself, despite having no kitchen in the two-room shack I rented from the mechanical dentist in town.

The shack abutted his cinder block, stucco-coated house. I often heard the whirring of his foot-operated drill, plumbing the buccal depths of some poor suffering soul. Thus, giving concrete meaning to the "mechanical" part of his title.

When I first arrived in country, I wanted to cook my own food. However, I soon realized that I would not be able to work all day and feed myself simultaneously.

It had nothing to do with Fram's not being connected to Paraguay's sparse electrical grid. I owned a two-burner table-top propane stove and a set of blue-enameled pots, plus a couple of plates, four forks, and two cups. As I found out preparing to make the doughnuts, shopping for food took the better part of a day. That's why, right after I arrived in Fram on that rainy, muddy day, I knew I needed to board someplace. That, and the fact Peace Corps forbade single women in the *campo* from staying alone. Which explained my living situation with the family of the mechanical dentist.

As for the doughnuts, after walking through the red mud in Fram's unpaved roads, I bought yeast from the local brewer, as well as some sugar. Oil emanated from a merchant selling soybean oil.

Back in my shack, I mixed up the dough and let it rise, then cut it into circles with two empty tin cans, making doughnut holes with an old tomato paste can. I fried the doughnuts, leaving them to cool on torn brown-paper bags, then glazed them. Piling the still-warm treats on a platter I borrowed from the dentist's wife, I first shared some with her and her two children. Then I stepped carefully through the mud, avoiding the pesky goose on the corner near the office, and shared the bounty with my boss and my boyfriend, Mike.

Word got around, so I fried doughnuts fairly regularly for people I knew in the village.

That probably was the only legacy I left.

Glazed Doughnuts

2¼ teaspoons active dry yeast (1 packet)

¼ cup lukewarm water

1½ cups warm whole milk

½ cup (1 stick) unsalted butter, cut into small cubes, softened

6 tablespoons granulated sugar

3 large eggs at room temperature

5-5½ cups all-purpose flour

1 teaspoon fine sea salt

3 cups powdered sugar

1 teaspoon pure vanilla extract

3–5 tablespoons whole milk

Oil for frying

Dissolve yeast in warm water in a small bowl. Mix warm milk, sugar, and eggs in a large bowl with a hand mixer. Stir in flour and salt. Beat together. Use a stand mixer or a food processor if you prefer. Scrape bottom and sides of bowl occasionally with a rubber spatula. Beat dough until it becomes smooth, about 5–7 minutes. Turn dough–it will be sticky–out onto floured work surface, knead for 5–6 minutes, making a smooth round ball. Put dough into greased mixing bowl, cover bowl with damp kitchen towel. Let dough rise in a warm spot until doubled in size, about 1–1½ hours. Turn dough out onto a lightly floured work surface, knead again for a few minutes. Turn back into greased bowl to rise until doubled, about 1 hour. Meanwhile, mix glaze ingredients.

Line a baking sheet with wax paper, set aside. Turn dough out onto lightly floured surface. With rolling pin, roll dough to about ½-inch thickness. Lightly flour a 3½-inch doughnut cutter, cut out doughnuts, placing them onto prepared baking sheet. Let rise for 1 hour, or until doubled in size. Save doughnut holes. Line another baking sheet with several layers of paper towels, set aside. In a large deep cast-iron skillet, add about 3-inches of oil. Heat to 375°F. Or use a Fry Daddy. Drop about 4 doughnuts into oil, making sure not to overcrowd the pan. Fry for 1–2 minutes per side, or until lightly golden brown. Remove doughnuts from oil, drain on paper towels. Let cool slightly before dipping tops in glaze. Let drip dry on a rack, placed over a parchment-lined baking sheet. Repeat with all doughnuts and doughnut holes, too. Makes about 18 3½-inch doughnuts, plus doughnut holes.

Pollo Rico

Everyone loves fried chicken. Don't ever make it. Ever.
Buy it from a place that makes good fried chicken.

~ Nora Ephron

"Complete unmitigated disaster" read the none-too-subtle rejection letter from the editor of Braniff's airline magazine. He was, of course, referring to Mom's pitch for an article about her trip to South America, the one she'd made to visit me in Paraguay.

I could vouch for that verdict: it *was* an unmitigated disaster of the highest caliber.

Naively, Mom didn't make any reservations for the entire three-week trip around South America. Open-ended plane tickets, yes, but nothing else. In the days before the internet, well, it was indeed naïve and foolish.

Things went reasonably well in Lima, Peru, where Mom flew in with my sister Paula to meet me. I'd been staying at the Riviera Hotel downtown, so with three more nights until we needed to check out, everything seemed normal, with no premonitions or other warnings of what was to come.

Once we arranged to fly from Lima to Cusco, a sense of adventure ignited our mood.

The grey granite of Cusco, ubiquitous in the walls and streets, lent that Andean city a somber air as a taxi driver drove us to a hotel, the best in town, he assured us. At last, he stopped in front of a stately colonial-style building, complete with arches and a heavy carved wooden door. We lugged our too-heavy, too-packed, too-big suitcases up the steps of the Hotel de Turistas, near Cusco's *Centro Histórico*.

When the concierge said, "*No hay*" in response to our request for a room, politely, but firmly, Paula sobbed, loud body-shaking, embarrassing sobs, cries that filled the lobby and reached the ears of the proper guests drinking coffee there. Worried about having to sleep on the street or worse, Paula couldn't take it anymore.

Seeing Paula sobbing, the concierge relented, rewarding us with a room on the second floor with three beds, bright with sunlight and bedspreads of woven alpaca fur, every hue of a painter's color wheel.

The sunrise in the morning over the ruins of Sacsaywamán to the north enchanted us. Typical of the Spanish conquerors, who invaded and subdued the Inca Empire in 1526, granite stones plundered from Sacsaywamán were used to build the cathedral and many walls in Cusco, including one on the north side of the hotel. The precisely cut stones fit together like a hand in a glove, perfect jigsaw puzzles created by talented indigenous stonemasons and skilled artists.

On a walk early the second day, as we moved along a narrow street near the hotel, we spied a native woman squatting nearby, leaning against a finely patterned wall of ancient stones, her voluminous skirts the color of rainbows. Soon a trickle of urine rolled toward us. Then, with a flash of her braids, she stood and walked up the sloping street, the large basket on her head wobbling with every step.

Not too far from where the lady did her business, we found a cheap, clean, and delicious place to eat.

Housed in a modern, white-stucco building, its trim the yellow of chicken feet, *El Pollo Rico* at first didn't inspire a lot of confidence in me. Concerned as I was about food poisoning and other sundry maladies so easily contracted when clean water was not the norm, I hesitated for a moment at the doorway. Formica-covered 1950s-style metal tables filled the small dining room, flanked by steamy floor-to-ceiling windows.

But the food smelled delicious!

Plastic baskets heaped with fried chicken arrived at the table. The cooks seasoned chicken with a tantalizing mixture of spices overlaying the crispy golden skin, tender meat underneath. With French fries and a Coke, the total cost of the meal came to $1.00 per person. And for Mom, ever the penny-pinching credit-card hater, that was good enough for her. We ate at *El Pollo Rico* at least once a day during our stay. And the people who worked there even packed us boxed lunches to take on our trip to Machu Picchu, too. It wasn't the Colonel's KFC, but it reminded me of the States.

I sorely needed a taste of home, I guess.

Peruvian Roasted Dry Mix for Fried Chicken

1 tablespoon powdered garlic

2 tablespoons kosher salt

4 teaspoons paprika

¼ teaspoon cayenne

2 teaspoons freshly ground black pepper

2 tablespoons ground cumin

2 teaspoons dried oregano

4 teaspoons sugar

6 chicken thighs

Vegetable oil

Preheat oven to 425°F. Grease a heavy baking sheet with shortening. Mix rub ingredients in a large deep bowl and set aside. Place chicken pieces in another deep metal or glass bowl, drizzle oil over them. Make sure to cover chicken entirely with oil. Then season each piece of chicken as evenly as possible with a bit of rub by sprinkling chicken with the rub until well coated all over. Place chicken on baking sheet, skin side down. Bake for 40 minutes. Halfway through cooking time, turn chicken. Serve with lots of piping hot French fries. Serves 3–4.

*Author and sister
Paula at
Machu Picchu*

Machu Picchu

Separating fact and fiction in Inca history is impossible, because virtually all the sources available are Spanish accounts of stories that had already been vetted by the Inca emperors to highlight their own heroic roles.

~ Mark Adams

The train lurched, a wild swing to the right, then left. Jagged green mountains rose through the white mist of the morning as the train chugged along the dual gauge track out of Cusco, Peru. Dedicated by Dr. Hiram Bingham, the "discoverer" of Machu Picchu, construction on the railroad began in 1913 and finished in 1948.

One of the most wondrous places on the planet, Machu Picchu represented a sacred world to the ancient Inca who built it, a pilgrimage site for the Tahuantinsuyo Empire to honor numerous deities, including Pachamama, the goddess of fertility and harvests. Rocks quarried nearby provided the stones for the vast ruins nestling atop the mountain, as well as for another site, Huayna Picchu.

At the Aguas Calientes station, a bus waited for people unable or unwilling to hike to the ruins. A gravel-topped road, a switchback, led to the ruins. There, alpacas and llamas ranged freely over the terraces and rubble of hundreds of walls and former houses, a city literally dead, filled with ghosts, which I was sure I would hear if I stayed there alone at night. I sat on a rock wall, my feet dangling over the edge, thinking that I'd never seen scenery so beautiful. Words failed me.

All too soon, the tour guides clapped their hands and called us back to the bus. Another dinner at El Pollo Rico, a night at the Turistas Hotel. We dreamed our way to the following morning when we boarded another train, this time headed across the high plains of the Altiplano, to Puno, Peru, on the shores of Lake Titicaca. Mom insisted she'd made reservations to cross the lake on a large ferry boat.

I took a seat on the left side of the train, facing the direction the train headed, and was rewarded with sights that I've never forgotten. Vast, flat land stretched like a yellow carpet, rolling all the way to the Andean foothills. Herds of llamas raced along the tracks, their white, beige, black fur flowing like locks of human hair as they whizzed through the cold, crisp air, their icy breath white in the sunlight.

The joy was short-lived. True to Mom's disastrous decision not to make reservations, no one stood at the train station in Puno with our last name written on a piece of cardboard.

Instead, lugging our enormous suitcases, we walked a mile in the dark cold until a kind family picked us up. Thanks to their concern for us, we ended up at the hotel where Mom thought we had a reservation. They'd never heard of us. Then, miraculously, the travel agent showed up for some reason—his office adjoined the lobby. He arranged for us to stay in a cheap guesthouse down the street from the train station, trying to smooth over the faux pas with promises of a delectable *desayuno* the following day, a breakfast fit for royalty. Tired, hungry, and cold, we mounted two flights of stairs to the room, the size of a walk-in closet. With one single bed and a thin sheet for a blanket.

Then another disaster struck. Altitude sickness overtook me.

Dulce de Leche

1 (14-ounces) can sweetened condensed milk

Preheat oven to 425°F. Open can and pour contents into a 9-inch glass pie pan. Cover pan tightly with heavy-duty aluminum foil. Then place pan in another, larger pan to create a water bath. Add water around the pie pan, about 1 inch. Bake for 1¾ hours, longer for a darker color, or better said, more caramelization. Cool and then transfer to a bowl. If lumpy, whisk. Use on croissants (*medialunas*, as they are called in Argentina), as frosting, or just plain *así no más!* Just like that. **Note**: There's another, easier way to do this. Remove the label from the can, submerge can in cold water in a tall stockpot, and bring water to a simmer. Let can simmer 2–3 hours. The longer can simmers, the darker the *Dulce de Leche* will be. Remove hot can carefully with tongs, place on a metal rack to cool completely. Open can when cooled. Store up to 1 week in refrigerator. That's it. Makes approximately 1 cup.

Coca Tea

There's always time for a nice cup of tea.
~ Mrs. Doyle

I turned over with a groan. Bright sunlight streaming through the window struck my eyes like tiny knives.

I was still alive. But I wasn't sure I wanted to be.

My stomach lurched suddenly. I dashed to the bathroom, with the expectation of vomiting for about the ninetieth time.

Being sick with altitude sickness was probably not all that unusual for foreigners passing through Puno, Peru. However, because we'd missed the trans-Lake Titicaca boat the night before, Mom, Paula, and I experienced one of the most hair-raising adventures of our lives. At that time, I had had many adventures, having lived in Mexico for six months and served half of my Peace Corps tour in Paraguay.

Emerging from the bathroom like a ghost from a crypt, I staggered over to the one twin bed in the room and flopped down into the fetal position, pulling the thin sheet up over myself and my coat. It was freezing cold. In fact, it was winter in South America. So there we were, three people crammed into one tiny room that had taken us forever to find the night before. Fortunately, all this took place long before *El Sendero Luminoso* appeared.

Mom and Paula slept on the floor, rolled in their coats, wearing all their warm clothes. Dressed in my warmest clothes and covered by a thin sheet, I spent the night in a delirious sleep, interspersed with recording-breaking sprints to hug the porcelain throne in the bathroom.

As bad as it was, it was still better than sleeping on the streets of Puno, which had seemed a real possibility after the fiasco with the boat.

All I remembered after that was the vague but frantic trip in the travel agent's car through the ancient winding streets of Puno, in search of lodgings. Stumbling up the stairs in the guesthouse where the travel agent dropped us, with one room available, I foggily recalled our dismay at the room and the decision that I, as the sick one, would sleep in the bed. As they say, the next thing I knew, it was morning.

Somehow, I got ready, unable to stand up or even sit up. Fearful thoughts raced through my mind as I dimly recalled that soon we were going to make the trip to La Paz via a hired taxi over the Altiplano on gravel roads. For ten hours.

Helped by Mom and Paula, I walked down the winding stairs to the guesthouse's dining room. The last thing on my mind was food. We sat at an empty table, nicely set with polished silverware, draped with a starched linen tablecloth. The waiter brought a lovely silver roll basket covered with a crisply starched linen napkin and filled with fresh cinnamon rolls. Quite a contrast from the disastrous room upstairs, to say the least.

Mom and Paula dug into the rolls, which were delicious apparently, smothered with white icing. Things I usually ate with abandon. But at that moment, I was a sick child. Mom urged food and hot, milk-laden coffee on me, rightfully saying that we had no idea when we would eat again.

I chewed a few bites of a roll before the gorge in my stomach rose in protest. My eyes darting left and right, I frantically searched for a bathroom. Spotting one, I dashed in and was violently ill again.

As I sat back down at the table, I felt the sickness engulf me once more, and there was no way I could make it back to the bathroom. Mom calmly removed the linen cloth covering the roll basket and stuck it under my mouth just in time. I quietly threw up the remains in my breakfast on top of all those lovely rolls. Mom just as calmly covered the vomit with the linen napkin. Laughing over the surprise awaiting the waiter when he picked off that linen napkin, Mom said it was time to go and get our gear, as the taxi would hopefully be waiting for us outside the guesthouse in ten minutes.

Following a blur of events, I ended up in the back of a battered taxi, my head lolling on the window, dimly aware that two young men about my age also shared the cab with us. Cheaper that way, according to Mom. We started off, leaving Puno behind, which was a step toward glory, in my opinion.

The endless nothingness that is the Andean Altiplano caught my attention from time to time whenever I opened my eyes and looked out the window. As long as I kept my head upright, my stomach stayed at an even keel.

When we got to the border with Bolivia, I could not get out of the car for the passport check. Mom took my passport inside and took care of the formalities. When she returned, she hinted that the men inside had had a good laugh over my passport because of the words "Peace Corps" inside the front cover. Oh yes, I told her, Bolivia recently ejected all Peace Corps volunteers for some reason. Maybe they'd been accused of spying. I couldn't remember. At that moment, I didn't care.

On we drove for endless hours over that gravel-roaded nothingness, avoiding sheer steep drops into crevices deeper than the Empire State Building was tall.

I recalled that the father of the Peace Corps doctor's wife, a missionary doctor in Bolivia, died going over one of those guardrail-deficient roadsides. From the number of trucks we met on the fettuccine-wide roads, I didn't doubt it. Although God played a very minor role in my days then, I thought about Him quite a bit that day. Majestic snow-covered mountains flanked plains and plateaus reaching into infinity, so it seemed. Even in my near delirium, the majesty of that desolate place impressed me.

Miraculously, we straggled into La Paz. Mom asked the cab driver to drop us off at a specific hotel. True to the previous pattern of our trip, no vacancy there. However, the concierge mentioned that a new luxury hotel had recently opened. Would we like to give it a shot? Luxury was something we were hungering for, so recklessly Mom said, "Yes!"

The concierge called another cab driver, who dropped us off at the Hotel Libertador, named for South American hero Simón Bolívar. There we found a lovely room and more. The Libertador's concierge immediately saw that I suffered from altitude sickness. He asked if we needed to eat and, if so, to please head to the dining room.

As I seated myself, a waiter placed a cup of pale green tea in front of me. The concierge explained it was coca-leaf tea that he served to many people with altitude sickness. At that point, I didn't care what it was, for I longed to get better. So I drank it, expecting some radical change in my mental capacity. Nothing happened. After a few sips of the tea, I was able to keep some soup down. Later that night, I downed another cup of coca-leaf tea.

The following day found me walking around in the thin air of La Paz with nary a problem, shopping in the markets for dried llama fetuses (essential for ensuring the good fortune of newly built houses), listening to Andean flute music in the evening, eating fried chicken and French fries. And anything else I could stuff into my mouth.

I was alive and glad of it!

Regarding coca-leaf tea, in my undergraduate studies of colonial Latin American history and nutrition, accounts proliferated about the effects of cocaine on the work capacity of the native people of the Andean region. From my brief and humbling experience, I understood for the first time that this drug was indeed a blessing for people living and laboring in such a harsh environment.

Indeed.

Coca Tea

1 teaspoon coca leaves, or 2–3 whole leaves

1 cup of water

1 teaspoon honey or brown sugar

Bring water to a boil. Add coca leaves to hot water, simmer for about 1 minute. Turn off heat, steep tea for 4–5 minutes. Strain tea into a cup, discarding leaves. Add sweetener, if desired. Serves 1.

The Pig

*Fortified by this far-from-subtle reminder to my spirit if not my liver,
I would head down one of the three alleys, sniffing my way
toward what smelled the best.*

~ M.F.K. Fisher

Screams woke me. I jerked back against the pillow, clutching the damp sheets with clenched fists. Had Señora Rodriguez gone off the deep end again? Was she lying face down in front of her stucco house, her elegant reddish-brown coiffure soaking in a matching puddle of terracotta-colored mud? It wouldn't be the first time that my landlady dropped her basket, as my paternal grandmother used to say about people who sometimes stumbled on the path of life.

Who didn't always get up.

Or maybe it was Gisella, the fourteen-year-old daughter, who snuck out at night under the window of my shack, giggling, shaking her long black hair, flashing her thick, sooty eyelashes at a boy. I was sure the boy had to be Eduardo, a drunk and a lout and a philanderer, very much like his father, the village mayor. Money and status talked no matter where in the world a person might be, it seemed.

Another scream, and I flailed at the mosquito net, kicking its limp ghostly folds away from the mattress. I pushed myself up, resting on my knees, and peered out the window, slowly. Ten or fifteen people circled an enormous pink sow, her swollen teats facing the blue sky, the chilly August air causing her breath to cloud up with each heaving pant. Trussed to a jerry-rigged platform of sawhorses and plywood boards, the pig strained against the rough ropes. A flash of silver in the sunlight, a knife slid across her quivering throat, another scream, long and drawn out, ending with a gurgle and a short bark.

Death.

The pig convulsed. My first experience with death up close. That was it. Quick. But not without trauma.

I slipped backward, my knees shaking so badly that I ended up on the wood-planked floor of my ramshackle shack, in a prayer pose, forehead pressing on one of the buttons holding the lumpy mattress together. After about ten minutes, sounds of laughter and chattering stirred me enough to finally move away from the bed. Off came my lace-trimmed baby-doll nightgown, robin's-egg blue, which one of the Anitas stole from my laundry when I lived in Doña Olga's *pensión*. On went a white long-sleeve blouse and beige skirt. Next, a brown corduroy blazer, wide wale, and then I was ready to face the morning. And death.

The pig was not a pig anymore. She lay in pieces, an "it" now, just a thing. A haunch there, intestines swimming in a cauldron of steaming water here. Blood everywhere, a vat of it, sloshing around in a metal bucket at the side of the table. The men drank beer, lots of it, from the slurring I heard. The women sipped thick red wine that arrived in barrels once a month, from Argentina, across the border.

I stopped near the well behind my shack.

Señora Rodriguez saw me. I raised my hand in a hesitant greeting. She picked out a lemon-sized piece of fried pork fat and handed it to me, dousing it first with a heavy sprinkling of coarse salt. Silence fell as everyone, from the priest to Gisella, stared at me. I sensed immediately that this fat also symbolized something akin to communion. The meat lying before me would feed many people in the year to come.

I bit into the sizzling hot piece of pork. Fanning my mouth, grease rolling down my chin, I chewed.

From death comes life.

Butifarra Sausage

5 pounds boneless pork shoulder, cut into chunks

1 tablespoon plus 2 teaspoons fine sea salt

1 tablespoon finely ground pepper, or to taste

1 teaspoon freshly ground allspice

¼ cup chilled sherry or Merlot

¼ cup ice water

Mix meat with salt, let sit covered overnight in refrigerator. The next day, mix black pepper and allspice with meat chunks. Grind to a medium grind. If meat is gristly, grind again. Place meat in freezer, until it is almost frozen but not quite. Add sherry/wine and cold water. Knead meat for a minute or two, until everything coalesces into a moist and sticky ball. From this stage, make links, if preferred. Patties work, too, and are far easier. Fry a sample, add more spice if need be. Makes 4 pounds.

Bus terminal in Encarnación

Goosed

I'm scared of the geese. When I was five, my mom took me down there to feed those horrible beasts and one of them nearly took my hand off.
~ Leah Rae Miller

Silly goose.

That thought ran through my mind the second I rounded the corner and glimpsed the enormous white goose preening her massive wing feathers.

Time seemed not to matter to her.

Every daybreak, her beak, the size of a boxing glove, transformed into a weapon. She and I dueled, like two dandies in a Jane Austen novel, I with my booted feet and a willow switch, she with what nature endowed her. A beak to end all beaks.

Silly goose.

I taunted her as I hurried to the office where I worked as a home economics extension agent in Fram, Paraguay.

My tune soon changed as she launched her substantial bulk at me, taking aim at my bare legs with her massive beak. I ran. She followed me, nipping at my legs. Finally, I reached the village's main road, Fram's equivalent of two New York City blocks, desperate to escape the enraged goose. Panting, I turned to check where the creature was. About 100 feet away, I spotted bobbing tail feathers and a telltale waddle.

In Fram, the night stars twinkled, faint and obscure, hinting of other worlds in their loftiness. Without electricity, days there ended when dusk crept up from the horizon, swatting down the sun. One blessing about living without electricity was that once the sun set, time abounded, to think, to dream, to ponder the old days, to let the juices stew, gazing at the stars.

At night, after work, I strolled through the soft green grass, a makeshift road as it were, leading past the rundown house on the corner, dodging the empty trough, alert. The white goose nested nearby, full of dried corn and fresh water. She, too, settled into the day's rhythm.

The creature lay still as I passed on my way home. Her eyelids sinking, closing like window shades, she drifted toward sleep.

A squeak of a honk emerged from the sleepy fowl's orange beak.

Silly goose, I whispered.

But then I looked at myself, far from everything familiar to me. Chased by a crazy goose, living in a run-down wooden shack, teaching women how to cook.

Really, who was the silly goose?

Duck Fat Potatoes

4 tablespoons duck fat, or goose fat if available

2 large russet potatoes, peeled, cut into 1½-inch chunks, parboiled

Fine sea salt, to taste

Freshly ground black pepper

Preheat oven to 400°F. Heat fat in a heavy oven-proof skillet until smoking. Toss in the parboiled potato chunks, fry until beginning to turn golden brown. Stir so that fat coats all pieces of potato. Roast in oven until potatoes turn deep golden brown, about 25 minutes. Halfway through cooking time, turn potatoes. Serve with roasted meat. Serves 4.

XIII a

MICHIGAN AND WISCONSIN

Although Daddy's father had ties to Wisconsin, I'd never lived there prior to marrying Mike Bertelsen in Holmen, Wisconsin. After our marriage, he and I attended graduate school at the University of Wisconsin-River Falls. I later earned a Master's degree in Library Science at the University of Wisconsin-Milwaukee. Of course, family history, routine family visits, weddings, and funerals often brought me back to the state. Food always played a huge role, especially in Milwaukee, with all the specialty grocery stores and restaurants.

Winter Road

Meatballs

Miracles are like meatballs, because nobody can exactly agree on what they are made of, where they come from, or how often they should appear.

~ Daniel Handler

On a cold, dreary day in early November, the tiny commuter plane landed at the airport in La Crosse, Wisconsin. Mike stood behind the wire fence, a knit cap covering his blond hair, smoking a cigarette as I eased my way down the icy stairs of the plane, gripping the ropy railing. As soon as we hugged, he said, "Mom wants to meet you right away. So does Dad."

He'd just flown back home from Paraguay because his father Knute had suffered a serious stroke. His mother Ethel called Peace Corps, a part of the U.S. Department of State. Mike received the bad news via a telegram signed by Henry Kissinger, Secretary of State. I'd returned to the United States a few months earlier, pining away for Mike, counting the months until his Peace Corps tour would be up.

A cramped elevator chugged up to the third floor of St. Francis Hospital. When the doors creaked open, we turned right and walked down a long hallway, past room after room, where patients languished in their beds, some alone, some with family members crowded around.

At last, we reached Knute's room, painted dull olive green, as most hospitals were in those days. A crucifix hung on the wall over the head of the bed. He lay there, his enormous farmer's hands splayed out on the crisp white sheet tucked up to his armpits. He smiled at me, the lopsided grin of a stroke victim, as Ethel rushed over to hug me. Mike's brother Ron and his wife Jan waved hello.

At that moment, my life's trajectory changed.

New family, yes, but also new foods. Such as meatballs, lefse, and lutefisk.

I don't remember exactly the first time I ate meatballs, Norwegian-style. It was probably our wedding day, on a cold January afternoon.

After a simple ceremony in Mike's parents' house, we headed to Drugan's supper club in Holmen, Wisconsin.

I think I ate my first Norwegian meatballs there.

There's no difference between supper clubs when compared to other restaurants, but somehow the name "supper club" conjures up steaming pots of substantial soups and thick winter-busting stews. Visions of warm farmhouse kitchens, and a mother's nurturing embrace, that's what supper clubs like Drugan's promise. Drugan's dishes tasted homemade and played a significant role in introducing me to Norwegian customs and foods.

Food like meatballs and lefse and lutefisk.

After lefse, Norwegian flatbread made with potatoes (see page 187), my mother-in-law Ethel's favorite food was meatballs, with gravy and mashed potatoes, sided with carrots or green peas or corn. I cooked these meatballs for the last dinner I ever made for her, served with lefse, mashed potatoes, corn, peas, and a salad. She never did take much to salads. We dimmed the lights in her dining area, lit a candle, and talked about everything. Oh, and there were no meatballs left.

Even Nikki the toy poodle snagged a few.

Meatballs

2 tablespoons unsalted butter

¼ cup finely grated yellow onion

2 eggs

½ cup whole milk

1 cup all-purpose flour

1½ teaspoons fine sea salt

¼ teaspoon freshly ground black pepper

½ teaspoon ground allspice

Pinch of ground nutmeg

I pound ground beef

1 pound ground pork or Jimmy Dean sage sausage

¼ cup finely chopped flat-leaf parsley

Vegetable oil for frying

Gravy:

> 2 cups rich beef stock or water from simmering meatballs
>
> 5 tablespoons all-purpose flour
>
> Pinch of dried thyme leaves
>
> Fine sea salt and freshly ground black pepper, to taste

Sauté onion in butter until transparent. Mix remaining ingredients in a large bowl and add onion. Roll into golf-ball size. Brown meatballs in skillet or in oven (cook at 350°F for 25 minutes or until browned). Once all meatballs have browned, remove them from the skillet or baking sheet. Place them, and any drippings, in a large pan, add water to cover, simmer gently until tender, about ½ hour. Make gravy, then cook meatballs in gravy for 15 more minutes. Serve meatballs with lefse and mashed potatoes. Serves 6.

Bertelsen extended family (Author and Mike on the left, second row to the top)

Lefse

Ole is on his deathbed. One day he smells the aroma of fresh lefse coming from downstairs. So he summons up the last of his strength and drags himself downstairs. He's at the table reaching for the lefse when Lena slaps his hand and says, "Ole, that's for after the funeral."

~ Ole and Lena joke

My mother-in-law Ethel passed the plate heaped with soft flatbread the color of pale cream, except for random brown splotched, like freckles. Lefse reminded me of flour tortillas. But when I bit into one, wrapped around glistening gravy-soaked meatballs, I knew I was eating something quite different. And quite ancient.

Many traditional foods like lefse trace their origins back to Viking days. Out of necessity, people learned to salt, dry, and smoke their food for preservation over the toe-numbing winters.

Lefse is a thin, flat bread, beloved by Norwegian Americans at holiday times. But its origins reveal a sad and somber story. Behind the knobby brown flecks and the grooves cut by special lefse rolling pins lies an odyssey of poverty, exile, and longing for Norway, the home country.

Women used to gather in Norway to prepare enough lefse to last for a year. Dried and stored in wooden barrels filling the *stabbur* or wooden storehouse, this lefse—called Hardanger—consisted of various flours and liquid ingredients. Potatoes didn't appear in lefse until the mid-1700s. Hardanger lefse became edible only by wetting and warming it slightly. Resembling hardtack eaten by sailors and soldiers at the time, lefse provided a crucial addition to the meager diet of Norwegian peasants and, later, of immigrants to the United States. In the early days of mass immigration in the late 1840s, a woman's worth could be measured by the thinness and lightness of her lefse, not her figure.

I used to worry that the lefse we ordered from Wisconsin for holiday dinners might go bad because the vendor only offered a two-day and three-day shipping service. When I learned women in the Old Country made lefse for an entire year at one fell swoop, I realized that a day here or there would hardly make a difference.

What more can I say about lefse? It's hard to make—it takes two to tango, so to speak—but is it ever worth it. Ethel owned all the equipment to make lefse, including the ricer, a cumbersome tool but guaranteed to remove all the bumps and lumps in the cooked potatoes. She and other family members began a tradition, making lefse every year for Thanksgiving and Christmas. For best results, make the dough—without the flour (add flour the day of baking)—before rolling and cooking it. The process flows more quickly when two people work together. Hence the tango.

That day, the lefse at Ethel's table came not from her rolling pin, but rather from the local grocery store run by her younger sister Gwen's husband Bill. Later, I learned to make lefse on my own, with a few hints from my sister-in-law Kay. Making lefse can't be done well without the right equipment. "Many hands make short work." Hands count as necessary lefse-making equipment. At least four will do.

Two to roll and two to cook.

A true community endeavor.

A symbol of community. And of endurance.

Lefse (Norwegian Potato Flatbread)

4 cups peeled, cooked, drained, and riced russet potatoes

4 tablespoons unsalted butter

½ cup heavy whipping cream

1 teaspoon granulated sugar

1 teaspoon fine sea salt

1½ cups all-purpose flour

Make sure potatoes are almost dry, by leaving them—drained—in the saucepan after turning off the heat. Stir occasionally until as much moisture as possible evaporates. Rice the potatoes. Place riced potatoes in a large bowl and beat in butter, cream, sugar, and salt. Cover bowl tightly with plastic wrap or foil and refrigerate overnight. When ready to finish the process the next day, stir in flour until well blended. Divide dough into 20 portions. Heat griddle to 400°F. On floured board, roll lefse with grooved rolling pin until almost paper-thin and about 10–12 inches in diameter. Bake on griddle until light brown spots appear on one side, flip, and briefly cook other side. Stack cooked lefse between waxed paper. Serve lefse, buttered, with meatballs or roast turkey. To freeze, fold lefse into quarters, stack, wrap well in plastic wrap, and place in freezer bags. Makes 20 lefse.

Wedding Day!

Lutefisk

Lutefisk: The piece of cod that passeth all understanding.
~ Norwegian joke

My mother-in-law Ethel grew up on a farm in western Wisconsin. She survived the flu epidemic of 1918, though her father Bernard caught it in his early thirties and lost all his hair. Life on a farm was no walk in the park, not hobby farming in the least. Farming demanded all hands pitch in. Ethel cooked most of her family's meals on a wood stove starting at an incredibly young age because her mother Ella suffered from severe asthma and couldn't do much. No electricity, no indoor plumbing, no central heating. The chill of Wisconsin winters in those days could crisp a person's nose hairs in seconds.

Unlike many Norwegians or those of Norwegian descent, Ethel hated fish. She grimaced at the mention of lutefisk, punctuated with "Ugh." Her dislike of fish eventually extended to the more luxurious varieties of sea life, such as shrimp and lobster. Once, when she visited us in Cedar Key, I treated her to lunch at a seafood restaurant overlooking the Gulf of Mexico. I mean, that is the real reason to be in Cedar Key, Florida! Unless deep-sea fishing for marlin fit on the agenda.

We sat on the balcony, balmy Gulf of Mexico breezes gently blowing through our hair, anticipating huge bowls of peel-and-eat 'em cooked shrimp. With the first bite, that familiar grimace appeared.

Ethel exclaimed, "It's off."

"No, no," I replied. "That's the way shrimp is supposed to taste," I insisted. Then I bit into one of the shrimp on her plate.

By golly, she *was* right. The shrimp *was* off.

A lingering ammonia flavor clung to our palates, and no amount of water could mask it. Despite the embarrassed ministerings of the restaurant owner, plying Ethel with new plates of fresh shrimp, nothing doing—no more shrimp was going down her throat!

My first taste of lutefisk turned out to be no more pleasant than Ethel's

189

shrimp. It was at a church supper on a cold December day. A rank fishy odor permeated the air in the church's basement. After singing the traditional meal prayer and blessing, everyone lined up, tapping their plates impatiently against their thighs or free hands. When I approached the woman serving the lutefisk, I nodded "yes" when she asked if I wanted extra melted butter. Mike told me the palatability of lutefisk improved with lots of it. I also asked for meatballs, as insurance against the lutefisk being inedible. I grabbed at least a dozen napkins, to be prepared.

I found a seat at one of the long tables, set my plate down, made sure I had a big glass of lemonade to swish my mouth with, and dug in. One bite and I was glad for the napkins. Into one went the half-chewed bite of fish, the rest covering the remains of the uneaten fish. I ate the meatballs and swigged some lemonade. Then, nonchalantly, I ambled over to the trash cans by the backdoor and scraped both napkins and fish as fast as I could into the barrels.

Since that day, I've thought a lot about how not all Norwegians included fish in their diets, popular tradition to the contrary. Ethel's Norwegian ancestors hailed from one of two landlocked regions of Norway, Hedmark. As a result, fish rarely appeared on their table. Especially not when they arrived in America in 1858. Most of those immigrants gravitated to the landlocked states of South Dakota, Minnesota, Wisconsin, and Iowa. Lutefisk, yes, but beyond that, very little fish, if any. Unless it came from nearby lakes or rivers.

Survival underlies the story behind lutefisk. At least it did in the beginning, when those first Norwegians arrived in America. But, as years passed, the dish became a nostalgic symbol of the Norwegian roots of settlers throughout the upper Midwest.

So what exactly is this stuff that Norwegian Americans swoon over and about which non-Norwegians say, "What the hey??"

Therein lurks a tale.

Over 855,000 Norwegians emigrated to the United States between 1820 and 1875. Most left because of the impossibility of farming Norway's mountainous, rocky soil. Only about 5,000 square miles of 125,000 could be put to the plow. Even then, huge boulders and rocks blocked the way. America's Homestead Act of 1862, meant to draw immigrants to populate the young country, encouraged many Norwegians to leave their homeland.

Social stratifications of Norway demanded the humiliating subservience of the poorer classes to the rich, something that few writers mentioned in their letters or diaries. As democratic movements sprang up like fairy rings after a summer rain—in Latin America, the United States, France—the peasants of Norway looked west and saw a way out. By sailing to America, they escaped the rigid feudal hierarchy of Old Europe.

And they brought lutefisk, immortalizing a poverty food that sustained them through bad harvests and arctic winters.

That sense of exile stayed with them for a long time.

Lutefisk

2 pounds prepared lutefisk

½ pound salted butter

Rinse fish thoroughly in cold water. Remove any scales. Cut fish into serving sizes. Since fish breaks apart during cooking, tie pieces into cheesecloth to maintain their shape. Place fish in cool salted water in a 5-quart saucepan. Bring to a boil. Cook approximately 10 minutes or until tender and translucent. Remove gently and serve with generous amounts of butter–to kill the taste, as Ethel would have said!

Christmas Cookies

I want to take all our best moments, put them in a jar, and take them out like cookies and savor each one of them forever.

~ Crystal Woods

Marrying into a family quite unlike my own charmed me. As did the culinary traditions handed down by my mother-in-law's two elderly aunts, Lillie and Helga. Both bakers of renown, both English speakers with discernible Norwegian accents, they'd come into the world with the sounds of that language all around them in that small Wisconsin town.

One winter day, it might have been February, the thermometer reaching 0°F if at all, I hiked through calf-deep snow to Aunt Helga's house. Helga stood at the door, a long silk dress of paisley fabric covering her slim body, her lively blue eyes twinkling, her long white hair drawn up into a sedate bun, every inch the proper lady, one with a huge heart. She reached out and hugged me. I breathed in a hint of perfume and fresh coffee perking away on her old white enamel stove. Behind her stood Lillie, sister to Helga's husband Carleton. Lillie once confided in me that she always felt upstaged by Helga's vibrant personality.

"Come, come," Helga gestured with her long, thin fingers, fingers which had for years rolled *krumkake* and pie dough and painted in the Rosemaling style, that most Norwegian of art forms. Plates and platters hung on the wall behind me, emblazoned in bold reds and greens and blues, trimmed with gold.

The two aunts perched at either end of a Victorian-era loveseat, while I sat on a stiff-backed chair, the colorful embroidered seat of which recalled a hard wooden pew in church.

They regaled me with stories of their early life as outsiders.

Born in Holmen, a Norwegian-American town in rural western Wisconsin, they told me that they didn't speak English until they attended the one-room schools prevalent in that area at the time. My husband Mike attended one of those schools much later, too. If the children breathed even a word of Norwegian at school, teachers smacked their hands with rulers and shamed them. Years later, as they relayed this to me in their Norwegian-accented English, I sensed their pain and humiliation.

They gifted me with handwritten recipe cards for krumkake, sugar cookies, and many other traditional Norwegian delicacies.

On December 23, "*lillejul*" or Little Christmas, Norwegian women cleaned house, baked, and scrubbed everything. Christmas food represented the very best of everything, whether from personal pride or as a sacred symbol of love for family and friends. Norwegian Christmas traditions dated to Viking days, when the Vikings celebrated *jól*. At this time, people sacrificed a hog and feasted on the meat. Farm animals traditionally received larger rations on Christmas Day, too.

Aunt Helga wrote down a recipe for making rosettes, but then said I could find the recipe and how to make rosettes on the box the rosette iron came in. That's probably the easiest way to learn, short of watching an expert like Helga making them.

I bit into cookie after cookie that day, admiring the sugar cookies most of all.

Whenever I baked Lillie's sugar cookies for the holidays in whatever kitchen I found myself in, memories of that snowy Wisconsin day surfaced.

I always whispered a silent "thank you" to Lillie and Helga, gone for many years, for their hospitality to me, a young stranger.

Aunt Lillie's Sugar Cookies

2 cups all-purpose flour

½ teaspoon cream of tartar

½ teaspoon baking soda

¼ teaspoon salt

½ cup unsalted butter, at room temperature

½ cup shortening, at room temperature

1 cup granulated sugar

1 egg

1 teaspoon pure vanilla extract

¼ teaspoon pure almond extract

Extra sugar for sprinkling on top

Preheat oven to 350°F. Sift dry ingredients together, set aside. Cream butter and sugar. Add egg, milk, and vanilla and almond extracts. Stir flour into creamed mixture. Mix well, until a soft dough forms. Chill in bowl in refrigerator about 1 hour, covered with plastic wrap. Make small balls of dough about the size of walnuts. Place on lightly greased cookie sheets about 2 inches apart. Using a flat-bottomed glass or another similar tool, grease the bottom lightly and then rub the glass bottom into a small plate of granulated sugar. Press down on each of the dough balls with sugared glass until the ball is about 1/8th of an inch thick. Take a fork, mark center of each cookie with tines, pressing down almost all the way to the cookie sheet itself. Sprinkle each cookie with granulated sugar. Bake for 8-10 minutes. Do not brown. Sprinkle cookies with extra sugar after removing from oven. Cool on racks until crisp. Freeze if desired. Makes about 2 dozen cookies.

~~~~~~~~~~

Aunt Lillie's Thumb-Cookies

¼ cup shortening

¼ cup unsalted butter

¼ cup brown sugar

1 egg yolk

½ teaspoon pure vanilla extract

1 cup all-purpose flour

¼ teaspoon fine sea salt

1 egg white

½ cup ground walnuts

½ cup of jam of your choice

Preheat oven to 350°F. Mix dough, roll into 1-inch balls. Roll in beaten egg white and then roll in walnuts to coat. Bake 5 minutes on greased baking sheet, remove from oven, make thumb imprint, fill hole with jam. Return to oven for 8 minutes. Cool on racks. Makes 24 cookies–this recipe can be doubled.

Windmill, Old Bertelsen farm

Spaghetti Mi Amore: Version 2

The simple tomato sauce is so cluttered with meatballs
you could stand the spoon up in the bowl.
~ Hannah Tunnicliffe

I climbed into the 1966 Oldsmobile, black and white and temperamental as a mule, the car whose pistons fused on a scouting trip to River Falls that Mike and I made in the dead of winter. And with no money for any emergencies and disasters that might befall us when we least expected it.

We struggled at first because we had no money for food for a few months either. At least not until payments came through from the assistantships we managed to finagle through the university. With the help of the U.S. government's Food Stamp program, we muddled through the first semester. When Mike's mom learned we were "living on the county," as she put it, she dug into her freezer and pressed packages of beef from their farm on us. She also packed a few jars of pickles and jam into a large box with the meat.

Now, headed to the one grocery store in that small Wisconsin town in that unreliable car, I clutched a small wad of bills in the pocket of my Navy pea coat, no match for the winter wind that day. But I owned no other wintery clothes.

Fifteen dollars, that's all we could spend on food each week. For that, I put up with a fussy, disorganized, and arrogant professor who never said "Please," "Thank you," or "Good job."

Fifteen dollars didn't go far.

Hamburger, spaghetti, tuna, rice, milk, corn flakes, frozen orange juice, white bread and bologna for sandwiches, laundry soap for the laundromat, shampoo and toothpaste, sanitary napkins. A six-pack of Red White & Blue beer for Friday nights. No fresh vegetables.

Spaghetti with peas on the side and garlic bread fed us that year. Since condensed tomato soup cost less than canned tomatoes or tomato sauce, I kept a half a dozen cans of soup on hand.

I cooked in a small kitchen the size of an average coat closet.

And that's what it probably was before the farmer and his wife remodeled the second floor of their house, on the outskirts of town, near a small river. The apartment suited us just fine. Large windows let in glorious light on sunny days in the living room, which was indeed the living room, as all living took place there. Upstairs in what had been the attic, we tossed a top mattress—no box spring—and slept on the floor, our few clothes hanging from hooks screwed into the beams like a dozen tiny dolls' arms.

What about the kitchen? Back to that.

A small four-burner electric stove with an oven just big enough to bake a pie in. Four shelves held our *batterie de cuisine*. A broom closet became a pantry for cases of canned vegetables from the Stokely Van Camp factory in Holmen—corn, green beans, and peas. A refrigerator with a small freezer at the top, where I swore more ice formed than outside the front door during a Wisconsin winter.

We ate at the flimsy card table that substituted for a dining table, a study desk at all other times. Poor in money, but not destitute in most other things. Fresh air, a purpose in life, and each other.

Spaghetti Mi Amore: Version 2

1 pound ground beef

1 tablespoon vegetable oil

½ small onion, finely chopped

1 garlic clove, peeled and chopped

2 (10.75 ounces) cans Campbell's Tomato Soup, do not add water

1 teaspoon Italian Seasoning

Salt and black pepper, to taste

Fry hamburger in oil until no longer pink. Add onion, fry until translucent. Stir in garlic, cook another 30 seconds. Pour in soup, season. Add water to desired thickness. Cover, let simmer 30 minutes. Meanwhile, cook one pound of spaghetti. Drain pasta. Top with sauce. Serve with green peas on the side and garlic bread. Serves 4.

Friday Fish Fry

*From 1920 to 1933, Prohibition prevented taverns from selling alcohol.
To keep customers coming to their businesses, Midwestern
tavern owners sold meals of fried fish.*

~ Culvers Restaurants

Like Ethel, I'd never much liked fish.

Shellfish? That's another matter.

But that changed somewhat when I first moved to Milwaukee for graduate school in library science. Because Fridays in that enormously Roman Catholic town meant fish fry at Turner Hall. Delicious fish fry, as a matter of fact.

Milwaukee's historic Turner Hall took its name from the German word "*Turnen,*" meaning gymnastics or physical fitness. Associated with the American Turners, a German-American athletic, cultural, and political association, Turner Hall symbolized "Friday fish fry" for me.

Most Fridays, we drove downtown for those fish dinners, intent on chugging some serious German lager, dipping our forks into hot bacon-studded potato salad, and biting into scalding hot fried cod fillets, an "all-you-can-eat" delight.

The Turner Hall fish fry recalled another fried fish I'd encountered in two unadulterated English places: London and Gibraltar.

Charing Cross, familiar to me because of Helene Hanff's *84, Charing Cross*. A book dealer and a spendthrift client and a series of letters … what could be more delightful? Hanff, a freelance writer, turned to a book shop in London in 1949 to send her books she couldn't find on the other side of the pond.

On a brief trip to London one December, shivering in a thin suede coat best suited for a warm spring day in Atlanta, I insisted on searching for that bookshop, Marks & Co. But no such book shop existed there anymore.

What there was, surrounding the Charing Cross tube station, were endless cheap eateries. Fish and chips shops. "Chippies," as the British called them.

The aroma of frying fish streamed into the cold, moist air. Like a cartoon character, I followed the scent with my nose until I stood in front of a steamed-up window, advertising Fish & Chips in bold black letters across the smudged glass.

I walked through the ramshackle door, tripping on the raised step covered with a stray patch of yellowed linoleum, originally white, coming undone. All but one table was empty. An older English couple, probably pensioners, sat at that lemon-yellow Formica table, she wearing a light green bandana over her greying hair, he bald and clutching a glowing cigarette in his left hand, a fork in his right. Both illuminated by the garish fluorescent lights above. The scene reminded me of Edward Hopper's painting, "Nighthawks."

We ordered at the cash register.

What appeared on the plate in front of me didn't match the aroma I'd chased in the street. The fish, soggy, gummy, the chips undercooked and raw-potato crunchy.

A few years went by. I forgot about Charing Cross and the dismal meal I'd eaten there.

On a trip back to Morocco, we detoured in Gibraltar. Climbing from the port area to the hotel we'd booked for the night, I noticed a small sign on a very narrow street, a terrace actually, advertising Fish & Chips. I ducked in, almost smashing my forehead on a low-lying wooden lintel. Since it was nearly no larger than a modern-day food truck, I almost walked out. But the owner enticed me with a bit of fried fish, like making friends with a stray dog or cat.

Oh my, sheer heaven burst in my mouth.

"I'll be back, I'll be back," I babbled.

That night, I led my family to my find. What delicate crisp batter, light melt-in-your-mouth fish, squirted with malt vinegar, crisp chips dipped in mayonnaise.

As I walked up the polished wooden stairs to the Turner Hall dining room and bar, I thought of Gibraltar. The fried fish, hash browns, coleslaw, horseradish sauce, and applesauce at Turner Hall were nothing like the English way with fried fish, which likely began thanks to Jewish immigrants in the nineteenth century.

But still, memory seemed brought me full circle, to a sense of home.

All it takes is one whiff. Then the memories flood in.

Batter for Fried Fish

1 (12-ounce bottle) of flat beer (open beer, pour into a bowl, let sit for at least an hour before mixing batter)

1 cup all-purpose flour, plus 2 tablespoons to thicken if necessary

¼ cup cornstarch

2 teaspoons baking powder, preferably aluminum-free

1 tablespoon fine sea salt

½ teaspoon freshly ground black pepper

Several dashes cayenne pepper or Louisiana-style hot sauce

Whisk flour slowly into beer–mixture will foam. Then add remaining ingredients. Let batter stand at room temperature for 1–2 hours. Mixture will thicken as it stands. Before using, whisk again to mix. Batter will be the consistency of heavy cream. **Note:** This batter stays crispy even after frying is done. Leftovers taste great, too. Makes about 2½ cups.

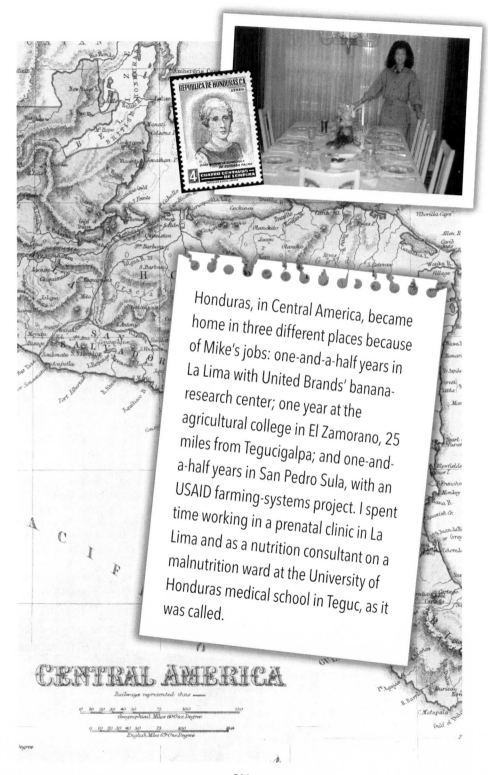

Honduras, in Central America, became home in three different places because of Mike's jobs: one-and-a-half years in La Lima with United Brands' banana-research center; one year at the agricultural college in El Zamorano, 25 miles from Tegucigalpa; and one-and-a-half years in San Pedro Sula, with an USAID farming-systems project. I spent time working in a prenatal clinic in La Lima and as a nutrition consultant on a malnutrition ward at the University of Honduras medical school in Teguc, as it was called.

Sign in Honduran Open-Air Market

By Way of Africa

… with a legion of cooks, and an army of slaves.
~ Lord Byron, "The Irish Avatar"

Christopher Columbus's voyages over 500 years ago created a collision of cultures, people, and foods on a scale never before seen in the history of mankind. Unfortunately, Columbus's "discovery" of America doomed thousands upon thousands of people yet unborn to become enslaved. Over the centuries, many millions of people worldwide gained economically and gastronomically, too, from those enslaved.

The fruits of Columbus's "discovery" soon showed up in the world's kitchens, from India to China to Europe to the Americas to Africa.

Consider the cooking traditions of those enslaved Africans whose traditions influenced the cooking of the Americas in many ways. Slavers, both African and European, wrenched people from the shores of West Africa, as Nora Neale Hurston wrote in *Barracoon: The Story of the Last "Black Cargo."*

In the Big Houses of plantations—be it in the islands of the Caribbean, Brazil, or the coastal plantations of Mississippi, South Carolina, Georgia, and Virginia—some cooking methods from Africa influenced some of the traditional European fare of the plantation owners. Seafood and rice dishes tend to predominate in this West African culinary heritage. Okra, peppers, *dendê* oil (palm oil), bananas, coconuts, rice, all these combined in the cooking pot. Huge black iron cauldrons stewed seafood *calaloos* (soups), fish stews, and shrimp gumbos. Fish fried in coconut oil, peanut oil, or lard, depending upon geography.

In the Caribbean, that taste of Africa still lingered, as I learned on my first trip to the northern coast of Honduras.

Chabelita's oceanside restaurant in La Ceiba looked like the last place on earth where a person accustomed to dining at Noma or Tavern on the Green would ever choose to eat. Double-screened entrance doors swung from rusty hinges, and neon-blue paint crinkled off walls. Neon-blue chairs, tables, walls, all assaulted the eyes. Two white wall fans the size of dinner plates swished at a tilt.

A smiling young waiter led us outside to the "dining room," a small thatch-roofed lean-to, where five other tables were already filled to capacity. The night, black as an obsidian blade, shrouded us as he lit two stubby white candles stuck precariously into two old wine bottles. The drip-drip of the candles kept time with the droning frogs hidden in the bushes. Candlelight flickered over the tattered, stained, simple menus.

There really was no choice.

Fried fish with French fries. The only dish on the menu.

Everyone knew that.

Soon the sound of laughter rose from behind the restaurant. Outside, a black iron cauldron the size of a whiskey barrel served as the kitchen, filled nearly to the brim with a mixture of red palm and coconut oils. Settled over a wood-charcoal fire, the pot gave off heady odors of hot oil and smoke combined with the aroma of salty sea air. Whole redfish, gutted and scaled, flung unceremoniously into the pot, floated in the oil, skin puffing, crackling. French fries gurgled in another pot. The cooks, all men of the Garifuna people, swatted at the fish with long metal hooks, turning them carefully, testing for doneness.

The Garifuna, shipwrecked or escaped enslaved people from West Africa, first settled in Roatán, one of the Bay Islands originally belonging to the British. Later, with Spanish support, the Garifuna moved on, to the mainland. Over 100,000 Garifuna settled on Honduras's northern coast in Tela, La Ceiba, and other cities.

After a long lull, the waiter laid a plate overflowing with fish and French fries in front of me. Crisp fish, eyes bulging with white frothiness, tart with lemon juice, sprinkled with salt, ready to eat. Tender moist meat hid under the crackling skin, rich with the taste of coconut, smelling of the sea. The sweet flesh melted like butter in my mouth, cutting through my hunger.

No one spoke. The mood in the lean-to turned languorous as a full tropical moon illuminated the cooks, living the traditions of their long-dead enslaved ancestors.

The heart of cooking lies not in dusty tomes, but rather in human souls. That's where true discoveries took place ... and hopefully, still do.

Fish in Coconut Sauce

Marinade:

> 1 garlic clove, mashed and minced
>
> 3 tablespoons lime juice
>
> ½ teaspoon dried oregano
>
> Freshly ground black pepper, to taste
>
> 2 pounds fish fillets, cod or another non-oily fish
>
> Flour for dredging

Sauce:

> ¼ cup peanut oil
>
> 3 garlic cloves, peeled and minced
>
> 1 medium yellow onion, chopped finely
>
> 1–2 hot green peppers, seeded and minced
>
> 1 bay leaf
>
> ¼ teaspoon dried oregano
>
> 2 cups coconut cream, not lite
>
> 2 tablespoons tomato paste
>
> Fine sea salt, to taste
>
> 1 tablespoon lime juice
>
> Whole lime, sliced paper-thin

Mix marinade ingredients, let sit for ½ hour. Strain, pour over fish in a glass baking dish. Marinate fish for 1 hour. Dry fish with paper towels, roll in flour, fry in hot oil until golden brown. Place fish on a warm plate. Set aside. Fry onion, garlic, and peppers in oil in same pan in which fish were cooked. Cook until onion is transparent and beginning to color. Add remaining ingredients, except for lime juice, cook for about 3–4 minutes. Stir in lime juice. Cook for another 3 minutes. Serve fish with sauce poured over the top, garnished with lime slices. Serves 6.

Fresh *Masa* and Pineapple *Chicha*

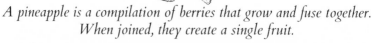

A pineapple is a compilation of berries that grow and fuse together.
When joined, they create a single fruit.

~ Suzy Kassem

To get to the *masa* seller's shack, I slogged along a narrow path of hardened mud, about twelve inches wide, bordered on both sides by deep watery ditches and tall scratchy grasses. Women often passed me, going the other way, back to their houses, large baskets balancing on their heads, the aroma of fresh *masa* or maize dough, seeping from the stained, clean cloths used to wrap it. One needed to balance quite often or otherwise fall into a ditch.

Elvira, the maid, usually went to get the *masa* because she knew exactly how much to buy for the day's tortillas. She'd pat them out by hand, clap-clap, whereas I needed a tortilla press, the knack of patting out *masa* somewhat beyond my skill set.

To cook the tortillas, I bought a pounded metal *comal*—a smooth, flat griddle—almost the first day I arrived in La Lima, the research branch of United Brands, formerly the United Fruit Company of such ill repute. Colonialism is a bad word these days, and it deserves to be. Still, my days in La Lima, Honduras, provided me with a whiff of a practice that'd been the norm ever since the Portuguese first set sail under the patronage of King Henry the Navigator.

Before I arrived in La Lima, I'd never employed a servant before. Mike and I were so poor we could hardly afford Comet to clean our one

Elvira

toilet in our apartment in Laramie, Wyoming. In fact, we could afford just one lone air conditioner for the house on stilts in La Lima. And that went in the small bedroom, where baby Erik's crib and our double bed filled the room.

Elvira's and my relationship evolved into one of parent and oldest/first child.

I don't recall how Elvira came to be the first maid I ever hired, but she wasn't the last. But, because she was the first, she stands out in my memories more than the others. Her main task was to clean the two-bedroom house assigned to us by the company.

Another of her tasks included babysitting Erik on the days I volunteered at the prenatal clinic at the company hospital nearby. Alison and Veronica, two English women, along with Ida, Honduran and married to an influential executive in the company, browbeat the hospital director into letting us use a stairwell on the first floor to do wellness checks for pregnant women who were either workers in the banana-packing plants or married to banana cutters. We checked blood pressure and other vitals regularly, something the male company doctors didn't bother with. And we dispensed nutrition and breastfeeding tips. Several women presented with pre-eclampsia, dangerous for both mother and baby. Fortunately, our clinic tagged them, and they received the care they needed. The stories these women told amazed me, some sad, some happy, and always poignant. One woman, age 29, arrived one day, her belly the size of two giant watermelons. Her intake chart read # of pregnancies: 12, # of live births: 12, # of live children: 12. And there she was, pregnant with twins.

One day, not long after I arrived in country, I bought a pineapple at the market in San Pedro Sula. It took twenty minutes to get to the market, driving in my unairconditioned pickup truck, windows opened wide, all the hot, sticky humid air causing me to sweat like a stevedore on the docks. By the time I pulled up to the market, the armpits, front and back of my robin's-egg-blue T-shirt dripped with perspiration, clinging to me, tight as a glove. People stared at me, obviously a foreigner, so I hurried along as fast as I could, ignoring the stares and smirks.

I pulled up to my house, wooden, painted white, on stilts for better airflow and cooling, such as that ever was in the torrid heat. Rigoberto, the gardener and Elvira's nephew, hurried to help me lug the straw shopping baskets filled with food up the stairs to the kitchen.

Elvira's eyes sparkled as she examined the pineapple.

"*Esta listo*," she remarked. "It's ready."

Since I did the cooking, I decided rice, beans, fried chicken, and corn tortillas would do for dinner that night, along with pineapple slices. When Elvira noticed me cutting up the pineapple, then tossing the skin, core, and other scraps into the garbage, she went berserk.

"¡No, no, no! Por favor. Para una bebida de piña," she told me, grabbing the pineapple pieces out of the garbage and putting them in the sink to rinse. "For a pineapple drink."

I handed her some aluminum foil, and she wrapped the pieces up like a mother swaddling her infant. Tucking the pineapple into her tote bag, she then proceeded to pat out tortillas, hands flashing, mouth smiling.

I gave the incident no more thought.

A few days later, I offered Elvira a ride home. I never knew how old she was, but her oldest granddaughter had turned ten a month before. I guessed Elvira to be around fifty. She probably was younger than that. She lived in company housing with her daughter and four grandchildren, because her daughter worked as a packer in the processing plant.

There, on the minuscule cement stoop serving as a porch for the dilapidated row houses, all topped with corrugated iron roofs, sat the remains of my pineapple, floating like a fetus in a large glass jar.

Elvira smiled, pointing.

"Chicha de piña."

It made sense to me. Something to drink with a bit of a kick to it, to take the edge off the days.

Waste not, want not.

Pineapple Chicha (Chicha de Piña)

Skins and core of 1 ripe pineapple, organic if possible, washed

3 tablespoons brown sugar, or to taste

2-3 quarts cold water

Combine all ingredients in a gallon glass container. Place container in the sun. Let it rest–covered with a thin, clean cloth–for two or three days, or until mixture begins to bubble and ferment. Strain and refrigerate. Serve with ice cubes. Makes approximately 3 quarts.

Plantains and *Tostones*

Plantain ripe, can't green again.
~ Jamaican Proverb

Votive candles in their tiny crystal glasses sparkled star-like as I climbed the long staircase to the Watsons' magnificent house. Like mine, it stood on stilts and glistened white in the moonlight that night.

The similarities ended there.

Dave Watson, a friend of Daddy's, headed *Química*, the research division at United Brands' banana plantation in La Lima, Honduras. Because of his position, the company assigned him the most opulent house in the expat compound. He and his wife Flossie threw memorable parties, including one when my parents visited us a few months after we arrived in La Lima.

Surrounded by nearly two acres of lush gardens only possible in the tropics, the white house rose high above the ground on stilts, flanked by two grand winding staircases on either side. French doors opened outwards, flaming citronella torches flared along the pebbled walkway around the curved driveway, where young men wearing well-pressed short-sleeved khaki shirts and matching shorts took charge of the guests' cars, parking them out of view.

Inside the house, twinkling white lights gleaming like night stars created a magical Cinderella-like atmosphere. A dozen maids in lacy white gowns, their hair wrapped in white headscarves, set overflowing trays of food on the long, gleaming mahogany table. Grilled beef, red beans swimming in a thick sauce flavored with garlic and *pimienta*, steaming white rice, and overly ripe yellow plantains baked with sour cream and creamy *quesillo*, dishes gobbled up by guests in a matter of minutes.

All the Honduran female guests lined up and filled plates for their men, then went back to serve themselves. When in Rome … .

Johnny Walker Red flowed like one of those chocolate fountains that became so popular later. At Christmas, every company employee from banana cutter to executive received a bottle of that liquid fire as a bonus.

But the most memorable part of the night was not the feeling of living in the colonial past.

It came in the form of crunchy-on-the-outside, but soft on the inside *tostones*, fried plantains chips. Sitting around a rustic wooden table, sipping beer, munching on too many *tostones*, listening to famed banana breeder Phil Rowe talking with Daddy about breeding bananas, everything seemed peaceful as the murmur of vices lulled me into a sense of oneness.

Suddenly Mom piped up out of the blue that bringing slavery back would solve so many problems in the modern world. A dead quiet hung over the table. I turned the color of Mom's poppy-red lipstick, wanting to sink into a hole, disappear into darkness.

No one said a word. Just silence. Then people stood and left.

Silence, a tool of shaming, shunning, and ostracism.

Creating the "Other."

Tostones

3 large green plantains

1-2 cups vegetable oil

Coarse sea salt, to taste

Peel plantains by making a vertical cut through the skin and peeling it back–doing this under running water makes it easier. Cut plantains into 1-inch-thick pieces. Soak plantains in heavily salted water until ready to cook. Dry in a thick kitchen towel before cooking, making sure to reserve the salty soaking water. Heat a 2-inch layer of oil in a heavy cast-iron pan or use a Fry Daddy or another fryer. Fry plantains in batches. When plantains begin turning light golden, remove from oil, place on a cutting board lined with paper towels. Smash each piece to about ¼ inch in thickness with a meat mallet. Put each piece in the reserved soaking water. Do not dry. Carefully shake off excess water, then put the wet pieces into the hot oil. Watch for spatters. Fry in batches in the oil again for an additional 4-5 minutes or until golden brown and crispy. Be sure not to get them too dark in color, more golden than brown. Place on paper towels when done. Sprinkle with coarse sea salt and serve immediately, dipped in a hot vinegary sauce. Serves 2-4.

Don Udo's Creamy *Jalapeños*

The only really good vegetable is Tabasco sauce. Put Tabasco sauce in everything.
Tabasco sauce is to bachelor cooking what forgiveness is to sin.
The next best vegetable is the jalapeño pepper.
It has the virtue of turning salads into practical jokes.

~ P.J. O'Rourke

Don Udo Van der Waag, a Dutchman, fell in love with the green mountains rich with jungle-like foliage surrounding San Pedro Sula. His eponymous restaurant started out as a casual bar where he scratched out the day's menu on a chalkboard. It soon became a restaurant frequented by wealthy local Hondurans and the growing expat community in northern Honduras.

Another Don, Don Pedro de Alvarado, founded San Pedro Sula on June 27, 1536. The original name was Villa de San Pedro de Puerto Caballos. Later renamed San Pedro Sula, from the Usula word meaning "valley of birds," the Spanish used the spot as a focal point for transferring goods from Nicaragua, El Salvador, and Guatemala to the coast at Puerto Cortés. However, persistent pirate attacks nearly destroyed that mission. The town, practically deserted by the nineteenth century, became a rural backwater until the 1920s. Then the United Fruit Company set up shop in La Lima and expanded their banana plantations, using Puerto Cortés as a hub for shipping out their bananas.

Don Udo's served dishes not to be found anywhere else in town, except maybe for the Hotel Maya Copán, and that was a stretch.

From the first moment I ambled through the gate into the verdant, leafy garden flanking the restaurant on three sides, the place enchanted me. High white stucco walls topped with embedded, shattered glass shards kept thieves and mischief-makers out.

Don Udo bounded over, arms outstretched. I thought he was going to envelop me with a paralyzing hug, pulling me to his grizzly-bear-like chest. But no, he aimed for our friends Tito and P.J., who'd invited Mike and me out for the night.

"Hello, hello," he bellowed. Tito whispered something to the Don, who stood back, sizing me up and down with a smile on his heavily bearded face.

"Come in, welcome, welcome," he said, a bit less loudly, throwing his arm around my shoulders, shaking my hand, and giving me two pecks on my cheeks, his beard tickling like a cat licking its owner's chin in the morning.

At the heavy Spanish colonial-style wooden table, I picked up a menu and discovered a dish I never knew existed: beef steak with a sauce thick with sliced jalapeños. Comforting, creamy, and sinful. As well as spicy hot. Eating it for the first time, surrounded by my friends' laughter, the atmosphere redolent of a French bistro, the dish sank deep into my bank of memories.

Surprisingly, that's what I thought of the night five-year-old Erik ran a fever of 105°F in the middle of a severe tropical storm. With Mike in La Ceiba on the north coast for work, I alone needed to deal with the crisis. I called Erik's pediatrician, who lived near the private hospital founded by physicians who'd trained in the United States. He told me to get to the hospital as fast as I could.

Clara, our maid, refused to let me go by myself, so we loaded Erik into the back seat of our ancient Honda Civic, an extra-small one with a non-working gas gauge. Off we went at top speed down the hill to the hospital. There a nurse jabbed a needle into Erik's buttocks so hard he screamed.

I needed to drive Clara back to our house because *her* five-year-old son Minor was asleep in their room.

On my way back to the hospital, the rain and wind intensified. Manhole covers blew off as I drove, my headlights the only lights on the road.

As I turned up the street to the hospital's parking lot, water poured into the car, high above the hubcaps. The engine died right there in the middle of the road. Frantic for news of Erik, I jumped out, put the car into neutral, and pushed it about ten yards into the parking lot, water halfway up my thighs.

The doctor put Erik on an IV to build up his fluids, deemed it a viral infection of some unknown variety, and said I faced an all-night vigil. As I sat watching over my feverish son, many thoughts came and went: hope, fear, sadness, anger.

When morning came, he woke and smiled at me, saying "Mama." I ran to him and hugged him, crying. I noticed then the stains on my white pants, black to the hip with the foulness of sewer pipes unleashed by the storm.

During that night-long vigil, strangely enough, I'd teased out the recipe for Don Udo's steak sauce. Every time I cook it, I cherish the memory of Erik's childish voice saying my real name after that nightmarish night.

Jalapeño Cream Sauce

2 tablespoons unsalted butter

¼ yellow onion, finely minced

1 garlic clove, peeled, finely minced

1½ cups heavy cream

3 tablespoons sliced pickled jalapeños

Fine sea salt and freshly ground black pepper, to taste

Sauté onion in a small skillet in butter for about 2 minutes over medium heat. When onion is translucent, but not brown, add garlic. Sauté for 30 seconds, then stir in cream and sliced chiles. Simmer until reduced so that sauce coats a spoon. Season with salt and pepper to taste. Spoon over grilled steaks. Makes 1 cup.

Left: Erik with a birthday piñata and right: Erik and the author hiking in a rainforest

Sambuseks

Honduras was the original "banana republic," and its poverty remains extreme.
~ Elliott Abrams

One afternoon, after Judy and I led a La Leche League meeting, we sat on her sunny, breezy veranda drinking tea served with crisp meat-filled pastries.

Not wanting to be greedy, I slowed down after gobbling the first savory triangle of phyllo filled with ground beef, seasoned with cumin and a strong hint of black pepper.

"Where did you get these?" I asked Judy, between mouthfuls of crisp pastry. "Does your maid make them?"

"Oh, no," Judy laughed. "My husband's cousin Miriam has a home business, sells them frozen in bags of twelve. Here, let me draw you a map to her house. Then, I'll call her, let her know you might be visiting."

A Jew from Brooklyn, Judy first arrived in Honduras to volunteer for an NGO (non-governmental organization/charity). Soon she met and married a Christian Lebanese man whose family emigrated to Honduras from Lebanon in the early 1900s, many of whom became community leaders in San Pedro Sula as doctors, lawyers, and businesspeople. She enjoyed the social standing granted to members of that community. Including giving people like me an introduction to kitchens like Miriam's, whose family—although Christians—still followed some of the old ways when it came to women.

Once the guard lounging in front of Miriam's rusty iron gate knew I was there for the food, I strolled up a winding path of inlaid grey stone to the backdoor of an opulent colonial-style house and pulled a string attached to a tiny tinkling bell. A maid appeared at the carved wooden door, dressed in white, her long shiny black hair covered with a white headscarf, her hand smudged with the telltale whiteness of wheat flour.

She held the door open for me. I stepped into a room with whitewashed walls, where a dozen chest freezers lined up against one wall, humming like a chorus of frogs perched on lily pads.

Looking at me quizzically, she motioned with both hands, palms up. The universal signal for "How many?"

"*Dos bolsas de sambuseks de carne de vaca, por favor,*" I responded.

She darted to one of the freezers at the end of the line and yanked out two bags of *sambuseks*.

"*Venticinco lempiras, por favor,*" she said, holding out her hand, dabs of flour and dough still visible on her fingers, despite having wiped her hands over and over again on her apron. "Twenty-five *lempiras*, please."

Back at home in the "American House," as I called it, I put the *sambuseks* in the tiny freezer compartment at the top of my refrigerator. It was not a house I'd have chosen. In fact, I never chose any of the houses I lived in all those years overseas, always arriving after project and team leaders made the big decisions.

The "American House" was no different.

Looking through the sliding glass doors in the kitchen to a dollhouse-sized patio where we never sat due to the heat, I watched Erik playing with Minor, Clara's little boy. Both jabbered away in the Spanish it took Erik one month to learn, and me years of study. That window was the only window in the entire house where it was possible to see outside because the owner chose frosted glass louvers instead of clear. Wall-to-wall carpeting made the house feel even hotter and damper. However, tile covered the floors in the bathrooms and the kitchen.

It was, in short, a house best suited for winters in Wisconsin. Even the dining room was carpeted. Food spills, though, became Clara's problems, not mine.

At least the air conditioning worked well.

In the afternoons, a few hours before dinner, I sometimes felt my stomach rumbling. To calm the growls, I heated a *sambusek* or two, placating body—and soul—with flavors that originated in a desert land almost 7,500 miles away from where I chewed.

Sambuseks

2 tablespoons extra virgin olive oil

1 pound ground beef or lamb

1 medium yellow onion, peeled, grated, and squeezed dry

1 teaspoon cumin

¼ teaspoon sumac

¼ teaspoon *za'tar*

Fine sea salt and freshly ground black pepper, to taste

Olive oil for brushing

1 pound phyllo dough, thawed

Vegetable oil for frying

Beaten egg for sealing

Fry meat in olive oil until pink color disappears. Add onion, cook for a few minutes until onion turns translucent. Add seasonings. Layer phyllo dough by placing one layer down, brush with oil. Repeat once more. Keep dough moist. Cut phyllo dough into 4-inch by 10-inch strips. Drop about 2 teaspoons of meat mixture in the center of each strip at the end and begin folding over to make triangles, edge to edge. Wet edges of phyllo with a small brush or a finger dipped beaten egg. Seal tightly. Heat vegetable oil to 375°F in a deep pot, begin frying the *sambuseks*. Drain on a rack over a baking sheet. Serve with hot sauce. Makes 12.

Author's house at El Zamorano

Erik and the author eating in the house at El Zamorano

Giving Thanks ... for a Cistern

... in other words, though the actors, techniques, and storyline shifted constantly, Honduras remained the quintessential banana republic.

~ Dan Koeppel

That Thanksgiving night, the last of our twenty-five guests left at eleven p.m. I sighed with relief. And not a little sadness. Friends and colleagues had gathered to wish us well as Mike's office began shutting down the farming systems project and vacating the "American House" where we'd lived for a year, the one with the glamor best suited for a magazine shoot, not appropriate for the torrid tropics.

In the torrid tropical climate of San Pedro Sula, cooking and serving the annual repast for twenty-five guests sapped my energy even more than the days of packing, yard sales, and anxiety about what would come next. As I stirred filling for the pumpkin pie and cubed dry bread for the herb dressing, anxious thoughts of the future raced through my mind. Such was the uncertainty that came with working as contractors for USAID and other aid organizations.

No crystal balls could have predicted what happened that night in Honduras, though.

When the headlights from the last car faded into the night, Clara came running out of the kitchen. I thought she might be agitated because she hadn't yet cleared all the dishes off the table and was afraid that I might be angry. But no.

"*No hay agua,*" she panted.

"No water?" I repeated. How could that be?

Clara ran to the neighbor's house and pounded on their maid's door. Same thing. No water. A water main burst when a too-heavy truck smacked into a pothole and sank into the road, down to where the water pipes nestled like worms in hiding.

It's a cliché, but my heart truly did sink.

"*Pero hay remedio,*" Clara announced, smiling. "There's a solution."

I stumbled out the kitchen door behind her to the patio. She pointed to a large cement square, topped with an even larger square, about four feet by five feet. I had no idea what I was looking at.

"*Es un aljibe,*" she said. Seeing my puzzled look, she tried another word.

"*Una cisterna.*" She paused. "*Hay mucha agua por ahí.*"

I nodded. If there was indeed a mysterious cistern down there, there would be enough water for washing off the caked-on gravy and grease on my grandmother's Mayflower Spode chinaware. Everything could be ready in time for the packers in the morning.

How to move the heavy cement top?

As that thought crossed my mind, the landlord showed up with his son and a cousin. Word had traveled about our dinner and all the guests and all the dishes. The men grunted and shoved the cement top to one side until enough room allowed us to dunk two plastic buckets into the swirling brown water below. For three hours we worked, lugging water, filling large pots to boil the muddy water, the color of milk chocolate, and smelling of fetid dampness. We scrubbed all the dishes in the boiled water, then dried them as best we could.

Eyes drooping like Dalí's watches, we spent another two hours wrapping the dishes and pots and silverware in packing paper. Air-freight boxes filled quickly.

When it comes to memory and most holidays, most of them run together, like a movie being fast-forwarded to the good parts. Memory goes thin.

That Thanksgiving was different, though. I indeed had something to be thankful for. The people around me who pitched in to help, whose names I no longer remember.

Pumpkin Pie

1 cup granulated sugar, or half granulated and half brown

1½ teaspoons ground cinnamon

½ teaspoon fine sea salt

1 teaspoon ground ginger

½ teaspoon ground cloves

¼ teaspoon freshly grated nutmeg

2 large eggs, lightly beaten

1 (15-ounce) can pumpkin purée

12 fluid ounces heavy cream

1 teaspoon pure vanilla extract

1 unbaked 9-inch deep-dish pie shell

Whipped cream for garnish, sweetened with powdered sugar and a dash of pure vanilla extract

Preheat oven to 425°F. Place pie crust in pan and flute edges. Mix all ingredients in a large mixing bowl, except for pie crust and whipped cream garnish. Pour pumpkin mixture into crust. Place in center of oven, set timer for 15 minutes. When time is up, reduce heat to 350°F, set timer for another 45 minutes. Check pie for doneness after 45 minutes by inserting a thin knife blade or wooden skewer into center of pie. If knife or skewer comes out clean, filling is done. Cool on rack. Serve garnished with whipped cream. Makes 1 9-inch pie.

The 100-Mile Cookbook

While she loved the whole idea of cooking elaborate meals,
her forte was in the reading of cookbooks.
~ Linda Wiken

Honduras offered a lot of excitement for the foreigner: fabulous snorkeling, gorgeous rain-forested mountains, and precarious politics. Dodging bullets had nothing to do with it. Not at all. Instead, thrills came with simple everyday things.

Such as getting mail.

Take my copy of *The Silver Palate Cookbook,* for example.

A loose notice tacked to my house's screen door in El Zamorano informed me that my cookbook had arrived safely at the Correo Nacional in Tegucigalpa after a three-month-long sea voyage. My mother-in-law sent it by slow boat because she, thrifty soul that she was, wanted to save me a few dollars on airmail costs, even though I told her that my life would be easier if she sent it by air.

Note that I would do just about anything to get a new cookbook when I lived in Honduras. Acquiring a new cookbook was as marvelous as winning the lottery, for me.

That day was a day like most others. Balmy weather, crazy and unpredictable drivers, chaotic electricity. I was due in Tegucigalpa late in the afternoon to consult on the malnutrition ward at the *Hospital Escuela.* But I decided to detour by the post office first and pick up the cookbook on my way to the hospital. So I drove the winding two-lane, twenty-five-mile highway to Tegucigalpa, admiring the pink and purple bougainvillea tumbling over the pastel-colored walls of even the poorest houses along the way.

Parking was always a problem in Tegucigalpa. As luck would have it, I found a partially empty parking lot near the post office and the central plaza. A leering parking attendant wedged my car between a shabby white Datsun with no left front fender and an enormous blue pickup truck with no right headlight. The lecher handed me my change and a parking stub, brushing my fingers with his oil-stained thumb. I thrust ten centavos in an old beggar woman's palm where she lay on the narrow trash-strewn sidewalk, then hurried down the street to the post office, dodging a mangy, beige-colored dog rummaging through a pile of rotten vegetables.

It was definitely a day like all others.

At the post office, my line seemed to be getting longer instead of shorter.

After twenty minutes, I was still the last person in line. Everybody else was butting in line in front of me. The saying is "when in Rome do as the Romans do," so I pushed. I elbowed a large lady in the ribs and arrived at the service window. They would have closed the window in the movies as I got there, but this was real life.

The girl working there said, "*Señora, lo siento,* but your package is across the river in Comayaguela, at the *Oficina de Rentas.*"

She continued eating a handful of greasy fried plantain chips.

Exasperated, I asked, "Where exactly is this *Oficina de Rentas, por favor?*"

It seemed that it was near the army post on the Calle Real.

"*Muchas gracias,*" I mumbled.

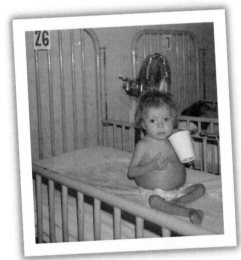

A patient on the malnutrition ward

Once outside, I wove my way through crowds of beggars and sidewalk vendors in the central plaza and claimed my car from the still-salacious attendant.

By now, my lateness on the ward was a given.

After a two-mile drive and many near misses with dented fenders and screeching buses, I found the *Oficina de Rentas.* Inside, I ignored two windows closest to the entrance. Then, down the hall, the sight of an astonishing warehouse-like room took my breath away. So amazing that I just stood there, with my jaw dropping into an "Oh!"

Parcels and packages and boxes and envelopes reached from floor to ceiling, hundreds of them balancing on rickety wooden shelves behind a wire fence, like a prison. Off to the side, seven people sat around one desk, gossiping. Six other desks lined the peeling walls, obviously belonging to six of the people crowding around the first desk.

"*Buenos días*," I exclaimed, showing my package notice to the older man sitting at the first desk. As if on cue, everyone else rose and returned to their posts. The man stamped my paper and wrote my name in a well-worn red notebook. Then, without a word, he pointed to the next desk.

I passed from desk to desk, either writing my name or having a paper stamped.

At the last desk, a bored-looking boy said I needed to pay fifty centavos for a permit to take the package out. I dug into my purse for a coin and held it out. Silently, he shook his head and, with his chin, pointed to the entrance. Looking out the door, I spotted the two windows I ignored earlier. I paid at the first window. That done, I returned to parcel heaven. The boy informed me I needed yet another paper.

"Where do I get that?" I asked, a slight touch of irritation shading the tone of my voice.

"At window number two," he grunted, fiddling with his nose. Funny, the man at window number one said nothing about window number two. So back I went. The paper was waiting for me.

By this time, I was getting rather anxious and bothered at the same time. If things went as usual, the tax on the book could be as much as the cost of the book. Or more. The clerk at the last desk stamped the paper I held in my hand. Without looking up, he said, "Tomorrow at two p.m. Your package will be ready."

With that, I forgot my resolution not to get angry, not to be impolite, and not to show impatience. I forgot for a moment that in the Honduran system, all these emotions stall works in progress like a stubborn burro on a mountain road. I squealed, "No, *por favor*, now please. I live twenty-five miles over the mountains. It's a long trip for me to come to Tegucigalpa. I want the package now."

The boy, no longer bored, grinned and shrugged his expressive shoulders. "*Impossible, Señora. Hasta mañana.*" Nothing more. Until tomorrow.

The best dodge ever invented was the word "impossible."

"All right, I will see you at two p.m. Tomorrow." I sighed.

With my temper at code red, I stalked out, sweat pouring down my face.

Needless to say, my rounds on the malnutrition ward did little to raise my spirits.

Upon returning to the *Oficina de Rentas* the next day—after again fighting it out for twenty-five miles on winding mountain roads replete with crazy drivers, drunken pedestrians, skinny beige dogs, bumbling cows, and stubborn burros—I approached the old man at desk number one again. With a trembling finger, he traced down the list in the red notebook.

"Ah yes, *Señora*, your name is here," he said. He stamped my copies of the various papers from the day before.

I moved to the second desk. Today, this man was much friendlier, too friendly, truth be told. I moved backward as he leaned toward me, talking about jewelry robbers on crowded Honduran buses. Nervously, I fingered my fake gold chain necklace, which cost all of ten dollars at Sears Roebuck. Stamping my papers, he told me to pay my tax at the bank.

"What?!," I sputtered, incredulous that there was more to be done. My five-minute errand of the previous day was turning into one of those nightmares where the dreamer never quite reaches their goal, where some new Herculean obstacle stands in the way.

"The bank, *Señora*, you must pay your tax at a bank. You must hurry. It is almost three o'clock, and banks close then. There is one on the corner. ¡*Rapido*! Hurry."

I thought, "Hurry? He is telling *me* to hurry?"

With a flourish, he handed me the tax form. I glanced at it furtively, fearful of the worst. Imagine my astonishment when I saw the tax was a mere two centavos! My astonishment quickly flipped to anger, as I realized that I had gone through all this for a tax of 1 American cent!

Huffing and puffing, I arrived at the bank barely in time to pay the two centavos. The teller stamped one of my papers and chuckled as I wiped rivulets of sweat off my face. I stood there silently, resigned to the wet moon shapes accentuating the shape of my armpits, too.

I rushed back to the *Oficina de Rentas*, handed the tax receipt to the man at window number one. Then, finally, the man at desk number one patted a tattered package and presented it to me.

"¡*Adíos, Señora*!" Smiling, he waved me off. "¡*Hasta luego*!"

There would be no next time if I could help it.

Elated, I skipped out the door and drove back to Zamorano. I had my new cookbook, 100 miles and 52 centavos later, counting the fifty I'd paid for the permit to take the package out.

The recipes turned out to be great, terrific, in fact. I considered making the caviar dip on page 36. But I couldn't find caviar anywhere. People suggested that I mail order it, but I demurred.

Springing someone from the slammer would be far easier.

Pound Cake

1 cup unsalted butter, room temperature

2 cups granulated sugar

5 eggs, room temperature

½ teaspoon fine sea salt

1 tablespoon fresh lemon juice

1½ teaspoons pure vanilla extract

2 cups unbleached all-purpose flour

Preheat oven to 350°F. Grease and flour a 10-inch bundt pan. Beat butter and sugar together in a large mixing bowl. Add eggs, one at a time, beat until mixed in thoroughly. Add salt, lemon juice, and vanilla–stir in well. Add flour, mix just until moist. Scrape batter into prepared tube pan. Set on middle rack of oven, bake for about 1 hour. If cake browns too quickly, cover top loosely with foil. When a skewer inserted into cake center comes out clean, remove cake from oven. Let cool for 15 minutes on a rack. Then remove from pan. Cool completely. Serve with berry compote, vanilla ice cream, or fresh strawberries and whipped cream, etc. Makes 1 10-inch cake.

Marcella and the Gamey Pork

Zamorano has many areas/spots that are host to species that are both native to the region and exotic from all over the tropical world.

~ Wikipedia

"Eduardo, if you have time when you're in Miami, could you bring back a copy of Marcella Hazan's *Classic Italian* cookbook for me?"

An architect from Guatemala working for the *Escuela Agricola Panamericana*, in Zamorano, Honduras, Eduardo planned on flying to Miami the next day, for a week-long meeting with suppliers

"Of course, happy to," he said as we stood by the long wooden table in the courtyard at the Casa Popenoe, a cocktail party honoring the Board of Trustees in full swing. "If you cook something for Margarita and me, that is!"

I turned to the table, loaded with *tostones* and small flour tortillas topped with refried beans and *crema*, grilled beef and chicken on skewers, and enough beer and Johnny Walker Red to start a small bar. After the debacle with my *Silver Palate Cookbook*, I looked forward to seamlessly acquiring a new cookbook.

Thinking of the cheese I needed for Italian cooking, I spotted Aurelio across the room. Originally from Peru, he ran the dairy department at El Zamorano. He oversaw pork butchering, too.

That's what I wanted to talk to him about.

El Zamorano grew and produced most of the food eaten by the students, who came from all over Latin American to this spot started by United Fruit Company to atone for their many sins in the region. Faculty and employees could buy directly from the various departments—dairy, meat, vegetables. A small store across from the school sold most of the extra food to the public.

The last pork leg I bought from the meat section tasted almost rotten, though I witnessed the butchering of that animal. But not the slaughter itself. That is where things went wrong, partially accounting for the gamey, foul taste of the meat. Boar taint, as it is called, occurs because of two compounds associated with male pigs—androstenone and skatole.

Aurelio apologized.

The next day, a student appeared at my kitchen door with a fresh pork leg and a large container of sour cream, as well as some fresh mozzarella. All accompanied by a short note from Aurelio, wishing me "¡*Buen provecho*!" Good eating!

About an hour later, Margarita knocked on the front door and handed me the cookbook I'd been longing for. She told me in the crisp Castilian Spanish of her homeland that she planned on going to Tegucigalpa in a few days, to buy some things for her baby Eduardito, and to shop at the central market in the big city, too. Did I want to go?

Of course! That day would be quite an adventure, as it turned out.

Pierna de Cerdo (Roasted Pork Leg with Sour Cream Gravy)

1 (10 pounds) pork leg, fat on

10 large garlic cloves, peeled, thinly sliced

2 teaspoons fine sea salt

1 teaspoon freshly ground black pepper

1 cup water

¼ cup white vinegar

1 pound (16 ounces) dairy sour cream

2 tablespoons cornstarch, mixed with 2 tablespoons cold water

Preheat oven to 450°F. Cut slits into pork all over. Insert garlic slices into the slits. Rub pork with salt and pepper. Place pork in roasting pan and put it into the oven. Let cook for about 45 minutes, then reduce oven temperature to 325°F, roast for another 5 hours. Remove pork to a platter. Make sauce by adding water, vinegar, and sour cream to roasting pan. Bring to a simmer, stir in cornstarch mixture. Simmer until thickened. If necessary, season with more salt and pepper to taste. Slice meat and serve with the sauce, passed separately. Serves 10.

Sandinistas

The church wanted us to give out food to malnourished children, but they didn't
want us to question why they were malnourished to begin with.

~ Elvia Alvarado

Sunlit fog shrouded the military khaki draping their hard, muscular bodies. For some crazy reason, when I spotted them, thoughts of gauzy bridal veils, foamy and pristine, crossed my mind.

Six masked gunmen stood in the road, legs spread wide, real live action figures balancing on unsteady ground. Automatic rifles pointed straight ahead. At us. Two women alone, on a mountain road in southern Honduras, the stomping grounds of renegade Sandinistas, the base of operations for U.S.-backed Contras.

Margarita slammed on the brakes. Her white Honda Civic shuddered, its fifteen-year-old engine sputtering, more a lament than a whine. We reached out to each other, our hands fumbling.

Our hands touching, she whispered, "Let me talk to them." The men strode toward us, fingers tapping on triggers, guns bobbing gently with each step. My head moved up and down, a universal wordless "Yes." My tongue filled my dry mouth, like a big wad of sugarless chewing gum. The kind I would spit out if I could.

But I couldn't.

As I turned to look at three-year-old Erik in the backseat, the muscles in my neck spasmed, sending a searing pain into my jaw. He stared at me, silent, knowing something was wrong. I put my finger to my mouth. "Shh," I mouthed. He burrowed deeper into his car seat.

"Quiet, stay still, don't move," Margarita ordered. Then she asked, "How's *mi hijito?*"

"He is playing grab-'em with his feet."

"One-year-olds do that." She smiled, for a second.

A loud rap on the window, the driver's side. Margarita flinched and scrunched lower in her seat, gripping the steering wheel. Something wiggled under my shirt. I wanted to swat at it, thinking that unseen insects crawled there. Only sweat, trickling ice cold down my ribs. I dared not scratch, dared not move.

"Open the window!" The man in the black ski mask barked.

Margarita rolled down the window and, in that instant, became an Oscar-award-winning actress.

"*Buenos días, señores*, how are you today?" She flashed the same brilliant smile that she reserved for both market vendors and the top brass at El Zamorano, where both our husbands worked.

Another gunman grabbed the door handle on my side and jerked the door open. Pointing his weapon at me, he gestured for me to get out of the car. I stumbled as I stood, clutching the door frame, my knees trembling as if I'd just finished running two miles. I snuck a look at Erik through the back window. His blue eyes bore into me, unblinking, large in his face. His thumb in his rosebud of a mouth, sucking. Quiet. Good.

I knew these men could kill us. I thought maybe they would. That image seared itself on my brain. The gunman pressed me against the car with the point of his gun, stepped back, and held the barrel steady, inches away from my heart. I kept my eyes on the weapon, not looking at his masked face, his dark leering eyes. Monster.

I vowed to pummel him if he moved even a centimeter toward Erik. If I saw that trigger finger pull back even a hair's breadth, I'd kick him first, right in the V of his legs.

The odor of his aftershave wafted into the air with every breath he took. Imagine patting on aftershave before emerging from whatever hole he woke in that morning, intent on terrorizing innocent women and children.

Margarita bumped into me as the first gunman pushed her next to me against the side of the car. We grabbed hands behind our skirts, our buttocks pressed against the white fender. Squeezing my clammy hand, she started talking again, her voice low, prayerful almost, reminding the men of their mothers, their sisters, their grandmothers. Somehow her voice conjured a saga of family, of ties to blood, to honor. To God.

The other gunmen faced us now, their eyes peering from their masks, their guns still trained on us. One reached for me, touched my left breast. My heart fluttered like a hummingbird, a *colibri*. I closed my eyes, tears burning beneath their lids. And wondered, a horrible thought pulsating in my brain like my throbbing heart: Would they rape us in front of our sons? Would they kill us?

A sudden breeze blew through the trees, whipping at our skirts, fluffing our hair.

In that moment, that breath of air, something changed. It was as if their leader woke from a spell and read my mind.

"¡*Vamos!*" he grunted. "Let's go!" With a glance at Margarita, he bowed his head, an *adios* of a sort, a tribute to her. My breath stopped in my throat.

Was it true that they were leaving?

I clenched Margarita's hand. Harder. I squinted through my right eye and saw the gunman who'd touched me hoisting his gun to his shoulder. The six of them turned and loped off into the woods, single file, silent.

Except for the rustling of the wind and the clack-clack of their guns, no sound rent the cool mountain air. Until the baby wailed. Margarita ran to the other side of the car. She clutched her son's little body to her heaving chest, peppering his head with small kisses, murmuring "*Te amo.* I love you" over and over.

Erik sat there, still soundless. Tiny tears coated his blond eyelashes. He held out his arms. I scooped him up, my sobs shaking us both. Holding our babies on our hips, she and I embraced with our free arms. Margarita slumped against me, her mouth trembling against my cheek.

"I did not know if they would listen to me. I spoke of my brothers, I called them, those brutes with guns, I called them 'brothers' too."

"You did good, you did so good," I said.

Margarita turned the key in the ignition. We rode back to El Zamorano, not saying a word.

We pulled into the circular driveway of my house.

"What are you having for dinner?" she asked.

"Probably red beans and rice," I said as I leaned over to hug her.

The nightmares came later.

White Rice, Honduran-Style

1 tablespoon vegetable oil

3 tablespoons finely chopped yellow onion

1 garlic clove, peeled and minced

1 cup long-grain white rice

1 teaspoon fine sea salt

2 cups water

Fry onion in oil in medium saucepan over medium-high heat until translucent and soft. Add rice, sauté until rice looks opaque white. Add salt and water, bring to a boil, reduce heat to low, simmer until rice is tender, about 20 minutes. Makes 3 cups.

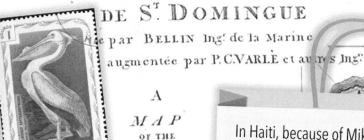

CARTE DE LA PARTIE FRANÇOISE.
DE St. DOMINGUE
par BELLIN Ing. de la Marine
augmentée par P. C. VARLÉ et autres Ing.

A
MAP
OF THE
ENCH PART
OF
St. DOMINGO

Note
Towns of the 1st rank are marked......1.
2.............................2.
3.............................3.
Parish & its chief Town bear the same
name........................§
Villages......................§
Places burnt by the Negroes
are coloured Yellow.

In Haiti, because of Mike's work with another USAID farming-systems project, I studied *Kreyòl* for a while. During the civil unrest after Baby Doc left Haiti, I also ran a small catering business called "Le Brown Bag," my customers mostly U.S. Embassy personnel and expat factory managers. Later, I designed a nutrition survey for the area surrounding Haut-Cap Rouge, near Jacmel. But all that came to an end when the Embassy evacuated all non-essential personnel due to increasing civil unrest.

Haitian Women with Beans and Rice

Sos Pwa Rouj

Haiti, it is said, is the place to discover how much can be done with little.
~ Wade Davis

Flickering lights in the darkness below outlined the curves of Port-au-Prince, a backward-facing crescent. Sounds of clapping and the singing of Haitians, happy to be coming home, drowned out the drone of the plane as it circled over the sparkling blue water of the Bay of Gonâve.

François Duvalier Airport was deserted, except for a half dozen armed men in blue-denim uniforms, dark aviator sunglasses covering their eyes despite the late hour. I remembered reading of Tonton Macoutes in Graham Greene's brutal, seductive novel, *The Comedians*. About Haiti under the dictatorship of Papa Doc Duvalier, it chilled me to the bone as I read it again and again over the years.

Nothing good would come of it if we looked suspicious or said something wrong. I edged away from the men as we grabbed our suitcases from the dilapidated baggage cart and shepherded Erik to the passport control desk. An old gentleman manned the desk, his sparse white hair jutting out from the top of his head, a smoldering cigarette hanging from his lower lip.

"*Bonsoir*," he mumbled, as he thumbed through our passports. "*Bienvenue à Haiti!*" With those words of welcome and a stamp of approval, we followed the rope line to the exit.

The night was humid, bats flying under the dim lights of the streetlamps, the air misty. A driver sent by the project waited for us, holding a crudely worded sign with our last name as he flicked his cigarette to the ground, smoke from the acrid tobacco hanging in the air like a tiny ghost.

"*Où voulez-vous aller?*" he asked. "Where to?"

"Turgeau," I said and handed him a piece of paper with the address on it.

"OK."

He gunned the gas pedal, the motor screaming like a beaten dog as we dodged people, donkeys, and more blue-denim-clad men with guns.

The project's apartment in Turgeau turned out to be a spacious, three-bedroom place, an expansive balcony overlooking leafy flame trees studded with red flowers and the azure deeps of the Bay of Gonâve.

The aroma of strong coffee woke us that first morning. When Celeste, the housekeeper, set down warm baguettes with rich, mango-yellow butter and fruit-studded apricot jam in front of me, I felt truly welcomed. I forgot those denim-clad men with the guns as dazzling sunshine poured through the gauzy curtains of the small dining room, burnishing everything in its path with a golden, almost magical glow.

Mike left for the office, his first day of work on the USAID-funded ADS-II farming system project headquartered in Damien, Haiti's equivalent of the USDA. The earthquake of January 12, 2010 destroyed Damien, along with all the agricultural survey data Mike's team collected by hiking segments all over Haiti, interviewing farmers. No such survey had ever been done before.

As I filled my mouth with a last sweet smear of jam, the doorbell trilled, sounding like the birds singing in the trees outside the windows. Ursina, the project leader's wife, strode in and bussed Celeste on both cheeks.

"Hello!" She tousled Erik's blond hair. "You, young man, will be visiting your new school today!"

At Ursina's request, Celeste surprised us that night with a typical Haitian dish—red beans in their own sauce—along with spicy fried chicken and fragrant white rice. Comfort food for many Haitians.

It soon became one of mine.

Sos Pwa Rouj (Red Beans in Their Own Sauce)

2 cups small red beans, soaked and parboiled in 6 cups of water for 2 minutes, left to sit 1 hour

2 tablespoons vegetable oil

2 garlic cloves, peeled and finely minced

½ cup flat-leaf parsley, minced

Fine sea salt and freshly ground black pepper, to taste

Cook parboiled beans in the water until tender, about 2 hours. Drain beans into a large bowl, reserving 3 cups of the cooking water. Take 1½ cups of beans and blend in a blender with some of the 3 cups of reserved bean water. Add puréed beans to remaining beans. Heat a heavy skillet over medium heat. Stir in garlic and parsley–cook slowly until garlic loses its harsh odor. Be careful not to let it brown or burn. Stir in beans and heat through, adding more bean liquid to make a creamy mixture if necessary. Season to taste with fine sea salt and lots of freshly ground black pepper. Serve over rice or cornmeal mush. Serves 6-8.

Street scene, Jacmel, Haiti

The Oloffson

Gods always behave like the people who make them.

~ Zora Neale Hurston

They called him Baron Samedi. He still walked at night. The sobbing beat of drums in the treeless mountains didn't keep him away. Perhaps the drums called him. That I did not know. I lay in bed at night with the memories. The nightmares. The fear. And other feelings, too.

In my reverie, Petit Pierre stood at the end of the long mahogany bar, the gouges in the gleaming wood hacked by the Tonton Macoutes not so visible in the dusky light. Joseph, withered and torture-damaged legs forming a tripod with the death's head cane he gripped in his left hand, was not there. I shivered. No, he wasn't there. He died.

I moved toward the bar, nodding to the beefy bartender, his smile punctuated by a glinting gold crown on one of his front teeth. "Good evening," I said, first in French, then in *Kreyòl*. I ordered. A skunky-tasting Haitian beer appeared in front of me in a flash. No ice, never. One of many rules not to be broken while living in most places in the world.

Petit Pierre snaked over to the bar, the last person to whom I wished to speak. I smiled, though, as he kissed my hand. I tried not to flinch at the warmth of his breath, the moistness of his lips on my skin, the tickle of his sparse mustache. He asked about any Embassy parties coming up, who would be there, who would not.

I said nothing.

Many unsuspecting women ended up in his bed, unaware that Aubelin Jolicoeur/Petit Pierre worked as a journalist. He was a staunch Duvalierist, too, in the pockets of the Tontons. A spy. First for Baron Samedi, the popular name for Papa Doc, who dressed like the Vodun god himself. Now his son, Jean-Claude, decided who lived and who died in this God-forsaken place. The dead souls haunting Haiti's notorious prison, Fort Dimanche, numbered in the thousands.

I excused myself, seeking to escape Petit Pierre's leering glances.

Wandering past the bar, through a narrow swinging door teetering on its hinges, I found a long hallway. I passed room after room, each named for a famous soul who slept at the Oloffson: writers, artists, actors, politicians. On the walls of chipped white paint hung dozens of colorful works of art. Statues and papier-mâché masks surrounded them. Vodun art. I shivered as I pushed through the bathroom door.

Not a believer, not me. Yet I felt something in the air, a sense of another presence. I laughed to myself. *Come on,* I whispered. *Vodun is not sorcery and "black magic."*

Instead of returning to my beer, I started down the elaborate staircase, built like the tiers of a wedding cake. Some of my friends stood at the foot of the stairs, gazing at the Hotel, mesmerized. Strings of twinkling lights hung from eave to eave, looking for all the world like a scintillating diamond necklace circling a bride's neck.

We returned to the hotel to eat and soak up the atmosphere, an ambiance Charles Addams once recognized as possessing sinister overtones. As did Greene. But was that sinisterness related to the hotel, the place, the art, or just shadows in my mind? A dream?

Old Cuba Cocktail

¾ ounce fresh lime juice

1 ounce simple syrup

6 mint leaves

1½ ounces Barbancourt Rhum

2 dashes Angostura bitters

1 ounce champagne

Mix lime, mint, and simple syrup. Add rum, bitters, and ice. Double strain into cocktail glass. Top with champagne. Serves 1.

More than Pineapples

Because in Haiti, so many people are poor, it's nothing to be ashamed of. And there's always a way to degaje, *to get by, even when you have nothing.*

~ Laura Rose Wagner

I loved shopping for food in open-air markets in Haiti.

Poking the tomatoes, prodding maliciously hot chile peppers, breaking off hunks of fragrant golden ginger, and deliberately bruising cilantro leaves to savor a whiff of that peculiar perfume, nothing beats food shopping (or buying perfume) for sensory experiences.

Shopping for food in a Third World country like Haiti offered perhaps the most intense immersion in all things olfactory. Rotting vegetation, open sewers, burning charcoal, dried shrimp with sightless beady black eyes, smoked fish chasing their own tails, the list of "smellable" experiences grows and grows beyond the pleasant pungency of ginger and garlic.

It is best to think of the odor of the market as symbolic of life itself.

With social unrest popping up from time to time, Haiti hardly seemed the place where shopping of any sort could be a consuming joy.

But it was.

True, vast piles of putrefying garbage shared space beside Petionville's grand Cathedral Square with the market ladies, "Madame Saras," as they called themselves, after the black crows that cawed incessantly from their perches on electric wires and tree branches. Flies crawled thickly over decomposing pineapples, and yellow skeletal dogs fought each other ruthlessly for the odd bony tidbit.

Each "Madame Sara" laid out her wares in small, symmetrical piles atop squares of torn, stained cloth, the original color difficult to determine. However, color ruled elsewhere. In the brightly colored headscarves worn by the women. In the carefully arranged tropical fruits. In the red tomatoes and bushels of leafy greens. In the baskets of cut flowers. And especially in the purple bougainvillea and flamboyant trees flowering red and yellow amid the cracked asphalt.

Successful shopping depended upon building a relationship with individual market women. While not friendship, this certainly imbued a sense of something more profound than a mere business deal. The best approach was to shop always with the same "Madame Saras."

Thanks to a memorable Haitian woman wearing a white spaghetti-strap tank top, one unforgettable day of food shopping stood out for me.

Weeks after the dictator Baby Doc Duvalier fled to France with the help of an American military jet, the markets flourished, and the streets filled with people moving to a new rhythm—light, confident, proud.

Petionville, high above the crowded Haitian capital city of Port-au-Prince and my last stop after a long day, glimmered that sunny afternoon, an eggshell-blue sky overhead. A soft, warm breeze rustled the dusty leaves of the skinny flamboyant trees nearby. With no demonstrations or new curfews announced by the U.S. Embassy, I felt my neck muscles relaxing as I swung my beige Isuzu Trooper into a parking space across from the cathedral. The one where Baby Doc married Michele "Dragon Lady" Bennett amid wall-to-wall gardenias.

One more errand, and I could go home to my house in Laboule, high above Petionville.

Returning from my weekly hoarding trip to the U.S. Embassy commissary near the port road in Port-au-Prince, I needed to pick up a few fresh ingredients: vegetables, carrots, and some lettuce. Stuff that could feed an average Haitian family of ten for a month jam-packed the back of my Trooper. As I climbed down from the Trooper, about twenty "Madame Saras" besieged me, shouting in *Kreyòl* to buy this papaya or that leek. This was not my usual market, for that one closed at around 1 p.m. My watch showed 2:30 p.m.

I approached the nearest "Madame Sara" selling carrots and asked her in perfunctory *Kreyòl* how much she wanted for them. By this time, quite a crowd had collected around me. Imagine the scene: me, the "rich" new foreigner driving a shiny four-wheel-drive vehicle, ready to buy something from somebody. It was like *La Borlette*, or the lottery—who would "win" my money that day? Warm bodies began pressing on me, heads craning over my shoulder to see what I bought, curious about how much I paid for it, maybe even glimpsing how much money lingered in my wallet and could perhaps be wheedled out of me. As bodies pressed closer, the odor of charcoal and sweat, warm sour breath, and the sweet scent of hair pomade filled my nostrils.

I also smelled my fear.

I was the only foreigner there. A privileged outsider. Although Duvalier's thuggish Tonton Macoutes no longer ruled the streets, daily civil unrest kept everyone on edge. A crowd of determined and increasingly belligerent market women surrounded me, gesticulating angrily and yelling at me when I shook my head at proffered moldy oranges and blackened plantains, gourd-like squashes and bunches of wilted parsley.

Paying for the carrots, smiling at everyone, I turned and attempted a quick getaway. Alas, I wasn't fast enough.

As I darted toward my Trooper parked about five yards away, a tall woman who could have been football player William "The Refrigerator" Perry's *doppelganger* approached me with two pineapples. They clearly should have been sold two or even three days before. The dark fermenting spots around the "eyes" attested to that.

"Madame, eight *gourdes* for these pineapples! Madame!"

I attempted to put her off by saying, "*Merci*, Madame, I don't need any pineapples today. Maybe tomorrow. *Merci*." I flung open the back of the Trooper to throw in the carrots and get the hell out of there.

Big mistake.

The pineapple vendor spied the food and supplies piled up in the back of my truck, and envy and resentment and anger seemed to overtake her reason. She lunged between the door and me. I could not shut the back of the Trooper and escape. Crowds of onlookers pressed me from behind, and this enraged woman stood solidly in front of me. Yes, I should have bought the pineapples and have done with it.

But I didn't.

I froze in place like a cornered animal.

Thinking fast despite my paralyzing panic, approaching a state of dissociation and movie-like slow motion, I pondered, "What am I going to say here before something really bad happens?" Finally, I managed to squeeze out a few words in my fractured *Kreyòl*, babbling like a child learning to talk but getting my point across anyway.

"Listen, I will come back tomorrow and buy something from you then. I promise. Now I need to get home and cook for my son." I gripped the door handle as she pushed the door at me, hard metal banging into my right hip bone.

At the mention of my son, she screamed that she had a baby and needed to buy milk for him, and for her, so that she could nurse him. She had to sell those pineapples to do that.

Then she did something that stunned me, and probably all the onlookers, too: she pulled down her white spaghetti-strap tank top over her bulging breasts, grabbed the right one with both hands, and squirted breast milk all over the food in the back of my Trooper.

Trembling like a frightened kitten, in my smallness I had the presence of mind to try to appear calm. I placed my hand on her shoulder, and looked her square in the eye, saying, "I *will* be back tomorrow, but please let me go now."

I subtly maneuvered her away from the Trooper, slammed the door, my key at the ready, walking determinedly with my hand still on her shoulder, assuring her of my sincerity. With shaking knees, I clambered into the front seat, smiled one more time at the crowd, and took off like a shot, cold sweat trickling down from my armpits.

The last thing I needed was bad blood between me and a "Madame Sara."

With trepidation, I went back to that market the next day, sought out the breast-milk lady, and bought from her the lettuce I had forgotten the day before, plus more. I told her my name, and she told me hers. Chante.

I bought devil-red tomatoes, misshapen carrots, juicy yellowish-red mangoes, tiny French haricot beans, plump purple eggplants, hot bonnet peppers, and other things from Chante many more times. And then street violence overtook civil law, and we fled Haiti, back to the United States.

Because we could flee, unlike most of the people in Haiti.

Just as Marcel Proust recalled whole memories with bites of *madeleines* dipped in tea, for me memory became the smell of sour milk that stubbornly clung to the Trooper, invoking flashback images of that day for quite some time to come.

The most enduring memento of that moment lay in the realization that no matter how long I stayed in developing countries, no matter that I'd lived in a shack in Paraguay as a Peace Corps volunteer, no matter that I worked as a nutritionist in humanitarian aid, I still would never, ever, really know what life is like for most of the world's people.

Intellectually, yes.

Viscerally, no. Never.

Otherwise, I would have bought those pineapples gladly, wouldn't I have?

Pineapple Salsa

2 cups pineapple, cut into bite-size chunks

½ red onion, diced

1 jalapeño pepper, seeded, deveined, finely chopped

Juice of two limes

Fine sea salt, to taste

2 teaspoons granulated sugar

1 bunch fresh cilantro, finely chopped

Mix all ingredients in non-reactive bowl (glass or stainless steel). Chill before serving. Serve with grilled chicken and pork. Good with black beans and rice as well. Serves 4.

Street market, Petionville, author driving

Mezze and Curfew

As we bounced along the dirt road winding through the hills, I could distinctly
hear the rhythm of drums and see fires on the distant mountains.

~ Captain Hank Bracker

Only now do I understand how happy the owner of La Phoenicia must
have been to see us sitting at his table that night, the snowy white cloth covering
it catching our breadcrumbs and dribbles from the *mezze* he served. No doubt
we resembled strangers happening upon an isolated Bedouin tent in a Middle
Eastern desert, seeking a haven from the chaos outside La Phoenicia's walls.

When we arrived, he did run to greet us, his actions recalling those ancient words of hospitality found in Genesis 18:1-5:

> *The Lord appeared to Abraham by the terebinths of Mare; he was sitting*
> *at the entrance of the tent as the day grew hot. Looking up, he saw three*
> *men standing near him. As soon as he saw them, he ran from the entrance*
> *of the tent to greet them and, bowing down to the ground, he said, "My*
> *lords, if it pleases you, do not go on past your servant. Let a little water*
> *be brought; bathe your feet and recline under the tree. And let me fetch a*
> *morsel of bread that you may refresh yourselves."*

Strictly translated, *mezze* means "hors d'oeuvre," conjuring up images of
boring little bits and pieces, drooping and dripping, reclining on stale crackers,
tasting distinctly of chemical preservatives.

Ignore the literal translation.

Culinary historian Claudia Roden's interpretation says it better, much
better:

Mezze are one of the most delightful features of Middle Eastern food—not
least because they are meant to be enjoyed in an unhurried way—indeed they are
almost a way of life. … The pleasure of savouring the little pieces of food is accompa-
nied by feelings of peace and serenity, and sometimes by deep meditation.

At first, finding *mezze* in Haiti appeared to be an impossible task, even though Lebanese immigrants began settling there as early as the middle of the nineteenth century. One day, soon after we arrived for our three-year stint in Haiti, a friend of mine called and relayed some interesting information: did we know that we could find Lebanese food in Petionville, too, along with excellent French cuisine, of course?

Weeks later, we walked into La Phoenicia for the first time. By the time we left, both the food and the owners charmed us, and we spread the word about that delightful, dreamy place.

Popular with foreigners and Haitians of a certain class, those with money, La Phoenicia represented the fusion that occurs whenever and wherever French colonialism left tracks, be it Lebanon or the French Caribbean.

Unlike some *mezze* in Lebanon, where a hundred different dishes with a hundred different tastes spread across the table, the simple *mezze* at La Phoenicia arrived on a simple-but-large platter. Tabbouleh (bulghur wheat salad with mint and parsley), hummus (puréed chickpeas with tahini/sesame paste and lemon juice), and *baba ghanouj* (puréed roasted eggplant with tahini/sesame paste), the basics, with many rounds of soft pita bread. Of course, there were *sambuseks*, or phyllo pastry filled with meat, which I'd loved when we lived in Honduras, where a large Christian Lebanese population livened up the local cuisine of red beans and rice. *Kibbeh* (ground lamb), too, cooked in a dozen different ways, fried, grilled, stuffed, served with yoghurt and mint sauce.

Five months after Jean-Claude Duvalier stepped on a jet and absconded into exile in France, we found ourselves indulging in Lebanese *mezze* once again. Two USDA consultants were in town, whom we knew well. They often flew into Haiti to assist Mike with his farming systems development project. It was one of those balmy summer Haitian nights, but now filled with widespread civil unrest plaguing Port-au-Prince and Petionville.

At a large table in the interior patio of La Phoenicia, drinking local beer, dipping freshly made pita bread into the *baba ghanouj* and the hummus, talking and laughing together, we shared the pleasure that good food and better company generates. Hidden away in that oasis—far from the destitute beggars, the lame, the tormented, and the infirm of the Haitian streets—on the other side of those high walls, we left behind for a brief moment the turmoil and suffering outside. The lacy wrought-iron gates of the restaurant sheltered us from the trauma of everyday life, where we struggled to help people marginalized by Haiti's rigid social system, a system keeping 90% of the population illiterate and destitute. At that moment, all seemed like a horrible nightmare forgotten gratefully upon an early morning awakening.

The promise of the slave revolt and the ensuing independence of 1804 never came to pass. The French left, yes. But then the Creoles stepped into French shoes, creating an oligarchy, declining to relinquish any power to the masses. Haiti's constant political unrest became like an enormous unmoving stone, never completely receding to the background.

That night no other guests appeared. Only us. In the patio of La Phoenicia, its pale and irregularly shaped stone floor and colonnaded archways shaded by giant flame trees bursting with red blossoms, we ate as if we were dining in a palatial villa, straight out of a dream world filled with trickling fountains and sweet-smelling breezes.

As for the grease spots we left on the white tablecloth, those could be considered our signatures in the owner's guest book. According to Daniel S. Wolk:

> *Among certain Bedouin tribes, it is customary, after dinner, for guests to wipe their hands on the sides of the tent. The hand marks of grease are not cleaned, and as the number of fingerprints accrue, the host points with pride at the canvas guest book surrounding him on every side.*

I'd almost finished dragging the final fragrant *kibbeh* through the last smears of a cumin-and-mint yoghurt sauce when the owner once more came running to meet us. This time his red face and flustered hand movements warned us that his words would not be ones of calm, peace, and welcome.

Jabbing the index finger of his right hand at his watch repeatedly, he gasped out the words, "You must leave, you must leave. Now! Now! Curfew in five minutes!"

Curfew. Violators shot on sight. No questions asked. No one immune from the sudden violence, no one free from on-again, off-again martial law or the whims of angry mobs.

Not needing more prompting, we jumped up in unison, throwing handfuls of brightly colored Haitian paper money, *gourdes*, on the table as we ran out of the restaurant. Faces blanching, the USDA consultants fumbled frantically in their pockets for the keys to the project jeep. They faced the farthest and the most dangerous route to safety. Four minutes remained until 8 p.m.

That night, that time, everyone made it to safety.

Yes, many things comprise *mezze*. But in our minds, *mezze* will forever be associated with that impromptu curfew.

La Phoenicia unfortunately no longer adjoins the plaza in Petionville, Haiti, in the shadows of the cathedral where Baby Doc and Michelle Bennett married each other on a carpet of gardenias.

Whether it stems from words or guns, violence always demonstrates its incompatibility with hospitality.

Baba Ghanouj (Eggplant and Sesame Paste Dip)

1 large eggplant, slender, ideally grilled until charred and tender, or under broiler in standard oven

¼ cup fresh lemon juice

¼ cup sesame paste (*tahini*)

2 large garlic cloves, peeled, finely minced

½ teaspoon ground cumin

½ teaspoon fine sea salt, or to taste

Paprika and cayenne, for garnish

Flat-leaf parsley, finely chopped, for garnish

1 tablespoon extra virgin olive oil, for garnish

Peel charred eggplant, removing any tough parts and seeds. Squeeze gently over a strainer to remove as much of the bitter liquid as possible. Chop roughly, put eggplant in a blender. Add remaining ingredients, except for olive oil, paprika, cayenne, and parsley leaves. Purée. Place purée in flat, shallow dish. Sprinkle with paprika, cayenne, and parsley. Dribble olive oil over the top. Serve with warm pita bread. **Note:** Use smoked paprika for a smokier taste, especially if not using an outdoor grill. Makes about 2 cups.

Foie Gras, Mais Non!

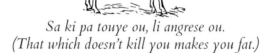

Sa ki pa touye ou, li angrese ou.
(That which doesn't kill you makes you fat.)
~ Haitian Proverb

I never liked liver.

For one thing, the gamey taste lingered on the back of my tongue a tad bit too long.

For another, the smell of liver frying in butter nauseated me. It was enough to gag a goat.

So how on earth did I end up cooking twenty pounds of goat liver one day in Haiti?

It was a long story.

The abbreviated version sounded pleasant enough.

I landed a job making goat liver *paté* for a development project dedicated to rearing goats on the central plateau near Hinche. Among other things, the project wanted to create a *paté* and market it to the French-influenced, wealthy Haitian elite. Proceeds from sales would help poor farmers by generating income. Testing would take place in an upscale supermarket in Petionville and at a butcher shop on Delmas owned by a French-Canadian.

The recipe I chose as the "guinea pig," Jane Grigson's *Pâté de Foie de Porc,* turned out well enough in the trial stages. But with goat liver as a base, I needed to add a little more oomph with a splash of brandy and *quatre-épices*—black or white pepper, cloves, nutmeg, and cinnamon or ginger—to pep things up a bit. The cost of doing it Grigson's way, unfortunately, precluded mass marketing.

So Sally, the project manager, handed me a recipe she thought would substitute well.

And that was where the arc of the story changed.

Shall I say that the uncensored version would include the part where I raced out of the kitchen, retching from the odor of all that goat liver sizzling and bubbling on the stove? For days afterward, every time I moved, my stomach muscles twitched in a funny and almost painful way.

Here's Sally's recipe exactly as I tested it:

1 pound goat liver, cut into thin slices

Butter or margarine for frying

3 tablespoons mayonnaise

2 tablespoon lemon juice

2 tablespoons butter (goat or cow)

1 tablespoon finely chopped onion

8-10 drops bottled hot pepper sauce like Tabasco

½ teaspoon. salt

½ teaspoon dry mustard

Dash pepper

Cook liver, covered, in butter/margarine, turning when brown. Put liver through meat grinder; blend with remaining ingredients. Place mixture in a 2-cup mold. Chill several hours; carefully unmold. Garnish with chopped hard-cooked egg, snipped chives, or snipped parsley. Serve with crackers or French country bread.

Not authentic *paté* at all, more like a spread. *Pas très authentique*, either. Nowhere near the buttery creaminess of authentic French *paté* nor *foie gras*.

Sally wrote the checks, so the recipe ruled.

The people who tasted-tested the *paté* reported that they liked it and would buy it.

But that never happened. Civil unrest in Haiti took a turn for the worse. The U.S. Embassy ordered all humanitarian-aid and non-essential personnel to leave, including us. The goat project closed down.

As for *foie gras*, on a foray once in the Foix area of France, I ate the real thing embedded in a *paté*—a big silver-dollar sized circle—and found it quite palatable. My tastes always ran toward champagne, while my wallet whispered "beer." Or put it another, more appropriate way: *foie gras* taste on a liverwurst budget.

Foie gras has come a long way from the days of chef Jean-Joseph Clause, who popularized *paté de foie gras* around 1779, during the reign of Louis XVI.

I've never cooked another smidgen of liver of any sort since that day in Haiti. Goat-liver *paté* still could be a thing. The farmers in Hinche and elsewhere deserve that opportunity.

Top: Author's house in Haiti, Rita and Pierre

Le Brown Bag

*It was one of the best kitchens I ever worked in, although
it was inefficient, inadequate, and often filled with flies.*
~ M.F.K. Fisher

Hal chugged a seemingly endless sip of his Prestige beer, the skunky-fla-vored swill popular with expats in Haiti. He opened his mouth as if to say some-thing. Instead, he took another bite of chicken, smothered in a cream sauce rich with chopped mushrooms and flecks of parsley, hints of tarragon. He chewed, cheeks moving in a slow rhythm.

Then he put his fork down on the table and leaned toward me, his nose nearly touching mine.

"You need to go into business," he slurred. "I'd pay good money to eat your food and not the slop in the hotel."

For a while, I'd been talking about a lunch delivery business with my friend Tito, who managed one of Hal's clothing factories in Port-au-Prince, where hundreds of seamstresses sewed slacks for Jos. A. Banks and other brands.

Hal slapped his hand down on the table. And pointed at me.

"Monday. I'm having a meeting with some shareholders. Bring me a lunch for eight people. Just sandwiches, and maybe a dessert. Yes, definitely dessert. How about that chocolate cake you made last time I ate here?" Another swig of Prestige, then he added, "Okay?"

This from the guy drinking beer with French food.

I had two days to get organized. The lunch came off well, so Hal ordered another for the following week, this time three days' worth of lunches.

Le Brown Bag, that's what I called the business, started with bang, thanks to Hal.

He surprised me with a rubber stamp and ink pad to use on the brown lunch bags I bought from a stationery shop on Delmas, one of the three main roads in Port-au-Prince.

Like many businesses, mine took off because of good timing. A few weeks after I started delivering sandwiches, mini salads, and simple desserts, the frustrated and downtrodden Haitian people protested against Baby Doc, the scion of the notorious Papa Doc, or François Duvalier known as the Vodun god Baron Samedi.

Because of the unrest, my clientele soon included several Embassy personnel afraid to venture out into the streets. Unwilling to bring lunches to work.

That left me to slice the crispy baguettes, so to speak.

I bought them every morning after dropping Erik off at school. Driving two miles down the winding mountain road to Petionville to the boulangerie and back, up through the morning mist, meant dodging the dozens of "Madame Saras" trudging to the market, as well as small pickups, called *tap-taps*, taxiing the more affluent to wherever they wanted to go.

I also concocted the sandwich fillings, salads, and cakes.

Most of the time, I moved about the vast chaos that was Port-au-Prince without much trouble. There might be the scent of burning tires in the air sometimes, down near the port where cruise ships no longer anchored. Crowds thronged sporadically at certain places, especially the Presidential Palace. A few days after Baby Doc Duvalier packed up and left, a mob tore down his house in Kenscoff with their bare hands, leaving mounds of rubble amidst a rare forest of pines.

Lieutenant General Henri Namphy succeeded Baby Doc, from February 7, 1986 to February 7, 1988. Namphy shared a bed, so to speak, with the Haitian oligarchy, a group of some thirty families who showed no interest in reform of any sort.

Euphoria at the regime change soon spun around to anger as it became clear that nothing had shifted for the poor people of Haiti, and the status quo remained intact.

One day Tito ordered twenty lunches for his staff because of escalating unrest.

While packing the coolers, Rita, an employee and friend who helped me, warned me to be careful, to stay away from the port road. But to get to the factory complex outside the city, I had to drive that road.

Revenge and retribution boiled over. People seethed with pent-up anger. They wanted revenge, retribution. Thus, the lives of many of Duvalier's former Tonton Macoutes ended on the port road. Necklaced with gasoline-soaked truck tires and set on fire, burned alive on the street, murdered for their past cruelty to their neighbors.

Despite all the violence surrounding us, Americans were not targeted. I took solace from that.

I smelled smoke from burning tires as I swung onto the port road, Tito's twenty lunches packed in the cooler in the back of my Trooper.

A barricade of tires blocked my way, but I kept going. The ragged men standing guard waved me on when they saw I was a foreigner, a *blan*. Then, at the opened gate to Tito's factory, a sizeable mob kept me from parking inside, as I usually did. The guard, his eyes wide, stuttered as he motioned for me to park by the outside wall on the left. I jumped out, my upper lip beaded with sweat, and not only from the oppressive heat.

About fifty yards separated me from the stairs leading to the factory offices, my usual delivery spot. I grabbed the heavy cooler and started moving through the mob, some armed with wide wooden clubs, some with machetes.

I was afraid. Terrified, actually. But I tried not to show it.

"*Excusez-moi, excusez-moi,*" I said, as I zigzagged through the hot, sticky, sweaty bodies, brushing skin, voices murmuring, voices shouting. And praying I would make it without someone bashing my skull in. I smiled as I went, trying not to bump people with the cooler. Most of the people there smiled back. I looked up, and spied Tito hurrying toward the staircase. The mob focused their attention on him. In that moment, I found a straight path to the first step. Tito almost carried me and the cooler to the top as one of his assistants pulled us in and slammed the door.

I had one more delivery to make and needed to leave. Tito took me to the head of the stairs and, in his fluent *Kreyòl*, asked the people to please let me go in peace. The crowd parted like the Red Sea. I stumbled through the salty, rancid, sweat-filled air. And collapsed in my truck, shaking. I drove off, realizing I was smelling my own sweat, too. In a blur, I handed the lunches to the man at the next factory, where all was quiet, and drove home as fast as I could.

When I walked into my kitchen, my stomach growled, but I felt no hunger. Rita heard it. She silently handed me a piece of the day's cake, the taste of cherries on my tongue reviving my spirits somewhat.

But there were no cherries in that cake.

Chocolate-Banana Cake

Unsweetened cocoa powder, for pan

1¼ cup unbleached all-purpose flour

½ cup unsweetened cocoa powder

1 teaspoon baking powder

½ teaspoon baking soda

¼ teaspoon salt

½ cup unsalted butter, room temperature

1 cup firmly packed dark brown sugar

1 teaspoon instant coffee powder

2 large eggs, room temperature

1 tablespoon freshly grated orange peel

1 cup banana purée, approximately 3 large ripe bananas

1 cup semisweet chocolate chips

Center rack in oven and preheat to 325°F. Grease a 6-cup fluted tube pan, then dust with a bit of cocoa powder. Put first 5 ingredients into a large bowl. Beat butter in another bowl. Add brown sugar and coffee powder to butter, whip until fluffy. Beat in eggs one at a time, beat for 2 more minutes. Stir in orange peel. Add dry ingredients alternately with banana purée, ending with dry ingredients. Stir in chocolate chips. Spoon batter into prepared pan and smooth the top. Bake until cake is firm to the touch in center, about 70 minutes or so, depending on the oven's idiosyncrasies. Cool cake in pan for 10 minutes. Turn cake out of pan and onto a rack to cool completely. Dust with powdered sugar moments before serving. Delicious served with super rich and creamy vanilla ice cream or whipped cream. Not bad plain, either. 8–12 Servings.

Gonâve Island

Little has been done to conserve Haiti's flora and fauna.
~ Britannica

As the boat roared away from the dock in Port-au-Prince, I thought of the lobster barbecue, the real buccaneer, that we signed up for on the isolated island of Gonâve, about twenty miles off the coast of Haiti. Ocean spray glittered in my hair, and sunscreen dripped off my nose as I swigged one of several musty beers I would guzzle that day, reclining on the deck of a large, powerful motorboat churning its way through the Bay of Gonâve.

Sympathetically tut-tutting as a few unfortunate fellow passengers hung green-faced over the railings, I hobbled across the deck toward the cooler. Was it the beer or the boat? Cracking open another icy bottle with a rusty opener, I eyed the receding shoreline that put me between the island and the "mainland." Being on that boat offered an entirely different perspective. Scrutinizing the mainland from the sea, I couldn't see the swarming masses of poverty-stricken humanity surging through the diesel-and-charcoal-smoke-choked streets of Port-au-Prince.

But I could see Haiti's majestic and denuded mountains, though, and thought once more how tragic the whole place was. Like Brown (or was it Jones?) in Graham Greene's *The Comedians*, I downed half my beer to drown those negative thoughts and walked even more unsteadily back to my perch.

After one more bottle of beer and several applications of sunscreen, I thought we were approaching the shore of Gonâve Island. As it turned out, almost. Just before reaching the island, the boat passed human settlements built on flat sheets of rock jutting at most a couple of feet out of the ocean.

Stunned, I watched the people who lived on these sheets of rock, thatched huts topping each slab of stone, cooking, hanging laundry out to dry, children skipping about. The few jobs around mostly related to fishing. Where did they get their water, their charcoal, their food if the fish weren't biting? Kevin Costner's film "Waterworld" had not yet been made, but those rock cities resembled

Gonâve Island boat tour

scenes from the film, dotting the sea at approximately half-mile intervals.

To my spoiled Western eyes, it seemed as if hell suddenly emerged from the deep.

I couldn't imagine the ennui of living in such miserable quarters. Did they sleep on damp beds at night? How did they fare in the tropical storms assaulting the Caribbean every year? Did they bury their dead in the ocean? My unspoken questions were endless.

I never did find any answers.

Feeling somewhat sobered by these thoughts, I studied the approaching reef-fringed shoreline of Gonâve Island, thirty-seven miles long and nine miles wide. The boat veered around the far southern end and chugged on for several minutes, finally docking about fifteen yards from a white sandy beach. Wearing tennis shoes to avoid coral cuts and sea urchins' spiny appendages, we gingerly slipped waist-high into the warm, gently lapping crystal-clear water, the bottom visible even when we stood up straight.

Fish of every color and hue fearlessly swam up to us, pecking softly at our legs with their bony mouths. As we waded slowly toward the beach, they darted swiftly away and hid in the crevices of the colorful coral.

As we reached the beach, we heard a jolting cry of pain.

Our friend Quentin, from New Zealand, unaware of the coral reefs, became so overwhelmed by the beauty of the water that he dove straight in and scraped his entire chest on the jagged coral. Bleeding from dozens of scrapes on his scrawny white, hairless chest, he staggered onto the beach, where the boat captain applied first aid.

In the meantime, we found the beer coolers again and plopped down nearby on a large blanket to watch the cooking preparations. Some men in a boat paddled up with baskets of live struggling lobsters. Dumping the baskets on the beach and taking their money, they left, but not before eyeing the women in their skimpy bathing suits.

Four Haitian men—crew members acting as cooks—dug shallow holes in the sand and piled wood into each. After dousing the wood with kerosene, they threw in lit matches. Eventually, both the fires and the sunlight warmed us. Once the flames gleamed crimson here and there in the ash, the cooks dropped large square iron grids over the holes. Grabbing lobster after lobster, they threw the still-living creatures onto the grids. Their dark shells gradually turned from black to ox-blood red over the white-hot ash.

Sensing that dinner was about to be served, we stood up and milled about, wondering where the table was, the dishes, the forks, etc. Out of seemingly nowhere appeared gourd bowls about eighteen inches in diameter and several inches deep. The cooks flung pieces of grilled lobster into each bowl. Then they handed each small group of diners wooden plates garnished with lime wedges.

The captain then demonstrated how to eat the feast.

Wading into the water, he stood with one of the large gourd bowls floating in front of him and a plate, too, a bottle of beer swaying on it in unison with the gentle waves. He dipped a piece of lobster in the ocean and squirted lime juice on the now-salted lobster pieces. With a flourish, he popped the lobster meat in his mouth, chewed, and swallowed. Lobster shells and lime rinds went into the ocean.

That was it.

Nothing to it.

No dishes to wash except gourd bowls and wooden plates. No tablecloths. No chairs. No tables. No napkins, just the back of my arm. Warm sunshine caressing my face. The taste of lime and lobster mixed with the saltiness of the sea. Cold beer.

Paradise, for me.

But not for the thousands of people living on the island. Water scarcity and isolation separated the people from the mainland, where they seemed to have been forgotten.

Though I prayed no one used the ocean for a urinal while we ate.

Grilled Lobster

4 (8-ounce) lobster tails

Salted water, as salty as the ocean

2 limes, cut into wedges

Heat grill to around 375°F. When ready, cut through top of the lobster shell and pry open slightly. Run a skewer through the center of each tail and place on grill. This helps to prevent tails from curling up as they cook. Cook approximately 5 minutes per side. Place lobster tails on plates along with a bowl of salted water and a few lime wedges. Pick out meat with fingers and dip in salted water, then squirt meat with lime juice. Nothing to it. Serves 4.

Street scene, Haiti

Revolution

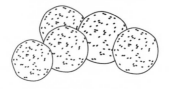

I am the Haitian flag. He who is my enemy is the enemy of the fatherland.
~ François Duvalier

Peggy touched my elbow at the Embassy Christmas party. Turning her back to the military attaché, a colonel we all knew as CIA, she flicked a strand of thick blond hair away from her blue eyes. Her nose pressed close to my ear as she leaned in, whispering, "Will there really be a revolution?"

I nod, "Yes."

She shook her head "No," back and forth, toddler-like. Her lips pursed, smearing pink lipstick across startling white teeth. A maid approached, offered us bubbly drinks. I snagged one and shifted away. Peggy followed me, hissing that I was wrong. Drops of her saliva sprayed across my nose as she spat out angry words.

"The intel doesn't point to revolution. People aren't radicalized. This isn't Central America, for God's sake."

I fumbled in my purse for a Kleenex.

Yes, there really will be a revolution.
*****

The dictator's wife chartered a Concorde, flew to Paris. Word on the street said she'd spent nine million U.S. dollars, Christmas shopping, money earmarked for Haiti's December gasoline imports. Endless lines at gas stations snaked around the pumps and down the roads. Gasoline left over from November sold out fast. Gas was lifeblood.

Haiti bled out, gut wounded.

Thuggish secret police, Duvalier's Tonton Macoutes, prowled the tense streets, their aviator sunglasses glinting like Christmas baubles, mirroring fear. Bloody machetes everywhere, moldering bodies filled gutters, bloating in the tropical heat. Fat turkey vultures roosted in sparse flame trees.

High above it all, in the mountains, the nightly pop-pop of gunshots whined through rocky crevices, decades of deforestation made visible in fleeting flashes of light.

Yes, there really will be a revolution.

*****

Pierre dug in the garden less. Instead, he stood outside the gate at my house, chatting with passersby in rapid-fire *Kreyòl*. Rita swept the tiled kitchen floors over and over as she whispered that Baby Doc Duvalier would be leaving. Soon. Her lips trembled as she spoke. How does she know? She shook her head. Talk meant danger. Best stay silent. And wait. During World War II, propaganda posters warned that "Loose lips sink ships." Here, loose lips guaranteed a prolonged and painful stay in the bowels of Fort Dimanche. Torture, a gun to the head, a bundle of bones in a pile of rotten garbage.

Yes, there really will be a revolution.

*****

The ambassador, a political appointee, threw a New Year's Eve party. Now he tread water in Port-au-Prince, in over his non-political head. Peggy sidled up to me. We grinned Stepford Wives smiles, all but curtsying as he passed by, patting us both on the back as he went. Her hands shook as she placed her empty drink glass on an empty tray offered by the maid. The same whispered question. "Do you still think there really will be a revolution?" I nodded, once again, "Yes. Really." I headed toward the punch bowl.

Yes, there really will be a revolution.

*****

The Embassy at last issued shortwave radios to USAID contractors. Our radio's constant beeps and burps signaled the coming of chaos. I silenced the chirping at night with a towel. And slept in a semblance of peace through the unceasing gun fire from down the mountain. My faith lay, right or wrong, with the Wackenhut night guards and our three dogs. Curfew confined us to four walls and dwindling food.

Still no gasoline.

Burning tires barricaded garbage-strewn streets in Port-au-Prince. Acrid smoke stained the air black. Frenzied, howling mobs smashed windows, tore down buildings with their bare hands, driven to madness by thirty years of repression, murder, and anger. Drums beat nightly, pulsating like a thousand hearts, eerie in the bleak darkness, summoning the god of war, Ogou. Streetlights turned blind as the power grid died. At dusk, the sun melted into the pinkness of the ocean and blackness seeped over everything. I read Graham

Greene's *The Comedians* for the sixth time, by the light of a candle.

Yes, there really will be a revolution.

*****

At the Embassy cocktail party a few days before Easter, Peggy tapped my shoulder. "How did you know?" I stared at her, then looked away. The colonel stood by the wall of windows overlooking the gardens thick with yellow-tipped birds-of paradise. I wheeled around to face her. "Because, my dear," I whispered, "Embassy people live in a bubble. The walls surrounding you are not only made of concrete."

The maid passed by with a tray of bubbly drinks. I grabbed one and raised my glass. She smiled.

Yes, there really was a revolution.

*****

February 7, 1986: The revolution came in the night—swift, quiet, deadly. A deal with France, a U.S. plane at the ready, a black Mercedes winding through funereal streets. Exile for the monster. Word spread like a raging flood. Dancing. Singing. Drumming. Hoping. Especially hoping. All dashed as the oligarchy sharpened its talons once again.

Salt Cod Acras

1½ cups salt cod, soaked, drained, deboned, and mashed

¾ cup all-purpose flour

1 teaspoon baking powder

¾ cup whole milk

2 tablespoons vegetable oil

2 egg yolks

4 egg whites, beaten until stiff

1 tablespoon chopped flat-leaf parsley

2 garlic cloves, peeled and minced

Pinch of hot red pepper, such as cayenne

Chopped fresh chile pepper, to taste

Oil for deep frying

Mix ingredients together, except for oil. Heat oil to 350°F. Form balls with 2-table-spoons-size soup spoon and dip into hot oil. Fritters should float, double in size, and brown in around 3–5 minutes. Serve hot with hot sauce and *Pikliz*, pickled vegetables similar to coleslaw made with vinaigrette. **Note:** *Acras*, or fritters, are found throughout West Africa and the Caribbean. They may well be the ancestors of hush puppies. Makes about 2 dozen.

Tap-tap, Haiti

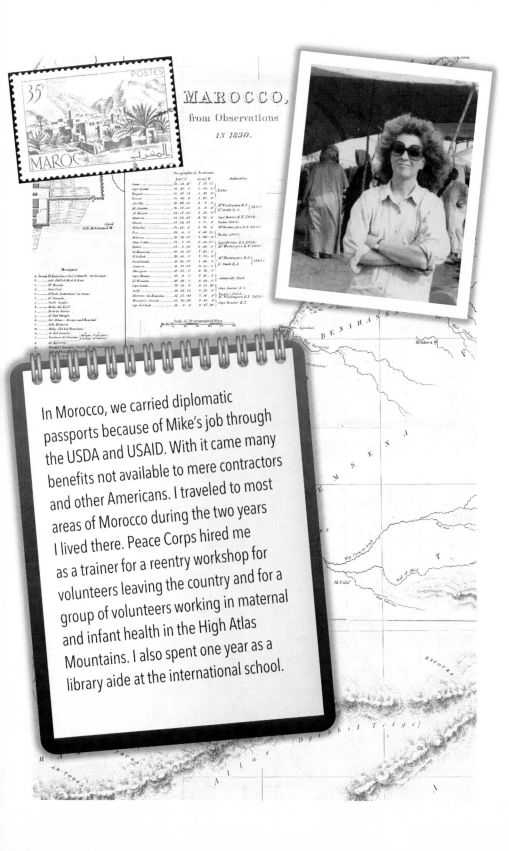

MAROCCO,
from Observations
IN 1830.

In Morocco, we carried diplomatic passports because of Mike's job through the USDA and USAID. With it came many benefits not available to mere contractors and other Americans. I traveled to most areas of Morocco during the two years I lived there. Peace Corps hired me as a trainer for a reentry workshop for volunteers leaving the country and for a group of volunteers working in maternal and infant health in the High Atlas Mountains. I also spent one year as a library aide at the international school.

Moroccan Market

Monkfish

She discovered a whole square devoted to seafood—squid and sea bass, shrimp, prawns, rock lobsters, octopus, sea cucumbers, and a pallet of unidentifiable slugs and snails, creatures with fluorescent fins and prehistoric shells ... .

~ Elin Hilderbrand

I first gazed at his ugly mug in French-influenced Morocco, more precisely at the Rabat fish market.

Like Beauty with the Beast, I fell in love.

His name was Legion—*Nomen mihi Legio est, quia multi sumus.*

Sea Devil

Crapaud

Baudroie

Lotte

Goosefish

Anglerfish

Poor Man's Lobster

With the slinky tail of an eel and the tooth-rich mouth of a shark, the monkfish incarnated ugliness.

Two-thirds of his body was skull. Tiny triangular-shaped teeth lined the rounded jaws that some call "Jaws of Hell," looking for all the world like miniature roadblocks. No fish, once inside that cavernous mouth, could flee, despite swimming frantically against those backward-pointing daggers. For the monkfish, life centered around its gaping vacuum-cleaner of a mouth, sucking in small fish, bathers' feet, and even the occasional goose. Burrowing into an underworld of muddy sand and eelgrass, luring small fish with its angling equipment attached to its head and centered between tiny marble-sized eyes, the monkfish itself often ended up ambushed.

This mottled-brown bottom dweller of the shoals put up a good fight when hooked. Yet fishermen didn't hesitate to throw this gnashing, thrashing fish back into the ocean. Often considered unwanted "trash fish," despite its appearance, the monkfish fed many poor fishermen's families.

I knew none of this when I peered into that toothy mouth in Rabat.

"What is this creature?" I asked Jane, my friend who'd studied at the Cordon Bleu in Paris.

"It's a monkfish." She smiled knowingly.

And added, "The tail is the prize. I call it 'poor woman's lobster.'"

The fishmonger rolled up the sleeves of his *djellaba* and grabbed the slobber-slimy and scale-less skin, bulldog-flaccid and loose. He peeled off the skin all in one piece, as quickly as a Follies swimmer removing her bathing cap. I bought the whole tail, the part with the sweet, white lobster-like flesh. That night, I lit a dozen large pieces of charcoal, uneven in shape and size, nothing like the briquettes sold at the U.S. Embassy Commissary.

And feasted on gorgeous, grilled unwanted flesh.

Monkfish Brochettes with Sweet Red Peppers

3 pounds monkfish tail, cut into 2-inch chunks

3 large red bell peppers, cut into 1½-inch squares

Olive oil for brushing

Fine sea salt, to taste

2 cups freshly squeezed orange juice

2 garlic cloves, peeled, minced

1/3 cup salted butter, cut into 6 pieces

½ teaspoon ground cumin

Red pepper flakes, to taste

Cilantro, finely chopped

Thread 24 bamboo skewers–presoaked in cold water for at least 30 minutes–by alternating pepper squares with fish. Be sure to allow about half an inch of space between pieces of fish. Brush with olive and salt to taste. Set brochettes on a baking sheet to rest until ready to grill. Prep grill about 45 minutes before cooking. If using oven broiler, start heating it 15 minutes before cooking.

Meanwhile, boil down orange juice and garlic until liquid reduces by half. Whisk in butter, piece by piece, until sauce thickens. Stir in cumin, red pepper flakes, and more sea salt if desired. Reserve about 4 tablespoons of sauce for brushing fish. Set remaining sauce aside. Place brochettes on grill, cook until brown in color and opaque. Brush with reserved orange sauce a few times. **Do not mix the brushed sauce with the rest of the sauce.** When fish is done, place skewers on a platter, spoon remaining orange sauce over them, and sprinkle with cilantro. Serve with an almond-and-raisin pilaf. Serves 4–6.

Erik and Mike climbing sand dunes near Erfoud, Morocco

Grain and Bread

*At the same distance from it is the city of Sala, situated on a river which bears
the same name, a place which stands upon the very verge of the desert, and
though infested by troops of elephants, is much more exposed to the attacks of
the nation of the Autololes, through whose country lies the road to Mount Atlas,
the most fabulous locality even in Africa.*

~ Pliny the Elder

As we neared the banks of the Bou Regreg River, Fatima pointed to the
large pink building to the right, surrounded by a chain-link fence as high as a
three-story building, razor wire undulating at the top. A deterrent to the hungry, to thieves, who would otherwise sneak over or through in the blackness
of night, as the oblivious guards stood around a sputtering fire, chatting and
drinking endless glasses of mint tea.

I spun the steering wheel to the right. My silver Peugeot 505 slipped
through the narrow open gate like a grey mouse squeezing under a door frame.

The aroma of raw wheat overwhelmed me as chaff danced in the air,
intensifying with every gust of salty air sweeping in from the Atlantic Ocean a
few blocks away.

Bread was, and is, sacred in Morocco. All scraps must be eaten, never
thrown to the ground, never tossed in the garbage. That explained the bits and
pieces of bread I often spotted left on windowsills, ledges, or any other flat surface where a starving animal or even a hungry child could nourish themselves.

Rituals attached themselves to this sacredness.

Every day, children or servants headed to the bakeries, carrying long,
narrow wooden trays covered with rising rounds of dough, each loaf slashed
on top with a family's unique mark. Otherwise, how would they know whose
bread they might be carting home?

The first step in this elaborate tradition required good, mold-free whole
wheat flour.

That was why I sat on a wobbly wooden stool in the grain market in

Rabat, the murmur of traffic matched by the sounds of the current of the Bou Regreg River, not more than fifty feet from where I watched the grinding of my grain. The flour made the nicest-tasting bread, even if it is soft wheat and not the hard wheat used for bread in the States.

I'd bought twenty kilos of wheat kernels a few days earlier, which we picked over sitting there in the market with the help of three Amazigh women, one veiled and the others not. Light blue Amazigh tattoos on their chins and their foreheads signified several things, including cultural identity. Formerly called "Berber," the proper name for their group was Amazigh.

The picking process took an hour and a half. The women began talking among themselves to pass the time. I, of course, understood not a single word they and Fatima uttered. Speaking Moroccan Arabic, they chatted away, as my sense of being an outsider deepened with every laugh and giggle. Every once in a while, the oldest eyeing me over the black veil covering her entire lower face.

I smiled and saw her eyes crinkle. A smile speaks volumes, no matter what language passes between people.

For those who did not grow their own grain or had no family members living in the *bled* (countryside) growing it, the old grain market in Rabat provided all the grain and other dried food necessary for life in Morocco.

The pink walls of the grain market sheltered more than huge mountains of wheat kernels; it was also an excellent place to buy lentils, chickpeas, white beans, whole- and split-broad beans, split peas, cornmeal, pasta, semolina, couscous, short-grain rice for risottos, and broken rice.

After the grain market, we stopped by the *souk*, or open-air market, and bought a large blue plastic tub for washing the grain. Once the grain appeared clean, we dried it in the sun for three days on the cement floor of my walled-in courtyard. Then we returned to the grain market, where the Amazigh ladies greeted us like old friends and ground the grain into flour for me.

After three hours, the women pronounced my flour ready and poured it into the large basket Fatima brought with us, lined with a clean white cloth. I drove back to my modernist house in Rabat's upscale Souissi neighborhood, where all the Embassy people lived.

With freshly ground grain, I knew the bran and other components would fast turn rancid in the summer heat. So I planned to store the flour in my freezer in 3-pound portions. Most flour and rice need to be sifted before cooking, a necessary step to rid them of weevils. Freezing helped to kill the pests, too.

We weighed and packed the flour into large, clear plastic bags, dated and labeled. Into the freezer it all went, crowding the rice and ready-made couscous, cut-up chickens and chunks of beef.

Plus a few rashers of bacon and other bits and pieces of pork I managed to buy from the French woman whose business possessed no sign, except word of mouth: "The white house covered with ivy."

Khobz (Moroccan Bread)

2 teaspoons granulated sugar

1 tablespoon active dry yeast

4 cups unbleached all-purpose flour

1 cup whole-wheat flour

2 teaspoons fine sea salt

¾ cup milk, room temperature

2 teaspoons sesame seeds

1 tablespoon anise seed

¼ cup cornmeal

Dissolve sugar in 1 cup of warm water. Add yeast, stir until dissolved. Let yeast sit about 5-10 minutes–it should look bubbly. In a large bowl, combine all-purpose flour with whole wheat flour. Mix in salt. Add yeast and milk to the flour. Mix dough with a wooden spoon, adding more water until it begins to come together, any-where from 1-2 cups of water depending on the flour. Dough ought to be sticky and wet. Scoop it out onto a well-floured surface, rest it uncovered for 15-20 minutes. Knead dough, adding a few more tablespoons of all-purpose flour if necessary. The final dough will be somewhat stiff but pliable. Continue kneading for 10 minutes. Add sesame and anise seeds toward the end of the kneading time. Divide dough into two equal rounds. Form each piece of dough into two round, dome-shaped loaves, about 2 inches thick in the center. Place dough on baking sheets sprinkled with cornmeal. Cover loaves with damp lint-free kitchen towels, place in a warm spot to rise until doubled in size. Preheat oven to 400°F. Before placing loaves in the oven, pierce top and sides of each loaf several times with tines of a fork. Bake for 25–30 minutes. A well-baked loaf should sound hollow when thumped with a finger. Cut into wedges and serve with *harira*. Makes two 8-inch round loaves.

Sister-in-law Kay Taylor, Habiba, and the author at a military cemetery in Khenifra, Morocco

Berber tents, southern Morocco

Pork Shop

Travelling, one accepts everything; indignation stays at home. One looks, one listens, one is roused to enthusiasm by the most dreadful things because they are new. Good travellers are heartless.

~ Elias Canetti

Every time I walked to the front gate to my house, its rusted hinges squeaking like tiny mice hidden in hollow walls, the piney smell of rosemary enveloped me. Thick, bristly, and rigidly trimmed in a way that reminded me of photos of Daddy's crew cut, this rosemary grew along the sidewalk, silent as sentinels. My long skirts always brushed against those tiny tongue-like leaves. So the scent of home followed me as I meandered through the labyrinth of Rabat's open-air market, where I bought fresh red meat and just-caught wide-eyed fish and ripe, juicy melons for my endless kitchen experiments.

That scent also enveloped me the day my friend Jane first introduced me to the Pork Lady of Rabat, who sold pork in a white house covered with ivy.

Hidden behind a small white wall, all the French cars parked on a quiet residential street in Rabat the only indication that something might be different about the place. The Pork Lady, whose name I never knew, was a brisk, no-nonsense, impeccably dressed French woman, a spotless white apron tied around her delicate waist, her blond hair twisted in a classic chignon. She looked as if she could move from abattoir to salon with a flick of the wrist as she shed the apron.

Every time I shopped there, I snuck through the door like a sinner on their way to confession. Nevertheless, I loaded up my basket with nearly every cut of pork resting on the immaculately clean trays in the glass display cases. Often.

The shop brought to mind the grilled pork loin studded with garlic and strewn with broken rosemary branches of a long-ago summer sojourn in southern France. When the taste of earth and smoke mingled with the lavender-scented air around me. When drops of red wine stained my lips. When rough linen napkins white as the pigeons bobbling at my feet slipped off my lap, falling on the stone floor of the bistro in a dark cellar. When the sound of barking dogs rang in my ears, as church bells tolled for Compline in the nearby monastery.

Eating pork in a Muslim country was sinful, but I couldn't help myself. I did bless The Pork Lady for making it possible, though.

Grilled Rosemary-Scented Pork Tenderloin

Fine sea salt and freshly ground black pepper, to taste

4 garlic cloves, peeled and mashed

1/3 cup Maille brand Dijon mustard

2 tablespoons fresh rosemary, coarsely chopped

2 pounds pork tenderloin

Olive oil

Mix salt, pepper, garlic, mustard, and rosemary. Rub mixture over pork, let marinate for 1 hour in a sealed plastic bag. Heat grill to 375°F. Brush racks with olive oil, place pork over fire. Let brown, but not burn. Remove pork from direct contact with the heat, cook via indirect heat. Be sure to close the grill lid. Check for doneness after about 25 minutes. Remove from grill, set on platter, let sit for about 10 minutes. Slice into serving pieces. Serves 4.

Fez medina, olive market

Chicken on the Hoof

*The camel never sees his own hump, but that of his brothers
is always in his eyes.*

~ Moroccan Proverb

A labyrinth, a medieval walking pattern, that's what the ancient market in Fez reminded me of. No map, only memory, could guide the visitor through the maze. That was why dozens of young Moroccan men always loitered around the Fez medina's main entrance. They possessed something I didn't: knowledge of the way out, the path to the end.

Walking through that thousand-year-old place mimicked a trip back in time. Except for the dim electric lights and tangled black wires crossing the narrow stone passageways, Fez gave me the illusion of traveling through centuries. Donkeys laden with terracotta pots and brass chandeliers clopped through, driven by men in long flowing robes, who would fit right in when Idris I settled his nascent Idrisid dynasty there 789 A.D. The occasional bad-tempered camel lumbered by, causing me to flatten myself against a wall to make room.

In contrast, the Rabat medina required no guides to lead visitors out of the labyrinth. It was in the Rabat medina that Morocco's culinary wealth first became apparent to me.

I walked through passageways there built not of stone, but of ordinary buildings flanked by makeshift tents and stalls. Mounds of spices fashioned into sharp-pointed cones, fish on ice, their bright eyes telling of their early morning demise in the Atlantic waters just offshore, lamb or mutton hanging bloody on hooks.

And chickens, dead and alive.

Fatima admonished me again and again to buy live chickens. The butcher would prep the chicken on the spot, but first, I needed to point out which chickens to slaughter.

"They taste better, more flavor," she'd say whenever I returned from the market with a plucked headless-and-footless chicken, killed by another's hand, not mine.

One day I set out to do that.

First, I took care to line my suitcase-size, straw shopping basket with a plastic bag in case there was blood. Then I chose a vendor to buy from, the fortyish man who always smiled at me and bowed, his right hand over his heart in greeting, gesturing to his pen of white-feathered birds. A small open wire cage allowed them a final sensation of fleeting freedom, their claws rat-a-tatting across a blue plastic tarp thrown over the cement floor. He sprayed the sheet often with a hose to remove any bird droppings, too.

I approached his stand, glancing at the birds strutting and pecking in the cage. The vendor asked how many I wanted. I held up two fingers. He grabbed two, stuck them into a blue plastic bucket, and placed the bucket on the scale, more or less guessing the weight because they squirmed too much. As he started to write the weight on a slip of paper, one of the birds cocked its head at me, peering at me, its eyes darting back and forth, wildly.

I couldn't do it.

I muttered, "*Non*," and waved, walked off, leaving the vendor perplexed, possibly offended.

About fifty yards away, I stopped in front of my usual vendor, whose chickens rested nude, plucked and dead, on the tile countertop of his stall. I held up two fingers, again. This time, I paid and put the chickens in the basket.

Once again, I realized something about myself: I couldn't kill my own meat.

But I was happy to let someone else do it.

Moroccan Chicken with Green Olives and Preserved Lemons

3 tablespoons extra virgin olive oil

3 pounds skin-on chicken legs and thighs, trimmed of excess fat

1 medium yellow onion, halved through the root and thinly sliced

4 garlic cloves, peeled and crushed into a paste with fine sea salt

Freshly ground black pepper

1 tablespoon sweet paprika

1 teaspoon ground cinnamon

½ teaspoon ground ginger

½ teaspoon turmeric

¼ teaspoon cayenne pepper

1½ cups chicken stock

1 preserved lemon, rinsed, peel removed, and sliced

1 cup green olives, pitted

1 tablespoon fresh lemon juice, or to taste

Chopped cilantro for garnish

Preheat oven to 325°F. Heat olive oil in a heavy Dutch oven. Brown chicken on both sides, remove to a plate, toss onion into remaining oil in pan, cook until translucent. Add garlic and spices. Stir for about a minute or until spices release their aroma. Return chicken to the pot. Pour in stock, add preserved lemon, bring to a boil, cover pot, and place it in center of oven. Cook approximately 1 hour or until chicken is tender. Uncover, add lemon juice and olives. Return pot uncovered to oven and cook for another 20 minutes. Place chicken pieces on a platter, pour cooking juices over them. Sprinkle with chopped cilantro. Serve with couscous. Serves 4–6.

The author and Sunny

Going to the Desert

Manage with bread and butter until God sends the honey.
~ Moroccan proverb

The call came a week before Ramadan began, the thirty-day fast in the ninth month of the Islamic calendar.

Peace Corps/Morocco wanted me to train nine Peace Corps volunteers in maternal and infant health and nutrition. When? In two days. Where? Near a small village called Ait Baha. In the Anti-Atlas, in the far south of Morocco, not far from Agadir, formerly known as Santa Cruz de Cap de Guè. Probably some other trainer backed out.

I boarded a small commuter plane out of Rabat and flew to Agadir, lugging one small suitcase and a briefcase bulging with papers and books. Ahmed, a Peace Corps administrator, picked me up at the airport in Agadir. In silence, we drove forty miles into the *bled*, or countryside, miles of nothing but sheep and goats and dry, parched earth.

We arrived at dusk at the training site, an as-yet-unfinished health clinic hovering on the edge of Ait Baha. My room would soon house the sick or the dying, windows instead of walls facing the corridor. Someone thoughtfully taped brown butcher paper over the windows. Giving me, the lone trainer, a bit of privacy. Though the toilet was down the hall, a typical hole in the floor, anything but private.

The first day of training ended fine. Late that afternoon, we Americans all piled into the Peace Corps Land Rover and chugged out into the *bled* to a site where the local community was building a school and a well. Ahmed wanted to check on the progress of the well project as long as he was in the area.

As soon as we stepped out of the Land Rover, dozens of skinny little boys surrounded us, staring. Then men arrived. Polite, seeing us neither as women nor as men, genderless as it were, they offered us, eight American women (and one man), strong, hot, bitter tea, wildly different from the tea of the city. The local women and girls were nowhere to be seen, as it was one of the most conservative areas of Morocco. Bidding our farewells, the Land Rover turned toward the snow-capped mountains, and we drove many more miles over rutted roads, the sun chasing us from behind.

Another Peace Corps-funded well project stood at the center of yet another small village where we finally stopped. Here, the local women felt comfortable enough to leave off their *haiks*, or face coverings. Lots of joking and teasing took place in Berber, which three of the Peace Corps volunteers spoke, the rest of us floating around like our tongues had been cut out, knowing only French and Moroccan Arabic. At the well, a turbaned man stood by his heavily laden donkey, and I knew I was witnessing an age-old scene that would not change any time soon.

Nestled in the foothills of the Anti-Atlas, the village was surrounded by breathtaking vistas down craggy valleys. The snow-capped High Atlas loomed to the north of us. As the sun set, stars peered from the blue-black sky, shining like sequins on a Moroccan bride's blanket. Unfortunately, the air became quite cold and bit like a lion, freezing us in our T-shirts and jeans.

And so we headed back to Ait Baha and the health clinic. On the way, I marveled at the bright stars, a sight I had rarely ever seen in the United States, what with all the light pollution obscuring the night sky.

That week I ate a type of Moroccan cooking I never dreamed of eating. Brains, tripe, and stews with mystery meat—I dreaded asking what was what. On the second day, tripe, a breakfast delicacy, exploded in the back of my throat. My gorge rose, and I kept gagging quietly into my section of the tablecloth doubling as a napkin. Of course, since I hated liver, that tripe brought me to my knees didn't surprise me at all. Of course, I'd eaten it before, when Doña Olga slipped it into stews back in my own Peace Corps days in Paraguay.

Argan oil, made from the seeds of an olive-like tree, proved to be another surprise, a good one. I loved it. Goats ate the fruit of the argan tree and spit out the seeds. Local people collected the seeds from under the trees, then pressed them to make the oil with its robust, nutty flavor, reminiscent of bacon fat!

Bread served as both the plate and the fork. As did my right hand. No eating with one's left hand, best left for doing one's private business. Cutting off a thief's right hand as punishment meant never eating again in community, because of that taboo against the left hand.

For a whole week, I never ate my food on a plate. Eating with my hands somehow felt more intimate than eating with metal utensils. Or even with chopsticks. More tangible, which describes the sensation of scooping up food with fingers, the touch of them against lips, the wiping of fingertips on cloth, the trickle of grease and sauce on my chin, all the sensations of touch. Aromas also became highlighted, redolent with the soft, subtle odor of wood smoke both in the air and the food.

That week, I grew to appreciate bread, too, as a life force, not something to be avoided for fear of not measuring up to a particular body type.

While going to the desert might have seemed simple, it became one of those experiences that clarifies many things, as it did for the Desert Fathers and Mothers, early Christians who escaped to the desert to commune more deeply with God. The whole concept of desert hospitality figured pre-eminently in desert cultures handed down for countless generations, as it was in Morocco. One day, I might be a stranger in danger of starving to death or dying of thirst in the desert. On that day, I would want food, I would want water. I would want nurturing, for it would save my life.

I would want someone to do unto me, as one of the least ones, as I would do unto them.

I hope.

Moroccan Cucumber Salad with Herbs

1 English cucumber, peeled and grated coarsely

2 teaspoons granulated sugar

1½ tablespoons freshly squeezed lemon juice

Fine sea salt, to taste

Fresh oregano leaves, crushed and minced, to taste

Flat-leaf parsley, minced, to taste

Fresh thyme leaves, crushed and minced (do not use stems), to taste

Black olives, seeded and slivered (DO NOT use canned black olives!)

Squeeze out excess water from grated cucumber by wrapping it in a towel and wringing it out like a wet rag. Mix lemon juice, sugar, salt, and herbs in a small bowl. Add drained, grated cucumber. Stir together. Spread grated cucumber on a plate, sprinkle with the olives. Chill before serving. Serves 4.

Ait Baha

When the stomach gets full, it tells the head to sing.
~ Moroccan Proverb

Stone by stone, I stepped gingerly across the shallow but rapidly flowing water. I focused on little but my feet as I navigated the large, round cement stones set like broken Roman columns into a low bridge. The Atlas Mountains loomed in the distant east and, to the west, if I could see far enough, would be Agadir and the Atlantic Ocean.

I stopped on one of the truncated "columns" and looked up, meeting the leering gazes of dozens of men crowding around on the bridge, gaping at us, Western women dressed in clothing that no respectable Moroccan woman would wear. Even though our bodies remained hidden under long denim skirts and wrist-length blouses or shirts, we still were exposed in a way that the local women never were, at least not in the countryside, which of course was where we were at that moment.

Our task was to buy ingredients for making low-cost but palatable weaning foods for infants and toddlers, using readily available ingredients from local markets in the region.

My foot suddenly slipped on one of the wet stones. A man grabbed my elbow to steady me. I murmured a "thank you" in Arabic, my eyes downcast, and was rewarded with a respectful, "It is nothing, kind lady," and we both made our way to the other side of the river. My group of nine Peace Corps volunteers and I headed toward the market. All we needed to do was follow the donkeys, who—like so many of the equine persuasion—seemed to know where they were going because they did it often enough.

The open-air market resembled most such markets in similar cultures. Unlike in many other markets, no women tended the stalls or the tables. Men and boys flogged the goods instead, a gargantuan variety of beans and spices and grains bursting forth from tall, narrow, white cloth sacks, rolled down around the edges to better display the wares of each merchant. Dust swirled like rising smoke at our feet as gentle desert winds blew. We slowly found every-thing needed for our experiments: red lentils, rice, chickpeas, cornmeal, cous-cous, green leafy vegetables that we'd not seen before, and other ingredients too numerous to list.

Clutching our purchases, wrapped in used brown paper or old newspa-pers or even in small plastic bags, we tip-toed across the river again, over the stones, making our way back to our headquarters in the now-vacant but soon-to-be-used health clinic.

Across a dusty main highway linking Ait Baha with the Sahara south of Morocco stood the kitchen for the clinic. Long, rough wooden tables lined the walls, a charcoal brazier serving as the stove. Lunch, it seemed, was soon to be served. We laid our ingredients on the tables with instructions for each recipe, washed our hands, and stepped outside to a small patio. On a small round table sat a tagine dish topped with the traditional conical "dunce" cap, as I thought of it.

We pulled up our chairs, as the Moroccan woman hired to cook for us proudly pulled off the cone top, revealing steaming yellow couscous drowned in fatty mutton chunks and well-cooked vegetables. So, in true community, we began scooping up couscous and meat and vegetable with our hands and shovel-ing the food into our mouths. Our Moroccan counterpart from the Peace Corps office in Rabat joined us, too. I looked on with amazement, and a good deal of queasiness, as he grabbed at the fatty sheep's tail and broke off pieces, smearing grease all over his beard as he ate.

My dislike of mutton certainly provoked my distaste, but as I thought lat-er about it, fat, and even meat, is in such short supply in most people's diets that the mere sight of it causes rapture and desire.

I witnessed such rapture that day. And I understood. Finally.

Couscous with Seven Vegetables

¼ cup extra virgin olive oil

2½ pounds beef chuck, cut into 2-inch chunks

1 large yellow onion, chopped

4 Roma tomatoes, coarsely chopped

1½ tablespoons fine sea salt

1 tablespoon ground ginger

1 tablespoon freshly ground black pepper

1 teaspoon turmeric

1 3-inch cinnamon stick

½ teaspoon saffron threads

Bunch of cilantro and flat-leaf parsley, tied

6 large carrots, cut into quarters

6 white turnips, peeled, cut into quarters

2 cups butternut squash, peeled, cut into 1½-inch chunks

2 red bell peppers, seeded and cut into quarters

1 small head green cabbage, cut into wedges, core removed

4 zucchini, cut into quarters

2 cups cooked chickpeas, from scratch or canned

½ cup dark raisins, soaked until softened in warm water, drained

1½ pounds instant couscous, cooked according to manufacturer's directions

Salted butter for couscous

Harissa

Brown meat in oil. Add onion, fry until golden brown. Stir in tomatoes, spices, and herbs. Pour in about 3 quarts of water, bring to boil, and then reduce heat to simmer. Cover and cook for about 3 hours. Remove herbs. Add carrots, turnips, squash, and red peppers. Cook 30 minutes. After 30 minutes, add cabbage, zucchini, chickpeas, and raisins to the tagine. Cook until vegetables are tender. Strain broth into a separate pan, cook down to about half the original volume.

Meanwhile, cook instant couscous. Spread couscous onto a platter, make a well in the center. Fill well with meat and vegetables. Pass reduced sauce and harissa to diners. Serves 4–6.

Ramadan

*It takes mind over matter to withdraw from food and drink
until sunset each day.*

~ Linda Hajj

Training in Ait Baha ended on the first day of Ramadan.

That morning, we drank sips of water at sunrise and a few bites of bread, for we non-Muslims decided to honor our host country and its people by following the fast that day, if not any other. At 2 p.m., we left Ait Baha, Bob Dylan singing "North Country Girl" on the car's cassette player as we drove across the vastness to Agadir. Lethargic and listless, we arrived in Agadir in the heat of the day, watching all the European tourists licking ice cream cones or drinking icy fruit drinks.

Finally, around 6:45 p.m., after driving around aimlessly, trying to pass the time until 7:15 p.m., when the sun was due to set that night, when a white thread and a black thread would look the same in the dying light, we stopped at a bakery selling Ramadan sweets. The cookies and tidbits available for breaking the fast at sundown tempt like gold and jewels, fried pastries stuffed with almond paste and dripping with honey or confectioner's sugar, covered with sesame seeds.

Like beggars, we packed small white paper bags as full as we could. Later, at the restaurant where we would break the fast, we lined the bags up along the edge of the table, sniffing them from time to time, salivating, looking at each other. And at the clock.

At 7:05 p.m., a waiter brought us *café au lait*. At 7:20 p.m., a cannon fired, signifying the end of the day's fast. We grabbed the bags and tore them open, stuffing cookies dripping with honey and other pastries into our mouths. The waiter appeared with *harira*, the primary break-the-fast dish served in Morocco at the first meal at sundown, a bean/meat soup, perfumed with cinnamon, rich with meaty broth, and soul-searing delicious. We ate. Silence.

Soraya, half-Moroccan, half-American, an administrative assistant for

Peace Corps, spoke. "Let us remember that the purpose of Ramadan is to make us realize what God has given us [water and food and family] and that none of it should be taken for granted. We should think of the poor, who suffer from hunger like this every day, for whom many days are a Ramadan with no end, since they might not always eat."

Despite the guilt I felt as she spoke, I gobbled my *harira* and pleaded with the waiter to flag down a cab to take me to the airport, not an easy task since even cab drivers must eat after the long first day of the fast.

I arrived home in Rabat at midnight, the streets filled with people celebrating the momentary respite from the rigors of the fast, which would last for another twenty-nine days, starting the next day all over again.

I woke early and ate my usual breakfast of bread, jam, butter, and coffee.

It was still Ramadan. The thought sat on my mind like a stone. I wasn't sure why.

At noon I waited for Fatima, my Moroccan housekeeper, to leave. I was hungry. I know she was, too. I could eat. And she couldn't. Or wouldn't. I felt extremely uncomfortable eating in front of her and others who practiced the month-long fast of Islam.

Ramadan certainly was an experience to savor. Food for breaking the fast, different in every country, always tasted sublime. But the sense and lessons of the fast remained the same regardless of place: fasting created real hunger, something some of us knew nothing about and reminded us, as Soraya mentioned, that all food is a gift.

Food must be reverenced, always, regardless of any religious proscriptions.

Harira

1½ pounds stewing beef, cut into small cubes (use lamb if you wish to be more authentic)

1 teaspoon turmeric

1 teaspoon freshly ground black pepper

1 teaspoon ground cinnamon

1 teaspoon ground cumin

½ teaspoon crushed saffron

¼ teaspoon ground ginger

2 tablespoons unsalted butter

¾ cup celery and leaves, chopped

1 medium yellow onion, chopped

1 cup flat-leaf parsley, chopped

1 cup cilantro, chopped

1 (2-pound) can tomatoes, chopped

Fine sea salt, to taste

¾ cup brown lentils

1 cup cooked chickpeas

1 cup fine vermicelli

Juice of 1 lemon mixed with 2 tablespoons flour (add a bit of water
if necessary to thin it)

Put beef, spices, butter, celery, onion, parsley, and cilantro in a large soup pot, stir
over low heat for 5 minutes. Tip in canned tomatoes and continue cooking for 10-15
minutes. Add salt to taste. Stir in 8 cups of water and lentils. Bring to a boil, then reduce heat, partially cover pot, simmer for 2 hours. When ready to serve, add cooked
chickpeas and noodles, cook for 10 more minutes. Stir lemon juice/flour mixture
into the stock. Season to taste. Ladle into bowls, dust with ground cinnamon, more
chopped cilantro, lemon juice, and black pepper. Serves 4-6.

Eid Al-Adha

The past is buried deep within the ground in Rabat, although the ancient walls in the old city are still standing, painted in electrifying variations of royal blue that make the winding roads look like streamlets or shallow ocean water.

~ Raquel Cepeda

Even without Islam, Moroccan culture would revere sheep. I saw examples of this every day as I made my way through Rabat's streets, markets, and public squares.

Like the American buffalo, their flesh and their wool provided sustenance and shelter. Sheep came into their own on the feast day of *Eid Al-Adha*, held seventy days after the end of Ramadan, commemorating Abraham's willingness to sacrifice his son Isaac to please God.

Over the years, many writers have attempted to capture the essence of the mass sacrifice of sheep.

In colonialism-toned language, Edith Wharton penned one of the more graphic stories of sheep sacrifice in *In Morocco*. She described how she and Inès de Bourgoing, wife of Louis Hubert Gonzalve Lyautey, the Resident Commissioner General of the French Republic in Morocco, attended a ceremony of the Sacrifice of the Sheep:

> *A sense of the impending solemnity ran through the crowd. The mysterious rumour which is the Voice of the Bazaar rose about like the wind in a palm-oasis; the Black Guard fired a salute from an adjoining hillock; the clouds of red dust flung up by wheeling horsemen thickened and then parted, and a white-robed rider sprang out from the tent of the Sacrifice with something red and dripping across his saddle-bow, and galloped away to Rabat through the shouting. A little shiver ran over the group of Occidental spectators, who knew that the dripping red thing was a sheep with its throat so skillfully slit that, if the omen were favorable, it would live on through the long race to Rabat and gasp out its agonized life on the tiles of the Mosque.*

Since not everyone raises a sheep for *Eid Al-Adha*, on the day before the feast the scramble begins to either find a sheep or to transport a previously chosen one home from the market or farm. Because the sheep must obviously be alive—the original concept of sacrifice demands that state of being—buyers devise any number of ingenious ways to get the sheep where they need to be for the feast.

People are out in great numbers, due partly to the marvelously cool morning, and because *Eid Al-Adha* takes place the next day. Yet, regardless of their financial constraints, every family strives to procure a sheep for the sacrifice and the following feast. An obligation for all believers, the sacrifice of a sheep places an undue burden on the poor, most of the time unless they pool resources with family or friends.

Thus, I spotted sheep everywhere, carried home to be someone's dinner via every mode of transportation possible. In a country where private cars were beyond most people's means, conveying a live sheep home demanded a great deal of inventiveness:

- slung around one's shoulders like a fur stole,
- pushed on a small flat cart with or without sides, tied down with rough ropes,
- thrown over a donkey and tied to its back,
- tethered on a rope, running pell-mell through a crowd with the purchaser's feet flying in a vain attempt to halt the fleeing animal,
- numerous sheep strapped to the roof of a bus and roasting prematurely in the merciless North African sun,
- wheelbarrowed through the Fez medina, hind legs serving as handles of the "wheelbarrow," gripped by the purchaser,
- carted in cars with the trunk door propped open just enough to refresh the sheep but at the same time preventing its escape,
- tied to iron rods on the sides of large *camions* or trucks,
- strung over the back "seat" (or front) of a moped,

and probably many other ways in places that outsiders never see.

The flesh of these sheep generally ended up in tagines or as *mechoui*.

It was on the second night of *Eid Al-Adha* that I first ate *mechoui*.

One of Mike's Moroccan colleagues invited us over for a feast of *mechoui*, whole roasted lamb served with cumin and salt. Two maids dressed in flowing white kaftans carried it out on a large brass tray, setting it down on a low-lying table. We, five or six of us, edged closer to the meat, all of us seated on ornate tooled leather ottomans, strong mint tea sloshing in etched glasses glimmering in the light of small brass lanterns hung on long chains from the high ceiling.

I was the lone woman at the table.

Watching the others, careful not to commit a faux pas, I tore off bits of butter-soft meat, dipping the small pieces first in ground cumin, then in salt. Silence ensued as everyone ate, left hands resting on their laps.

It was the only time we ever enjoyed such an invitation, an intimate meal in a private home.

Our host hoped that Mike would recommend him for a new position.

Mechoui

5 pounds lamb shoulder, deboned and slit in spots with a sharp knife

4 tablespoons unsalted butter, at room temperature

4 garlic cloves, peeled and mashed

2 teaspoons fine sea salt, or to taste

1 teaspoon freshly ground black pepper, or to taste

1 teaspoon ground cumin

½ teaspoon crushed saffron threads

¼ teaspoon turmeric

2 tablespoons extra virgin olive oil

Fine sea salt and ground cumin for dipping cooked meat

Mix butter, garlic, spices, and oil. Rub butter mixture over meat, pressing some into the slits. Heat oven to 250°F, place meat in greased roasting pan. Cover tightly with heavy-duty foil and pan lid. Cook meat for up to 9 hours. Once meat is tender, remove foil and increase heat to 475°F. Let meat brown uncovered in hot oven for about 30 minutes. Baste with cooking juices to speed browning. Remove meat to a platter. Serve with cumin and salt in little bowls for each guest. Traditionally served with various salads and bread. Serves 4-6.

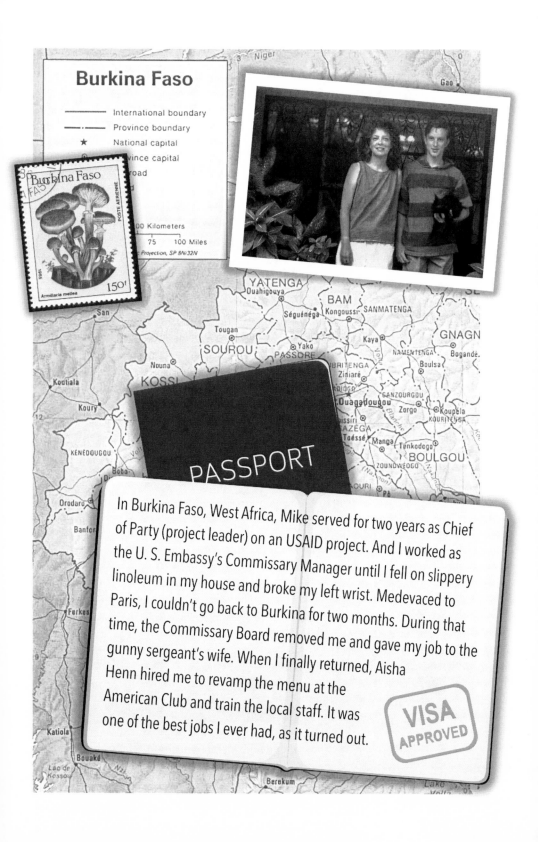

Burkina Faso

——————— International boundary
——·——·— Province boundary
★ National capital
●ince capital
oad

00 Kilometers
75   100 Miles
Projection, SP 8N/32N

Burkina Faso
POSTE AERIENNE
1985
150f
Armillaria mellea

In Burkina Faso, West Africa, Mike served for two years as Chief of Party (project leader) on an USAID project. And I worked as the U. S. Embassy's Commissary Manager until I fell on slippery linoleum in my house and broke my left wrist. Medevaced to Paris, I couldn't go back to Burkina for two months. During that time, the Commissary Board removed me and gave my job to the gunny sergeant's wife. When I finally returned, Aisha Henn hired me to revamp the menu at the American Club and train the local staff. It was one of the best jobs I ever had, as it turned out.

VISA
APPROVED

Burkinabe Woman Cooking with a Child Strapped to Her Back

The Cook

Food gained by fraud tastes sweet to a man,
but he ends up with gravel in his mouth.

~ African Proverb

Ouagadougou, the capital city of Burkina Faso, was the last place on earth where I expected to know anyone. But through a somewhat circuitous route, I did.

Shortly after I arrived, the Embassy's Community Liaison Officer called to say that she'd be sending a man to my house for an interview as a servant. Highly recommended by previous Embassy personnel, nothing but praise. Even a few words about love.

That was how Michel slunk into my life, through one of those other-wordly coincidences.

A light knock alerted me that he'd arrived. I opened the heavy wooden door. My first glimpse of him revealed a sweaty man with an earnest air about him. Long black pants pressed, shiny, almost frayed, at the knees. White short-sleeved shirt buttoned up high on his neck.

"Bonjour, Madame."

A gold front tooth glinted in the sun as he spoke. With shaking hands, he held out his letters of references, five pages of worn paper, folded and refolded many times, streaks of red dirt and sweat puddling around the wilted edges. His nervousness resonated with me. I'd been desperate myself. Just like that.

I was desperate then. For a gardener to tame the desert wasteland outside my door.

There was a catch, however.

Not one of the letters described Michel as a gardener.

"Cook."

"Cook."

"Cook."

I read that word again. And again. I should have said to him, "No, you're not a gardener. Sorry. No. *Au revoir."*

My life would have been quite different if I hadn't let my heart, my sympathy run away with my reason.

One look at the barren landscape of that rental house strengthened my resolve. High brick wall or not, I wanted something more than a few scraggly unhappy flame trees. I wanted someone who would "make the desert bloom with flowers," aided by a few measly gallons of the rusty water that flowed like cold molasses from the house's faucets.

I didn't need a cook. Why was I talking to this guy?

I stared over Michel's head at the dust coating the tiny leaves of the flame trees, red flowers not yet in sight. Diesel fumes wafted through the hot, dry air. The roar of truck motors and grinding moped gears on the other side of the garden wall drowned out my whispered "No."

Then a signature on the fifth letter somersaulted off the page at me.

John Fleming! I remember that name, I do. Could it be? Yes.

John Fleming! A former classmate since kindergarten, he was also from the same small university town in eastern Washington as I was. The guy who worked with me on the mock United Nations every year, the guy I dueled with in the annual U.N. essay contests. Former political officer at the Embassy. Small world.

There I stood, facing Michel, with John's letter in my hand, his words heaping praise on Michel and his cooking and his industriousness.

How amazing! What a coincidence!

Fate nudged me forward.

I showed Michel the kitchen, too small to be a walk-in closet in a modest American house.

He would clean the house and wash the dirty dishes, plus the laundry. And make orange juice from fresh oranges first soaked in water tempered with a small amount of bleach. I emphasized that I cooked most of our food.

He started work the next day. Soon I learned that Michel's birthday fell on the same day as mine. The ties that bind tightened.

Many days I regretted hiring him.

For Michel approached nearly every chore with the intensity of a Jack the Giant Killer, though he stood no higher than a corn stalk at the end of a droughty summer. When he made orange juice, he bore down fiercely on the juicer, pulp and juice splattering everywhere, all over the red-tile counters, the white walls, the flagstone floor. Dishes shattered in the wake of his haste. Bleach spots speckled T-shirts and towels like polka dots.

Weeks passed. I soon learned that Michel could not cook. In my heart, I cursed John Fleming for his mendacity. Nevertheless, I gritted my teeth and bore it.

Fate, ever the Lorelei, stepped in again.

One rainy July morning, Michel stood in the road in front of my house, gabbing with neighborhood servants. Meanwhile, in my study, rainwater drenched my most precious Moroccan carpet. I ran to yank the rug away from the gushing water but slipped and fell instead. My left wrist banged hard on the linoleum-covered cement and splintered into dozens of tiny pieces beneath skin and muscle. The Embassy medevaced me to Paris. French doctors worked out the puzzle of all those pieces, putting me back together, a Humpty Dumpty success story for once.

Orders from on high decreed that I couldn't return home for two months because of the severity of my injury and the lack of adequate follow-up care in Burkina Faso. Thus, I was forced into medical exile at my parents' house in Florida. There I pined for my home in Burkina Faso.

Michel reigned as king of the kitchen during my two-month-long absence.

One night, he served Mike and Erik a can of warmed-over button mushrooms and popped some popcorn. Another night they stared at cold oatmeal swimming in condensed milk. Yet another night they spooned up a can of chicken noodle soup mixed with a can of New England clam chowder.

They begged me to come home. Once I received the all-clear from my doctor in Florida, I boarded the first plane I could.

When I walked into my kitchen after my release from exile, Michel smiled. "*Bonjour, Madame. Comment ça va?*"

I smiled, just to be polite, not feeling it.

We fell back into a routine. One day, though, he refused to buy enough fabric for a new mosquito net. He informed me that I was wrong about the amount needed. I decided then and there to demote Michel. Because of my anger at him. For breaking one dish too many. For the oranges. For the ruined clothes. For the mosquito net. For lying about being a cook. For the agony of my broken arm.

I assigned him to day-guard duty.

And I hired another cook. Houseboy, actually.

Every day Michel sulked, sitting on a folding chair in the garage. He'd lost face. Guilt crept up on me from time to time. I chose not to fire him, unwilling to leave his family destitute. I kept hoping he'd quit. But he didn't.

Six months later, we left Burkina Faso. I wrote a bare-bones character reference.

I thought I'd never hear of Michel again.

But the story didn't end when my Air France flight took off from Ouagadougou on a hot June afternoon.

As Fate would have it, I attended a high school reunion in my hometown a few years later. John Fleming showed up, goofed around with the rest of the guys who'd played basketball in high school, the cool boys. I sidled up to him and said, "Hey, John, remember Michel? From Burkina?" John looked at me, his forehead scrunching. Then he grinned. "Good ol' Michel. Tell me, how are you acquainted with that conniving bastard?"

I informed him that, thanks to his letter of recommendation, I'd hired Michel, the cook who could not cook.

"Why did you write that glowing letter if he couldn't cook?"

John stared at me as if I'd grown a second head.

"Well, no one ever tells the truth about the servants, you know."

Yes, I know.

Greens in Peanut Sauce

1 pound greens (kale, spinach, sweet potato leaves, collards, turnip greens)

½ teaspoon fine sea salt

6 plum tomatoes, chopped

¼ cup peanut powder (grind roasted peanuts in blender or mortar and pestle)

1 medium yellow onion, finely chopped

Cover greens with boiling water, add salt. Cook until softened over medium heat. Layer tomatoes, peanut powder, and onions on top. Do not mix. Simmer over low heat for 15 minutes. Stir, simmer for 15 more minutes. Serve with cornmeal mush or other grain preparation like *fufu*. Serves 4 as a side dish.

Za'atar

Knowledge is like a garden—if it is not cultivated, it cannot be harvested.
~ African Proverb

I saw him before he saw me.

Laughing, smiling, he gestured to a friend on the other side of the road.

At the stop sign, I sat in my rusty Peugeot, beige as the dusty road beneath me. I could not turn right because mopeds and bicycles had the right of way in Ouagadougou. Otherwise, I might bump into a moped rider. Besides, the oncoming traffic never seemed to let up on the road, the one I wanted to ease on to. From there, I planned to make my way to the Lebanese bakery with its fragrant *Man'oushe*, flatbread embellished with olive oil and *za'atar*.

I searched the rearview mirror with anxiety gnawing at me. I simply could not move my car in any direction. Yet the young man, still laughing raucously with his friend, still did not see me.

"Look, look," I screamed into the air. I honked my horn, but so many horns blared for no reason there. He still didn't see me.

And then he did, moments before he would have plowed full-bodied into the back of my car. He swerved to the right, frantic now, and managed to hightail it around me enough to avoid a body slam.

But he propelled straight into my right side mirror, hitting his right shoulder with unbelievable force, the thwack of the impact loud enough to raise the dead, as the saying goes. The mirror flew over the top of the car like a pheasant roused from the bushes, landing with a thud on my side of the car.

Stunned, I fully expected a crowd to converge on me, keeping me from getting home. Or worse. I remembered what Doc said in Paraguay. "Don't stick around in case of an accident."

To my shock, the young man stood up, his eyes frightened not by his injury but by me. He darted around my car and picked up the mirror. He handed it to me through the window, his hand shaking, bowing and apologizing in French.

"Are you OK?" I asked, and he nodded. "*Bonne chance,*" I said. "Good luck."

At that moment, I spotted the opportunity I'd been waiting for. I turned right and sped off to the bakery, *my* hands shaking.

That night's *Man'oushe* was the last I enjoyed for over six months. Fear kept me away from the street of the accident. Sure that people would recognize me and my distinctive curly red hair from that day, I stayed away

But I always wondered about that young man, what became of him.

Flatbread with Za'atar

1 tablespoon dried thyme leaves, crushed

1 tablespoon ground cumin

1 tablespoon ground coriander

1 tablespoon toasted white sesame seeds

1 tablespoon sumac

½ teaspoon fine sea salt

Extra virgin olive oil

1 pound pizza dough

Mix all spices. Store in a tightly sealed jar in refrigerator or freezer. To make *Man'oushe*, preheat oven to 450°F. Place rack at lowest level of oven, heat a sturdy baking sheet or use a pizza stone on the rack. Roll out dough to about ¼-inch thickness. Brush with olive oil, sprinkle with a few tablespoons of *za'atar*. Bake approximately 15 minutes. **Note:** Most grocery stores carry premade *za'atar*. Serves 4.

Out of Africa

Those who are at one regarding food are at one in life.
~ African Proverb

It didn't take long for the red dust to coat the white Nissan Patrol 4WD like the sugar crust on a *crème brulée*. Thick. Crunchy. Slightly gritty.

"Look like we here," said Moussa, our driver, his Moré accent glossing the familiar English words.

He turned the Patrol off the long straight highway at Koudougou. Two weeks after arriving in-country, not yet used to the 120°F heat and the blazing sun overhead, pulsating like an overheated car's exhaust pipe, we were deep in the bush, 60 kilometers from home. The gas station at the edge of Koudougou was the first one I'd seen since we left the outskirts of Ouagadougou.

Enigmatic Burkina Faso, landlocked, a back-of-the-beyond former French colony in Francophone West Africa, then called Upper Volta, sits on the cusp of the Sahel, dry, hot, with scarce vegetation, redolent with the native religion of animism, tempered by Islam and Catholicism.

As I learned, it was a unique manifestation of all three that we were heading toward, a memorial mass and village feast in honor of Mike's colleague Daniel's father, on the second anniversary of the revered chief's death.

Once the Patrol left the asphalt, the tone of the day changed. We couldn't flee back to Ouagadougou and the security of the foreigners' relatively opulent residential zone. The rutted road ahead bore the scars of past rains, not unlike the fissures of ritual scarification running down the sides of the faces of Mossi tribespeople. Like a whirlwind in our wake, the dust rose higher and higher. People trudged along the side of the road, drawing their flowing white robes around them, struggling to keep from breathing the choking dust swirling around them.

On and on Moussa drove, past forty-foot-high baobab trees looming over the road like sentries, their swollen trunks giving birth to puny limbs. Small brown-and-white goats frolicked in scrubby fields as tiny child herdsmen chased after them. Horizon and sky merged seamlessly into vast crimson nothingness.

As the truck approached the outskirts of the village, undulating crowds of singing villagers flanked each side of the road. Dancing their way into the village, they stopped at a row of enormous terracotta cauldrons, each holding probably five gallons of red sorghum beer. Men and women alike drank this frothy sourness, using dried gourds cut in half as bowl-like drinking cups.

Nearly everyone in the village wore clothing cut from the same pink robin's-egg-blue and lime-green plaid cloth. Like the plaids of Scottish clans, this cloth identified people as part of an exclusive group, relatives of the dead chief. As one of the chief's twenty-five sons, Daniel enjoyed plenty of company.

Moussa parked the Patrol alongside a Land Rover idling next to several donkey-drawn wooden carts. He pointed to the crowd and said, "You go that way."

Stepping down from the high running board on the Patrol, I immediately regretted wearing sandals instead of bush boots. Dirt seeped between my toes and lodged under the straps. Not wanting to touch my feet, I simply shook each foot as hard as I could and started walking toward the church, following the women in their ankle-length *pagnes*, wrap-around skirts that are cousins to sarongs.

When Daniel invited us to the ceremony and explained the significance of the event, I'd pictured a small, European-style Catholic church. One with a bell tower built of stone, men dressed in black suits and women wearing the wide-brimmed straw hats and flowery print dresses common in the French countryside.

Well, I couldn't have been more wrong.

Off toward the end of the village, the nearest family compounds about 100 yards away, stood the church, unlike any I'd ever seen. Round as one of the huts in the family compounds scattered around the village, topped with a thatched roof, the cement-walled church contained cement pews about a foot off the ground, eight inches wide. These pews circled the altar. Two white Belgian priests stood at the doorway, their tanned faces contrasting sharply with the snowy whiteness of their vestments.

Pushing our way through the crowd and into the church, we squeezed ourselves in between several excited children and a sedate older woman wearing regal robes of local cloth she might have worn any day of the week. Mass started with throbbing native drumbeats as the procession marched in. A choir of young girls wearing tie-dyed *pagnes* and white blouses erupted into a frenzy of dancing and singing. Hips swaying and shaking, heads thrown back, throats opened like howling wolves, their joy in the music and the day took my breath away. The drums moaned and screamed along with them. Back and forth, the girls bent in time with the beats.

Intoxicated by the sounds and the dancing and a, well, lack of inhibition, my toes tapping the dirt floor, I whispered to myself, "My goodness, it's all I can do to keep from jumping up and dancing, too!"

Then an old woman—naked from the waist up, wearing nothing but a tattered gray *pagne* around her hips—darted into the church, yelling and moaning. The priests stopped the service and motioned for someone to be quick about getting her out. Two men grabbed her and dragged her to the door, her withered breasts swinging like empty pastry bags. The priests resumed the Mass as if nothing had happened.

Daniel found us as we stood perplexed in the middle of the crowd leaving the church.

"Sorry, sorry, I had to help my mother for a minute," he said as he led us to a thatched lean-to, where we sat for a while, watching people drinking sorghum beer and shooting an antique French musket, a dead ringer for an illustration in an old history book. And, on the wall of the hut behind us, a picture of the dead chief stared at my back. Set into a red-mud wall, his portrait was flanked on one side by a bas-relief crocodile. On the other, a snake. Sacred crocodiles, I later learned.

"I'm starving," I thought, as several women dressed in the pink-lime-green plaid cloth dragged in crates of soda and beer. Following them were more women carrying bulky, dented aluminum pots of rice and chunks of meat, seasoned with fermented locust-bean seeds—an acquired taste to be sure. Cucumber and tomato salad. Millet/cowpeas/greens dumplings soaking in an oily but delicious peanut sauce.

"What do you think?" I asked the Frenchman sitting next to me, "Do you like it?"

"Not bad, but I'm more worried about eating the salad," he said, pushing the salad off to one side under a slice of baguette.

"Well, we have to eat everything, or they'll be insulted," piped up John, another of Mike's colleagues and a former Peace Corps volunteer who'd served in Burkina.

So I ate. And wiped my plate clean with bread.

Then came the moment to greet the new chief, Daniel's oldest brother.

"This way," Daniel said as he walked beside us toward the hut with the photo of his dead father.

Approximately sixty years old, his collarbones angling out from the base of his neck, the new chief stretched out on a shocking-pink lounge chair. His kaftan, cut from the clan plaid, hung from his shoulders. A high-brimmed pink crocheted hat sat on his scalp, an unlikely crown, incongruous in the heat.

Seating us in the circle of people around the chief, Daniel motioned for a young girl to bring a gourd filled with sorghum beer. I sipped the sour yeasty froth and passed the gourd to the person on my left. Then, one by one, we rose and greeted the chef by semi-kneeling, a sort of half-hearted genuflection. Then people from the village filed in and paid homage by crouching, kneeling, or even prostrating themselves on the ground in front of him. The whole scene reminded me of writer Isak Dinesen, also known as Baroness von Blixen, meeting the Kikuyu chief in the film "Out of Africa."

The Belgian priests had disappeared, nowhere to be seen.

As we left the chief's compound, the sun sat low on the horizon. It was time to start back to Ouagadougou.

Walking through the village at dusk, observing all the people chatting happily, at first I didn't notice the wrinkled older man. Draped in a goat-skin cape, carrying a skinny ridged gourd, he lugged a canvas bag filled with long sticks. A younger man followed behind him, riding a donkey, playing a traditional three-stringed gourd instrument. I stopped to let them by, wondering who they were. As they passed, the old man turned to face me, running one of the long sticks over the ridges of a dried gourd. Making loud rasping noises, staring at me with wide-opened eyes, both men then cried out in unison. As I hurried away, their eerie screeching faded, but it still raised goose pimples like small hard pellets all over my body.

Moussa waited patiently for me by the Patrol.

"Moussa, what on earth was that all about?" I asked.

"Oh, he witch doctor. Not want us here," Moussa said in his soft, velvety voice.

I climbed into the Patrol. Through the dark and silent African night, Moussa drove us home to our house in the foreigners' zone. Another world entirely.

Rice with Meat

2 pounds beef, sliced into 12 pieces, and tenderized with a mallet

1 teaspoon fine sea salt, or to taste

½ cup peanut oil

1 large yellow onion, chopped

3 garlic cloves

2 large tomatoes, chopped

2 tablespoons tomato paste

1½–3 teaspoons crushed red pepper

1 cup rice, 2 cups water, ½ teaspoon fine sea salt

Salt meat, brown it in ¼ cup hot oil in large pot. Remove from pot, keep warm. Add half of chopped onion and garlic to oil, cook until softened. Stir in half chopped tomato, 1 tablespoon tomato paste, crushed red pepper, and 2 cups of water. Simmer until water is almost evaporated. Add browned meat to tomato mixture, simmer gently until stew is thick and meat is tender. Add remaining chopped onion and tomato. Stir in remaining tomato paste. Cover and let simmer while rice cooks. Meanwhile, cook rice with 1 teaspoon salt in 2 cups of water for 15 minutes in a separate pan. Cover pan, simmer for another 10 minutes, or until rice is tender. Serve meat with rice. Sprinkle with chopped green herbs of choice. Sop up oil and sauce with bread. Serves 4–6.

Michel

Celestine

Hold a true friend with both hands.
~ African Proverb

Blending as they did into the green leaves of the crimson flowering flamboyant trees looming over the crumbling mud-brick wall, it was hard to spot the bottle-green chameleons. Dozens of these "ground lions" perched in the crevices of the wall surrounding my house in Ouagadougou, their red throats puffing in and out like bellows stoking a fire.

I envied the chameleons more each day—their food came to them, snatched up quickly with long projectile tongues. They just sat and waited, scanning their world through their beady black eyes, sleepily opening and closing like two tiny ball-and-socket joints.

I envied the chameleons. Yes, I did.

For me, getting food meant a daily running of the gauntlet. So many desperately poor street vendors out there, on the streets. All women, all grabbing at me, pawing at me, shrieking at me, "Buy my vegetables, Madame! *Madame!* *S'il vous plaît!*"

I wanted to avoid the streets.

I wanted home delivery of vegetables.

I wanted to be like a chameleon.

I wanted my food to come to me.

I wanted to blend in.

I don't remember when she started coming to me, this Muslim woman riding astride a rusty blue moped, her serpentine tie-dyed green gowns flowing like bridal trains behind her, always green, clean, starched, and prim. Sparse, wiry black hair peeked out from underneath her enormous and flamboyant matching green head-tie. A big straw vegetable-laden basket, its fraying edges like tendrils of a young bean plant, swayed behind her on the moped, strapped down with a worn rope. Vegetables lurched and rolled in the basket as she rode the pot-holed street where I lived.

I never learned her real name, so in my mind, I named her Celestine. She never called me anything but "*Madame*," and I called her "*Madame*," too.

Two women from opposite sides of the earth.

Placing the heavy basket on her head, Celestine walked gracefully through the iron gate toward my front verandah, sashaying like an anorexic ballet dancer performing a *chassé*. Vegetables poked out of the top of her basket, like so many baby birds peering cautiously from their nest. Scrawny limp carrots, mushy tomatoes, wilted cabbages, yams coated with shriveled brown skin, small red peppers so hot a simple touch scalded fingers, tiny juicy oranges, and now and then a soft mango or a bruised pineapple carpeted with flies sucking out the sweetness. Never was there much more than that, until the rains came, that is.

Sometimes she brought a few scraggly parsley sprigs or maybe a slice of a pumpkin-like squash, and always some mysterious green leaves the size of an elephant's ear, rolled up like a Jimi Hendrix poster, tied carefully with burlap string saved from a coffee-bean bag.

Setting her basket on the top step of my tiled porch, Celestine's thin cold hands extended first toward me in greeting. This took place always after a polite, delicate cough, a hint of embarrassment, and gratitude for the glass of iced water I presented to her, in our private version of a Japanese tea service. I took the glass from her and pushed my empty market bag forward, its floppy straw craw ready to receive food, from this woman whose dark eyes I met only by craning my neck, as if to peer at a spider web at the top of a doorframe.

Squatting in that graceful way no Westerner ever easily musters, heels flat on the ground, taking each vegetable from her basket like a cat moving her kittens from one home to another, Celestine carefully placed each vegetable in my basket, apologizing for the bump on this one, the bruise on that one. Soon the mound of produce reached the "it's-time-to-talk-price" level.

"*Combien?* How much?" I asked.

She sighed, straightened up, her gaunt face shiny with beads of sweat from the effort, her sparkly, fevered eyes blinking away a fly.

"For you, Madame, the price is ... ."

Waving my hand impatiently, I smiled, saying nothing. I knew the price was too high. But this slim woman whose cheeks resemble chiseled ebony more and more every week, whose discreet cough sounded deeper and wetter every time I saw her, needed the money. I sensed her unspoken want. The bargaining game I wouldn't play with her.

I dug through my money envelope and handed her a wad of colorful paper money and a few coins, placing it all in her skeletal hand, wondering if I would see her next week as I said, "*À la prochaine.*" Until the next time.

The weeks passed as the long dry season extended into July, nearly starving even us, the foreigners. Only U.S. commissary food sat in my cupboards, cans and bags and boxes stamped ominously with expiration dates from before last year's Christmas. No matter. Food was food. We ate. And we dreamt of our grandparents' gardens, of their kitchens, of holiday tables laden with abundance. We were the lucky ones. At least we ate. The local people were not as fortunate.

But still, Celestine arrived at my gate every week with a few token vegetables. Each week she diminished a little more, her walk less a dance than a trudge. Seeing her fading away reminded me of films of the liberation of Nazi concentration camps. Each time she stood at the gate, those images haunted me, creating mental snapshots of emaciated, walking skeletons.

One week, Celestine didn't come. Another week passed, and she still didn't rattle the gate.

I began finding mummified chameleons on the mud-brick wall, brittle bones piercing through thin dried green skin. I began to think that being a chameleon was not all that great after all.

I went back out on the streets again, running the gauntlet of pawing, frantic vegetable vendors. I asked them about Celestine, describing her lithe figure, her walk. Dark eyes looked away. No one knew anything. From their silence and apparent fear, I sensed that AIDS had brushed me, albeit lightly, with its insidious terror.

Every time I read that increasing numbers of AIDS victims were women, I imagined Celestine. Tall. Dignified. Strong. Brave. Performing small acts of hope to go on living by selling vegetables to a foreigner.

Dead.

Shamefully, I recalled washing my hands over and over again, careful not to touch myself anywhere until I washed my hands almost raw, careful to sterilize Celestine's water glass every week. Careful not to get too involved.

Mea culpa.

Tô (Cornmeal Mush)

3 cups (about 1 pound) millet, sorghum, or corn (maize) flour

2 quarts water

Fine sea salt, to taste

Bring water to a boil in a large pot over high heat. Add salt to taste. Stir in ¼ of the flour quickly. Try to avoid lumps by stirring constantly. Reduce heat. Cook for about 5 minutes, still stirring constantly. Take out a ¼ of the mixture, set aside. Add remaining flour little by little, a cup at a time. Mix flour in thoroughly with each addition. Stir in the rest of the flour, finishing in 5 minutes. Mix in some of the set-aside mixture if the mixture in the pot gets to be too thick to stir. Cover pot, cook about 10 more minutes over low heat. Tô should be a stiff, smooth paste, too thick to stir. Remove from heat. Serve warm or cool with any sauce, soup, or stew.

The author's house in Ouagadougou and the author with a guest

Tomatoes and Dust

It is not the cook's fault when the cassava turns out to be hard and tasteless.
~ African Proverb

The phantasmagoric hot August days of my childhood seemed far away as I squatted in the dust under a dry-season, white-hot sky in West Africa, re-membering the luscious tomatoes Daddy grew in our backyard garden. Staring at five scrawny plum tomatoes arranged pyramidally on the ground in front of an African market lady, I sensed the bad news immediately. But I asked anyway, my fingers crossed behind my back like a 4-year-old kid.

"*Madame, vous n'avez plus de tomates?*"

"No, Madame, no more tomatoes," she answered.

Standing, I counted out several bills, colorful paper money, torn in so many places, covered with the ubiquitous red dust of the southern Sahara during the Harmattan. I handed it all to the *marchande*. Placing the tomatoes gently into my straw market basket, the market lady beamed, her beautiful white teeth a testimony to the wholesome diet she ate. When she could.

In heat hovering at 120°F in the shade, I trudged from one market lady to another, buying as many tomatoes as I could find. Five runty tomatoes just wouldn't cut it for a feast for twenty-five people. As a Westerner newly arrived in the country, I was learning firsthand the near impossibility of feasting during the dry season, another epiphany of sorts. Food simply does not exist in large enough quantities, no matter how much one might wish it were so.

Miracles happen. Sometimes.

Money helps, a lot.

That day, I brought home enough tomatoes for a feast fit for a king. Or at least for the village chief coming to our house.

That night we would eat Fiery West African Tomato and Chicken in Peanut Sauce with Spinach after all. I could hardly wait.

Chicken in Peanut Sauce with Spinach

3 tablespoons peanut oil

6 chicken thighs, trimmed of excess fat, rinsed and patted dry

1 large yellow onion, finely chopped

3 garlic cloves, peeled, sliced, and lightly crushed with the side of a cleaver or large knife

1 piece of fresh ginger the size of a quarter, peeled and lightly crushed with the side of a cleaver or large knife

1 small hot green pepper, seeded and minced

6 large plum tomatoes, coarsely chopped

1 teaspoon fine sea salt

½ teaspoon freshly ground black pepper

¼ teaspoon cayenne pepper

½ teaspoon paprika

½ teaspoon curry powder

½ teaspoon dried thyme leaves

1 cup natural peanut butter

8 ounces fresh spinach leaves

Fresh cilantro leaves, chopped, for garnish

Heat oil in a large, heavy-bottomed pot over medium-high heat. Place chicken pieces skin-side down, fry until golden. Flip pieces over, brown the other side. Remove chicken from pan, set aside on a large plate. Add onions to pan, fry until translucent and golden in color. Toss in garlic, ginger, and hot green pepper. Cook for another minute or so, until garlic turns golden. Stir in tomatoes, cook for about 3 minutes. Mash tomatoes with a potato masher or other implement. Mix in salt, black pepper, cayenne pepper, paprika, curry powder, and thyme leaves. Stir well. Pour in 2 cups of water. Add chicken, making sure to cover pieces with the broth. Reduce heat to low, simmer uncovered for 10–15 minutes. Using a bit of broth from the pot, thin peanut butter, stir well. Add half of peanut butter mixture to stew. Reserve the other half of the mixture for the spinach. Cook, covered, until chicken is tender, about 40 minutes or so.

While chicken cooks, rinse spinach, and immediately add it to a large skillet over high heat. Stirring constantly, cook spinach until all leaves wilt. Remove from heat instantly, dump spinach into a colander. Run cold water over spinach and drain. When cool enough to handle, squeeze out excess water from spinach and set aside. Before chicken is done, place spinach in a heavy-bottomed pot, gently stir in reserved peanut sauce, warm mixture over medium-low heat, uncovered, making sure that mixture stays moist. Add a few tablespoons of water if mixture gets too dry. Ladle sauce over white rice, placing a piece of chicken on side. Garnish chicken and rice with chopped cilantro leaves. Spoon spinach near chicken. Pass **Fiery West African Tomato Condiment** (see below) around the table and dribble some on the chicken if desired. **Note:** This dish freezes and reheats well. Serves 4–6.

Fiery West African Tomato Condiment

3 tablespoons peanut oil

5 large garlic cloves, peeled and finely minced

3 habanero peppers, seeded, and finely chopped (leave seeds in for more heat)

8 large plum tomatoes, cut into quarters

Salt and freshly ground black pepper, to taste

Heat oil over medium-high heat in heavy-bottomed skillet. Add garlic, sauté for about 30 seconds, or until garlic turns slightly golden. Add peppers, fry for another 30 seconds, stirring constantly. Slip tomatoes carefully into oil to avoid splattering. Sprinkle with salt and pepper. Cook for 2 minutes, then lower heat. Simmer uncovered until oil separates from tomatoes. Store refrigerated in covered container for up to a week. Use as a condiment with any African main dish. Also good with grilled meats. Makes 2½–3 cups.

Chicken Yassa, Side of *Tô*

You should know what's being cooked in the kitchen,
for otherwise you might eat a forbidden food.
~African Proverb

It took a dinner party in Ouagadougou to teach me another important lesson about food and culture.

The news that their boss, my husband Mike, was inviting everyone in the office to a dinner at his own house seemed to set several people on edge. Because the dinner would not be at a restaurant, where the food would be cooked and served by Burkinabe, anxiety about pork and other matters surfaced. Over 61% of people in Burkina Faso identified as Muslim. Generally, people's names, like Michel, who worked as my houseboy, reflected their religion, Christian names as opposed to Muslim names, as in the case of Bourani, the gardener.

What to do?

My friend Jean, from Ghana and married to a Burkinabe, suggested we visit one of the catering companies she knew. Of course, people coming to the dinner would happily eat that food. But not the food of a strange woman from a country on the other side of the world. Not Muslim, either.

I hopped in Jean's Jeep, the sun a blinding white disk hanging high in the cloudless blue sky. She drove through Ouagadougou's dusty, winding streets to the outskirts of town and parked in front of a flimsy bamboo wall. Walking through the entrance, what I saw amazed me.

There's no other way to put it.

On either side of the entrance sat enormous aluminum vats positioned over pits filled with wood charcoal fires burning below, small boys feeding charcoal to keep the embers going. Women holding long, narrow wooden paddles stirred the food cooking in the cauldrons. I counted at least twenty of these stoves, ten on each side.

We walked from pot to pot as the owner, speaking impeccable French and dressed in an elaborate headdress and matching dress of the shiny colorful tie-dyed fabric popular among upper-class women, explained what was cooking in the various pots.

"How many people will be coming?" she asked.

"Maybe fifty," I said.

"Then perhaps you ought to serve six different dishes with *tô* and yellow rice on the side," she suggested. "A dozen baguettes, too," she added.

That's what I did.

On the day of the party, I made several dozen *sambusas*, ground-beef-filled pastries based on a recipe from Julie Sahni's *Classic Indian Cooking*. Michel shredded cabbage and onions and carrots for the Chicken Yassa I'd ordered from another caterer.

The first caterer filled large plastic buckets with the food about an hour before the guests arrived. The project's driver, Moussa, lived in the neighborhood near the caterer, and offered to pick up all the food. He helped me put everything into serving dishes. I worried that the food wouldn't be hot, but he brushed away my concerns.

"*Pas de probleme*, Madame," Moussa assured me. "Not a problem, Madame."

As the guests arrived, laughing, at ease, making their way to the beer or the Fanta, I stood on the veranda of my cottage-like house, eyeing the tables covered in white linen cloths and the Tiki poles strung with twinkling white lights. The sun set in a blaze of red fire, and a coolish breeze blew, the aroma of jasmine masking the smell of burning charcoal streaming from our neighbors' cooking fires.

People filled large white plates with everything, from beef and spinach to calabaza and dried fish. They heaped on pieces of Chicken Yassa, drowning the crisp grilled chicken with Michel's slaw.

As the night ended, and as the clock struck midnight, the guests left. Bourani took charge of the cleanup of the outside tables. I stepped inside to pack up the leftover food for Michel and Bourani to take home to their families, while Michel handled the dishes.

Imagine my surprise to see just five *sambusas* left on the platter.

Chicken Yassa

½ cup peanut oil, or any cooking oil

1 chicken, cut into serving-size pieces

4 yellow onions, sliced

½ cup lemon juice, from approximately 4 lemons

½ cup cider vinegar

1 bay leaf

4 garlic cloves, peeled and minced

2 tablespoons Dijon mustard

2 tablespoons Maggi cubes, crushed, or soy sauce

1 chile pepper, seeded, deveined, and chopped

Cayenne pepper or other ground red pepper, to taste

Freshly ground black pepper

Fine sea salt

½ green cabbage, shredded

2 carrots, peeled and shredded

Mix everything in a stainless-steel or glass bowl, except for cabbage and carrots. Let marinate in refrigerator a few hours if time is pressing or overnight. Remove chicken from marinade when ready to cook. Save marinade. Grill over hot coals until chicken is browned but not done. Alternatively, brown in skillet in oil until golden but not done. Sauté onions in 2 tablespoons hot oil, add reserved marinade. Bring to a boil and cook for 10 minutes. Add chicken, lower the heat, cover pan, cook until chicken is tender. Add cabbage and carrots, cook for 3 minutes. Remove chicken and vegetables to a platter. Reduce sauce more if necessary. Pour sauce over chicken. Serve with rice or *fufu*. Serves 4–6.

Dried Fish and *Soumbala*

If you find no fish, you have to eat bread.
~ African Proverb

English explorer, Richard Francis Burton, quoted a Yoruba saying, which never made sense to me until I discovered that smoked fish played a big, important role in the cuisine of West Africa:

"It is as hard as the eye of a (smoked) fish, which the teeth cannot break."

Best said when attempting to deal with any problematic matter.

For a landlocked country, markets in Burkina Faso featured a fantastic plethora of dried or smoked fish and shrimp.

Before refrigeration, people naturally either ate everything all at once or developed technologies to handle the inevitable problems of rotting, with the subsequent loss of scarce food resources. Another possible benefit of fish consumption lay with a possible anti-sickling effect. This is significant for many people with African roots suffering from sickle cell anemia.

Smoked and dried fish, and other seafood such as shellfish, supplied flavoring as well as protein, too. I soon realized that smoked, salted pork no doubt replaced the smoked, salted fish in the diets of enslaved Africans in the southern United States.

The first time I set foot in Quagadougou's chaotic Central Market, I had no idea what I was seeing, aside from a few vegetables and fruits, meat and poultry.

I learned that most Burkinabe cooks used smoked and dried fish sparingly in their cooking, close in technique to the Italian tradition of using anchovies to add another layer of flavor to certain dishes. Or like smoked and salted pork products in some traditional American dishes.

My bewilderment and avid curiosity about the strange—to me—ingredients piled on counters and bags at the Central Market led to a meeting with Asitou, the friend of a friend. Her husband was a doctor. She agreed to guide me through the market and teach me what I wanted to know about cooking going on behind closed doors and high walls.

In addition to fish, Asitou told me that Maggi cubes seasoned many stew-like dishes, or "sauces." But so did traditional fermented products such as *dawadawa*, also known as *soumbala*, made from the fermentation of African locust beans (*Parkia biglobosa*).

I was ashamed to admit this, but with my first bite of rice flavored with *dawadawa* at an official function in Burkina Faso, I nearly gagged, thinking a dead mouse might have gotten into the rice somehow. I pushed it off to the side of my plate and would have left it there, uneaten. However, that day some women on the other side of the room were watching me, like vultures eyeing a dying animal crawling across hot sand. So I relied on the old tried-and-true trick of my childhood when forced to eat something I didn't like. Grabbing a bottle of beer with one hand, balancing the metal plate on my knees, I forked a massive bite of rice, tossed it as far back in my mouth as I could, bypassing tastebuds for the most part. Then I chugged a huge swallow of beer and washed the rice down with minimal effect on my taste buds.

No one knew what I'd done, so no one felt slighted. My plate was clean, as was my conscience.

Smoked Fish with Vegetables

¾ cup palm oil or half palm oil and half vegetable oil

2 yellow onions, peeled and finely chopped

3 garlic cloves, peeled and finely minced

1 Scotch Bonnet pepper or habanero, seeded, deveined, and finely chopped

4 fresh medium Roma tomatoes, peeled, seeded, and chopped

1 pound smoked white fish, skinned and boned

¼ teaspoon freshly ground black pepper

1 teaspoon fine sea salt, or to taste

1 pound fresh spinach, washed, drained, cut into shreds

Heat oil over medium-high heat in a heavy skillet. Add onions, cook until translucent, then add garlic and hot pepper. Cook for about 30 more seconds as garlic releases its aroma. Stir in tomatoes. Cook 5–10 minutes. Add 1 cup water, fish, pepper, and salt. Lower heat and simmer 10 minutes. Stir in spinach. Cook 5 more minutes until spinach is wilted. Serve with white rice or *tô*. **Note:** This dish is nothing more than a version of *Maafe*. Use low-salt canned diced tomatoes if the tomatoes in the market are hard. Serves 4.

Top: Village street scene and left, cooking fufu with greens

The American Club

Even the best cooking pot will not produce food.
~ African proverb

After breaking my left wrist in a terrible fall in my house in Ouagdougou, I returned in-country after two months of recuperation in the United States. I'd been the Commissary Manager before my fall.

The Embassy Board removed me from my job while I was gone and gave it to the gunny sergeant's wife. It crushed me that no one seemed to have any compassion for my suffering. But I needed to return to the Commissary to pick up my personal items. I had no idea what I would be doing with my time once that was done.

I swallowed my hurt pride and made arrangements with the new manager.

The day I returned to the Commissary, I first picked Erik up from the International School. Then we drove through the dusty streets to the U.S. Embassy, dodging shoeshine boys and Chiclet sellers and children abandoned to the streets to eke out a living as best they could.

To enter the Commissary, people had to walk through the Embassy motor pool, across the street from the Embassy itself. Dozens of Burkinabe men of all ages worked in the motor pool. One of them saved a cat's life when he found her quivering under the hood of a Jeep. I adopted her and called her Heidi. He always asked after her. Others joked with me as I walked through their workspace when I was the Commissary Manager. Still others were related to Michel, my houseboy, whose finger I'd saved by insisting that a local doctor not amputate the badly infected flesh and pleading with Paulina, the Embassy nurse, to save the finger. To do so, she recruited a young French doctor doing his national service in Burkina Faso. After two weeks of daily debridement and other treatment, the only reward he asked for was a bottle of Johnny Walker Black!

I parked my car next to the Embassy, darted in to pick up some mail, and then started across the dirt road to the motor pool, waving off the beggars who camped out by the low-lying wall surrounding the white stucco building.

As I pushed open the gate to the motor pool, quite a sight greeted Erik and me. All the men in the motor pool clapped and sang and smiled as we made our way through the center of two lines they'd formed, a pathway stretching from the gate all the way to the doors of the Commissary. By the time I got to those doors, I was crying. It touched me so much that those men, most of whom I barely knew, welcomed me home like that.

Out of the blue, as the saying goes, a few days later my Moroccan friend Aisha called me one day, on a molten December afternoon in Ouagadougou. Her call changed a lot of things for a small group of people, including me.

I didn't know that when I heard her calm voice that day.

"You know Dave, the guy at the Club's restaurant?" she asked.

"Yes, of course," I replied. Everybody knew Dave, the flamboyant, long-time manager of the U.S. Embassy's American Club, trickster, possible embezzler of funds. And a terrible cook. His hamburgers tasted as if someone mixed in some ground sawdust, or—at the very least—some mystery meat, something best not to ask the origin of. The rest of his menu hadn't changed in fifteen years.

"I just fired Dave and have asked Isouf to become the manager, but he needs some help to do it properly," she added. "Would you be willing to take a consulting job and train him and the new staff? The menu needs shaking up."

"Gee, that sounds interesting! I'd be delighted to see what I can do," I said.

"I thought what they did to you was unfair, so it will be great working with you," she explained.

And thus began some of the most rewarding months of my life.

After a week, with the new three-person crew interviewed and hired, it was time to go hands-on. Isouf, Mathieu, Catherine, the cooks. Osei, the waiter. While they all possessed cooking skills, they didn't know American cooking other than hamburgers. Americans posted in Burkina Faso, far from home and from other American communities in West Africa, wanted—and needed—a taste of the mother country.

One of the things they craved was Mexican food. Flour tortillas, refried beans, guacamole, beef or pork carnitas, quesadillas. Desserts. Especially pie. Apple. Coconut Cream. Chocolate Chess.

I taught Isouf how to make all those. And more.

Daily, he cranked it out, much to the acclaim of the Americans. Breakfast plates came garnished with a slice of fresh orange and omelets, too. Sometimes

Isouf, who did the marketing, had trouble finding everything needed for a full menu, but with daily specials, he did fine. A brilliant cook, he needed me to show him once how to do something new.

Aisha stopped by one Saturday morning, soon after I started work. She gently informed me that I needed to be less like a drill sergeant and more like a mother.

"Patience and kindness," she admonished me.

A week or so after that well-deserved dressing down, the tension in the kitchen abated somewhat. That is, until Aisha, on another inspection visit, announced that the Embassy scheduled the West African U.S. Softball Tournament in Ouaga over Memorial Day weekend. Moreover, participants from other U.S. Embassies in West Africa learned of the Club's Mexican food. Trembling, I told Isouf that the crew needed to prepare almost 300 meals a day for three days, starting in two weeks.

If the Club kitchen were anything but what it was—a small room about twelve feet by fifteen—that many meals a day would have been a piece of cake. But with one four-burner gas stove and a stovetop griddle, two large refrigerators, and an upright freezer, it took the crew everything they could muster to keep the pace with orders when the big weekend arrived. To make things harder, the young Marines never seemed to stop ordering beer and eating until the doors closed, around 10 p.m.

Isouf, Mathieu, Catherine, and Osei rose to the occasion and pulled it off in grand style. The whole endeavor boosted their self-confidence.

As with all postings, ours had to end. I packed up most of my kitchen equipment. Before I left, I presented Isouf with a big box of practical items: large stainless-steel bowls and kitchen implements—spatulas, measuring cups, spoons, and baking sheets.

Many years later, I learned that Isouf still managed the Club's restaurant. A sure sign of his success: he owned two cars. The rest of the crew still worked for him. Except for Osei, who seemed to have been imbued with a bit of Dave's spirit, skimming off the top of the meal checks.

Flour Tortillas

½ cup vegetable shortening or lard

4 cups all-purpose flour

2 teaspoons fine sea salt

1 cup warm water, or more

Work shortening/lard into flour by hand, until it resembles fine cornmeal. Add salt and mix well. Stir in warm water until a soft dough forms. Knead for 3-4 minutes. Dough will soft and pliable. Put dough into a plastic bag, seal, leave at room temperature for about 2 hours. This relaxes the gluten and makes dough easier to roll out. Divide dough into 8-12 equal-size balls. Let sit for about 5 minutes, covered. One by one, roll out the rounds into circles as thin as possible. Bake each on a dry heavy skillet until brown flecks appear on one side, flip and cook briefly on second side. Stack in a warm towel. Use for burritos or soft tacos. Store in refrigerator or freezer in plastic bag. Makes 8-12.

The American Club kitchen crew

le Havre

BRETAGNE MAINE

OCÉA

CARTE GÉNÉRALE
DE FRANCE
divisée
par Gouvernements

etttée et assujettie aux observations
Astronomiques
par M.Bonne, Mgr de Mathém?

A PARIS,
hés Lattré, Graveur, rue St. Jacques,
a la Ville de Bordeaux, 1771
avec Priv. du Roy.

Recipe

France turned out to be a haven from the hardships of living in Africa, especially Burkina Faso. I returned to France many times, eventually traveling throughout most of the entire country. I also studied for several weeks at Le Cordon Bleu cooking school in the 15th arrondissement, seafood and sauce, and charcuterie. In 2011, I won a Julia Child grant from IACP to study the ways immigrants might be changing French cuisine and food habits. I lived for a month in a garret on the Île Saint-Louis in the middle of Paris.

Peeling Potatoes, France

Le Cordon Bleu

The preparation of good food is merely another expression of art,
one of the joys of civilized living ... .

~ Dione Lucas

What food-obsessed person in love with France doesn't dream, at least sometimes, of attending culinary school in France? Or doing a *stage* at some respected restaurant either in Paris or the provinces?

Le Cordon Bleu Paris, the same cooking school attended by Julia Child, still sold dreams. It now occupies a starkly modern building in Paris's 15th arrondissement and didn't at all resemble the quaint place where Julia out-onioned a cadre of G.I.s dreaming of becoming chefs.

Julia wouldn't recognize the commercialization there now.

It was still a palace of dreams, one where frying onions or sizzling sausages perfumed the air, where I instantly crossed over to another side of existence, rising above the drama of failed relationships, the pain of tight budgets, the heat of summer. A place where art reigned and beauty sustained souls.

Unless that soul belonged to a lobster.

Dreaming the dream, I convinced myself to sign up for two short courses at Le Cordon Bleu: Fish and Their Sauces, as well as Charcuterie. In the former, dishes such as *bourride* captured my attention. In the latter came lessons on making passable *galantines*, *ballotines*, white sausage, and blood sausage. The highlight of the charcuterie class was the gallon-size vat of pig's blood the chef poured into scraped pig intestines by standing on a stool and funneling the dark rose-colored liquid. Blood sausage, not a favorite of mine.

Lobster starred in the first fish class.

And not just any lobster. My lobster.

The one I couldn't kill with a deft thrust of the knife.

It looked so easy when the chef demonstrated the process in the morning's lecture. But when I picked out my lobster for *Homard L'armoricaine*, the enormity of what I needed to do caused me to hesitate.

A lot.

The creature lay on the white tiled countertop, its black claws bound with white kitchen twine. Its tiny eyes followed my movements. As I came close to it with a sharp chef's knife in my right hand, grabbing the tail with my left, its eyes waved back and forth, frantic at the dawning knowledge that it could not defend itself. It wiggled, arched its head, making the sweet spot of death a moving target.

I stabbed. The shot did not go home. The beast writhed violently as tears trickled down my cheeks. Another stab. More writhing. The chef stood behind me, grabbed a mallet, and bashed the creature's head.

My eyes red from crying, I finished the recipe. Chef tasted it, mumbled something like "*Bon*," and moved on. I couldn't bring more than a tasting spoon to my lips.

That lobster caused me to discover something about myself, again: I can't kill my own food. I can't.

But I am okay with someone else doing it.

"Hypocrite," I whispered to myself as I changed out of my stained uniform in the locker room. The light of the Paris dusk seemed a little less vibrant as I walked back to the Hotel Mars at 117, Avenue de la Bourdonnais.

Escoffier's Homard à L'armoricaine

Recipe exactly as it appeared in A. Escoffier's *Guide to Modern Cookery*, published by William Heineman in 1907 in London.

The first requirement for this dish is that the lobster must be a live one.

Cut the tail into sections; remove the claws and crack them so as to facilitate the removal of the flesh after cooking; split the carapace in half lengthways and remove the sac which is found near the top of the head (this usually contains a little gravel). Place the creamy parts and coral from the head on one side and reserve for use. Season the pieces of lobster with salt and pepper. Heat 4 tablespoons oil and 30 g (1 oz) butter in a shallow pan until frothing, place in the pieces of lobster and fry quickly on all sides until the flesh is well set and the shells have turned a good red colour. Drain off the fat by tilting the pan on one side with its lid on, then sprinkle the lobster with 2 finely chopped shallots and 1 small clove of crushed garlic. Add ¼ dl (1 fluid ounces or – U.S. cup) flamed brandy, 2 dl (7 fluid ounces or – U.S. cup) white wine, 1½ dl (5 fluid ounces or – U.S. cup) Fish Stock, 1 tablespoon melted Meat Glaze, 150 g (5½ ounces) roughly chopped flesh only of tomato or 1½ tablespoons tomato purée, ½ dl (2 fluid ounces or ¼ U.S. cup) Sauce Demi-glace, a pinch of roughly chopped parsley and a touch of Cayenne pepper. Cover with the lid and cook gently for 15 - 20 minutes. When cooked, transfer the pieces of lobster to a dish, remove the flesh from the sections and claws and place them in a timbale or deep dish with the two halves of the carapace on top standing up against each other; keep warm.

Reduce the cooking liquid to 2 dl (7 fluid ounces or – U.S. cup) and add the reserved creamy parts and coral chopped together with approximately 15 g (½ ounce) butter. Reheat and pass through a fine strainer. Reheat again for a few minutes without allowing it to boil, then add away from the heat, 100 g (3½ ounces) butter in small pieces. Pour this sauce over the lobster and sprinkle with a little roughly chopped parsley.

Le Cordon Bleu

323

Angelina's

I would be me, yes, in Paris, I would be me.
~ M.F.K. Fisher

For anyone who's walked through the streets of Paris on a rainy winter day, a cold wind whipping passersby's coats above their knees, umbrellas upending as in Bugs Bunny cartoons, Angelina's tearoom loomed as a welcome respite.

That's precisely what I felt when I followed the guidebook's starred review of Angelina's, founded in 1903 by Anton Rumpelmeyer and his son René at 226 Rue de Rivoli.

Walking through driving rain, I passed 228 Rue de Rivoli. And shuddered for a moment. The Hotel Meurice. And shuddered some more. The Hotel Meurice, the spot from which the Nazis ruled "*Gross Paris*," where a German general named Dietrich Hugo Hermann von Cholitz defied Adolf Hitler, who demanded "Is Paris burning now!?" as World War II came to an end. Although the Nazis requisitioned the hotel after they marched into a subdued and beaten Paris in June 1940, General von Cholitz recognized the beauty and historical importance of the City of Light. So instead, he chose to leave it intact for future generations, knowing that he'd be detained by the Allies.

Across the street, deeply embedded into a cement-and-stone wall, brass plaques commemorated dead Resistance fighters, the *Macquis*. Thoughts of those tortured *Maquis* briefly overshadowed the pleasure of passing through the glass double doors of Angelina and smelling the aromas drifting in the air.

Drenched, hair slicked to my forehead, I wound my way through dozens of tables, through crowds of chattering tourists, wishing I looked as French as the ladies sitting along the wall, their proper black dresses and shining ivory-hued pearls draping their thin necks.

With her chin, a waitress dressed like a stereotypical French maid pointed to an empty table. I sat, the small round table about the size of a large pizza. I thanked her in my best French, "*Merci, 'mamselle*," as she handed me a menu and hustled off to the kitchen.

Saliva pooled under my tongue, and my taste buds quivered in anticipation as I smelled the aroma of chocolate hanging in the air. I ordered. Angelina's house special. Hot chocolate, of course. But not just any hot chocolate.

L'Africain.

There was also the *Mont Blanc*, a confection worthy of God and all the saints.

On my first visit, I wanted only the signature dish.

When the waitress set the steaming silky chocolate in front of me, foaming and spoon-thick in a pristine white pitcher, I poured it into a small demitasse cup and brought the cup to my lips. I was glad to be sitting down. Swooning came to mind, so rich and luscious was that miraculous confection. Images of Bernini's St. Teresa fluttered behind my closed eyelids. No, it wouldn't do to faint in ecstasy.

Tourists who stumbled upon Angelina's on the Rue de Rivoli in Paris got a hint of what drove earlier clients such as Coco Chanel wild: thick, unctuous hot chocolate in white porcelain cups, topped with layers of whipped cream, smelling strongly of cinnamon and requiring a spoon to scoop up what is essentially a melted candy bar of pure chocolate.

For over 300 years, the Western world only knew chocolate as a drink like Angelina's and a nuanced taste in certain meat dishes. However, nuns in the sweets-producing convents in New Spain produced various concoctions other than the usual drinks, including the legendary *Mole Poblano*.

Descendants of those sweets sparkle behind gleaming glass cases inside the entryway to Angelina's.

Opéras, aptly named. Small, compact layered cakes, flamboyant, enough to make a body sing with joy. Chocolate. With a tiny fleck of gold leaf resting atop rich ganache. I bought a dozen, to gorge on later in my small airless hotel room near the Champs de Mars.

As I walked by that wall across the street, and touched the brass plaques, I murmured a silent prayer for the dead souls who saved Paris from burning.

Hot Chocolate Like Angelina's

3 ounces fine-quality semisweet chocolate, chopped

3 ounces fine-quality bittersweet chocolate, chopped

¼ cup water, room temperature

3 tablespoons hot water

3 cups hot milk, divided

Granulated sugar, to taste

Whipped Cream, if desired

Over low heat, combine chocolate and ¼ cup water in a double boiler, heat until chocolate melts, occasionally stirring until creamy and smooth. Whisk in 3 tablespoons hot water to thin mixture. Pour equal amounts into 4 large cups or mugs. Stir ¾ cup hot milk into each mug. Add sugar and whipped cream to taste. Serves 4.

The author in Aix-en-Provence

A Round of Brie

... The more I learned, the more I realized how very much one has to know before one is in-the-know at all.

~ Julia Child

The French do food well. Scenery, too. Wine. History. *Bien sûr!* Washing machines? *Mais non!*

Frankly, when it comes to household appliances in France, I'd rather walk a plank on a pirate ship than turn a knob.

I've always been pretty mechanically illiterate. I've never stayed in a Paris apartment where I felt genuinely comfortable with the machinery. My garret on the Île Saint-Louis offered no respite from the annoying peculiarities of French washing machines. It resembled the monster under the bed I feared in childhood, except this one leered with one Cyclopean eye and emitted a real growl.

The truth was that I sweated, a lot, as I scampered around Paris studying immigrant foodways, taking the crowded metro to the Bibliothèque nationale de France. Temperatures hovered above 80°F.

Not to mention that seven pairs of underwear went only so far.

The moment came.

I needed to wash clothes. Had to. I pulled out the landlord's instructions, typed on a worn sheet of paper:

Washing Machine: There is a washing machine in the bathroom. [Note: The bathroom?!] *There is no dryer—the French believe dryers cook their clothes—they hang to dry. To operate the washer, load the clothes. Put a little less than one scoop of detergent into the drawer on the upper left. Close the drawer and the door and turn the "Programme" knob clockwise to one of the three areas within the three large blocks (approx. the 2 o'clock, the 4 o'clock or the 7 o'clock positions—heavy duty/ normal, permanent press and permanent press/fine, respectively). Pick the temperature you want (anything above 70 degrees is going to nearly boil your clothes). Make certain the "vitesse d'essorage" button is set to "1000" (i.e. top pressed in) and then push the Start/Stop button (which is next to the "Porte" button).*

IMPORTANT: When the washer finishes the "arret" light will come on. Do NOT push any buttons until you have turned the knob, counterclockwise, back to the Arret *position (i.e. the Noon position on the dial), and then push the "Porte" button to open the door. Finally, with the door open, push "Start/Stop". (Any other combination of steps is likely to lock the door with your clothes inside and force you to wash them all over again.)*

Always that word—IMPORTANT—followed by a clause warning of the dire consequences wrought by a finger rebelling against the task at hand. So, with the instructions firmly ensconced on the bathroom counter, I dug around in the cupboard and came up with the detergent.

Two blobs of detergent in each cellophane wrapper. I guessed that meant it was OK to use both. Concentrating hard on the instruction sheet, I pulled out a little drawer in the side of the machine. Some water sloshed about in the tiny soap cubicle, but I ignored it. Instead, I cut open the cellophane packet and plopped the tablets into the water. They dissolved like Alka-Seltzers, speaking of which I felt as if I needed a couple of those myself. And I hadn't even baked my Brie or uncorked my new bottle of Riesling yet.

Then came the part where I wished I knew a rocket scientist: the KNOB. Reading the instruction sheet out loud, I closed the door and pressed the correct button. I turned the KNOB, and presto!

Water poured into the machine! It works! A miracle!

But wait! Oh no, I forgot to put the clothes in!

Two hours later, the sparkling clean washing machine stopped. So I started all over again, penciling in additions to the instructions: "Be sure to put your clothes in first!"

Of course, by then, I was well on my way to needing a few Alka-Seltzers for real. I'd emptied my wine glass a few times and scraped up the last of the Brie with a hunk of baguette as I listened to the music of that snarling machine.

Baked Brie with Apricot Jam

1 (8-ounce) round of Brie

¼ cup Bonne Maman apricot jam

2 tablespoons sliced almonds

Heat oven to 400°F. Place Brie in a small, greased casserole dish just a bit larger than the cheese itself. Top cheese with jam and almonds. Wrap snugly with foil, folding edges over and pleating foil to seal. Place small casserole in pie pan or another baking dish. Bake approximately 25 minutes, or until center oozes. Unwrap and serve in the dish with sliced apples, crackers, crostini, or crudités. Serves 4 as an appetizer.

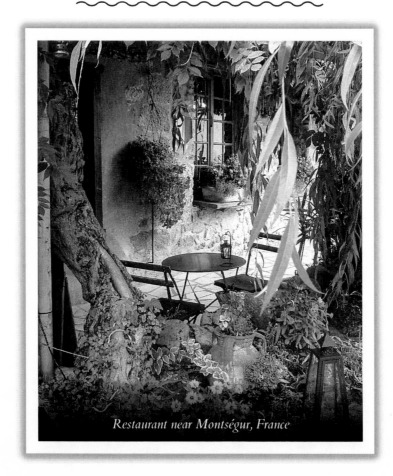

Restaurant near Montségur, France

Tarte Flambée / Flammekueche

Even apocalypse looks less dire when viewed over a plate of bacon.
~ Stephanie Stamm

One cold, rainy day in October, in front of a fireplace in a small *weinstube*, or bistro, in Strasbourg, France, I heard my stomach growling. But I couldn't face another round of choucroute, that heavy Alsatian love ode to the pig and the cabbage.

Fingerprints from earlier guests were visible on the greasy laminated plastic menu. One dish stood out: *Flammekueche*, also known as "*Tarte Flambée*." I ordered it. Plus a bottle of Alsatian Riesling, never mind the particulars of vintage and *terroir*.

Arriving on a board, thinner than plywood and softened by years of service, the *Flammekueche* bubbled like a lava pit. Bacon, cut into lardons, trembled from the heat of the fiery womb that birthed it, sputtering drops of fat into the air. The bread crust, slightly blackened by licks of flames in the wood-burning oven, looked as thin as meat pounded for scaloppine.

My maiden bite of *Flammekueche*, or "flame cake," convinced me I'd found a keeper, a recipe that I needed to engrave in my mental cookbook. I rolled up each piece like a crêpe and ate like a famished peasant. Not hard to do since *Flammekueche* is Alsace's version of "all you can eat." If there were a Guinness Book of Records for *Flammekueche* consumption, top mention would go to a person who put away three at one sitting. An impressive feat since the average *Flammekueche* measures approximately twelve inches by seventeen inches.

According to François Lassus's *Les hommes et le feu de l'Antiquité à nos jours: Du feu mythique et bienfaiteur au feu dévastateur*, fire and myth carved deep grooves into the ancient cultures of the area. Humans and fire, warmth and devastation. *Flammekueche* symbolized well-being, home and hearth, and, yes, security.

Flammekueche entered Alsace's repertoire of recipes through the ingenuity of farm women in the Bas Rhin region of what is now Germany. The key ingredients—bacon, onions, farmer cheese or quark, cream, and flour—filled farm larders, at least in good times. Each farm wife boasted a different recipe, but the basic ingredients remained the same. Rolled out thin, the dough used in the dish served as a thermometer for bread baking. If the *Flammekueche* cooked up in one to two minutes, that signaled that the oven burned hot enough for baking the weekly bread supply. Near Pfulgriesheim, eight miles northwest of Strasbourg, cooks made a creamier version of *Flammekueche*, called *Flambreeli*.

First mentioned in culinary literature in 1884, not until 1968 or so did restaurants in Strasbourg begin selling *Flammekueche* to the hordes of tourists gawking at the city's puff-pastry-like Notre Dame cathedral, its sandstone walls glowing pink in the nightly sunsets. A *Confrérie de la Véritable Tarte Flambée d'Alsace* formed, to set standards for *Flammekueche* sold in Alsatian restaurants. Nowadays, French homemakers buy ready-made *Flammekueche* in supermarkets, produced by companies such as Pierre-Schmidt.

Julia Child never mentioned *Flammekueche* in her luminous masterpiece, *Mastering the Art of French Cooking*. And her role model, Madame E. Saint-Ange, failed to do so in *her* masterwork, *La Bonne Cuisine de Madame E. Saint-Ange*.

I stored the memory of that Strasbourg meal in my mind for a long time. Until one cold, snowy day in Virginia, when I turned memory into reality by using a pizza stone instead of a wood-burning oven and ricotta instead of quark.

As for wine, a California Riesling did the trick just fine.

Tarte Flambée / Flammekueche

1 medium sweet onion, sliced no more than ¼-inch thick, preferably 1/8-inch thick

½ cup plus 2 tablespoons whole-milk ricotta

½ cup plus 2 tablespoons *crème fraîche* or sour cream (if using sour cream, add 1 tablespoon of flour to keep it from thinning out)

Fine sea salt, to taste

¼-½ teaspoon freshly ground black pepper

½ pound slab bacon, cut into pieces the size of wooden matches

½ pound bread dough

Parsley, minced finely, for garnish

Place a baking stone on lowest rack in oven and crank up temperature to 450°F. Remove all other racks in oven. Grease a baking sheet with sides at least ½-inch high. (No baking stone? Don't worry. Use the pan.) Mix onions with ricotta and *crème fraiche*/sour cream. Add salt and pepper. Let mixture sit for at least 15 minutes. This melds flavors a bit and onions loosen up. (For a less strong onion taste, blanched the sliced onion in boiling water for about 1 minute. Drain on paper towels.) Roll dough thin, fit it to baking sheet, and smooth dough out up to the edges of pan. Spread cheese/cream mixture over dough to the edges. Put bacon all over the top so that the whole area is well covered. Grind more black pepper over everything, to taste. Bake about 15-20 minutes, until dough is crisp around the edges and bacon sizzles. Remove from oven, sprinkle with parsley, and cut into squares. Serve right away! Remember the wine! Makes one.

Top: The author in her garret on the Île Saint- Louis, Paris

Left: The author and Erik on the Atlantic coast, France

Chartreuse

The price of peace and solitude has been unending struggle.
~ Roy Andries de Groot

Sometimes certain books speak to my soul, over and over again.

Roy Andries de Groot's masterpiece, *The Auberge of the Flowering Hearth*, spoke to me deeply when I first read this rapturous travelogue and cookbook. Like a chef cooking down *jus de lis*, de Groot captured the essence of a place—L'Auberge de L'Atre Fleuri—a small restaurant in France's Alpine region, where a man could stand nearly upright inside the large fireplace. Two older ladies, the Mesdemoiselles Artaud and Girard, worked culinary magic with their hands, creating memories so strong that de Groot wrote this tribute to them and their way of life. A way of life that no longer exists, making de Groot's book an example of what culinary historians call "primary research material."

I nearly cried when I came to the last page, where he described a 1911 Cognac of Gaston Briand poured at his last supper at The Auberge: "The soft velvet, the delicate power, the aromatic excitement of this ancient spirit are almost beyond description. It was a climatic curtain."

The End.

I didn't want it to end. I wanted a sequel!

From that moment, I plotted to visit the place that inspired de Groot, who slowly went blind from a blast during the London Blitz, to pen such rubyesque words on the page. He captured the essence of the high granite peaks of France's Savoie without seeing them, relying on his wife's words and descriptions gleaned from other traveling companions.

Shortly before my first trip to Europe, I re-read *The Auberge*, touched with feelings welling up in me as I sank into de Groot's sensual prose, larded with recipes and observations on the taste of this dish and that dish. Yet, slyly, he didn't include the slightest hint of where L'Atre Fleuri could be found.

All he mentioned was St. Pierre de Chartreuse.

So, because of one book, we drove through emerald-green forests, following D912 and the Isere River in the shadows of the French Alps, seeking La Grande Chartreuse. The morning sun blazed through the still-crisp air. Jewel-like bubbles shimmered in the light, dancing on the river's surface, gleaming like clusters of the frozen grapes used to make ice wine.

Before we turned off D912, we passed through Chambery, the home of French writer Jean Jacques Rousseau. I briefly considered reading his 1762 *Du contrat social* or his *Confessions*, published twenty years later. Rousseau angered both French and Swiss powers-that-be and spent his remaining years in exile.

The irony of his life story versus that of the monks at La Grande Chartreuse did not escape me.

At St. Pierre de Chartreuse, I stood on the grey granite gravel of the parking lot, under a towering pine tree, gazing at the monumental, white-walled buildings of the monastery of La Grande Chartreuse, as austere as its surroundings. St. Bruno arrived there with six other men and founded the monastery in 1084 A.D., where silence still rules: no one speaks.

Bruno followed the Romans, who founded St. Laurent de Pont and a few huts in another area, called *catursiani*, meaning "little house where one is alone in an isolated and wild place." From this word comes "Chartreuse." And the name for the Carthusian order.

Throughout history, the Carthusian order suffered persecution, especially during the French Revolution and afterward, because of popular identification of the Roman Catholic Church with the *ancien régime*.

Yet monks still concoct the liqueur they began making over 400 years ago, although nowadays not on the monastery's premises. The recipe for Chartreuse emerged from a mysterious manuscript donated to the monks in 1602 by Marshal d'Estrées, a courtier of French king Henri IV. Today, the distillery—where over 130 medicinal plants go into the recipe for Chartreuse, yellow and green—is located in nearby Voiron.

The monks built a new monastery about two kilometers away to maintain their privacy. Visitors to La Correrie can buy bottles and other souvenirs at the gift shop there. At the same time, visitors can tour models of the stark cells where the monks live, see how their food is passed through a small cupboard in the cell walls—much like prisoners, actually, and walk through the tiny gardens outside each "apartment" or cell where the monks grow flowers. A prie-dieu, or prayer stand, stood off to one side in each cell.

The long, silent cloister provided much to ponder.

The hard wooden beds, which testified to the asceticism of the monks.

The coarse, white raw-wool habits the monks wear.

The twelfth-century chapel with wooden seats for the monks to sit on during Mass and prayers.

The peace of the valley.

I understood all too well the attraction of the place and the lifestyle. But most people could not live as monks do.

I wondered if those Carthusian monks drank their product. After all, the founder of the Benedictine order, St. Benedict of Nursia, allowed his monks a liter of wine a day.

I couldn't wait to sip Chartreuse on ice, so we bought a bottle of the eponymous green variety and stashed it in the trunk of our car, waiting impatiently for nightfall.

Having learned a profound truth the night before, thanks to a mosquito-infested, mildew-festooned room, we reserved a room in a modern Ibis Hotel, quite similar to a Day's Inn in the United States. A sorry lesson hammered home by Holiday Inn's refrain: "The best surprise is no surprise."

Gambling on the fact that we were in France, ergo the food must be good everywhere, we naively ate in the dining room at the hotel. The food spoke French linguistically: tarragon chicken, hamburger steak, potato salad, beet salad, smoked herring, marinated fish. "Linguistically" was the extent of the Frenchiness of the food. We could have been eating anywhere in the world where tourists congregate. Wine, on the other hand, the French do well. So we chose Domaines des Causses et Eynes (a Côtes du Rhône).

Back in our room, its smallness typical of bargain-basement-priced one- and two-star French hotels, I scrounged up a couple of shrink-wrapped plastic glasses. Grimacing at the idea of drinking a liqueur made from a centuries-old recipe out of plastic glasses, I nonetheless poured the green gold over a few ice cubes. The ice glistened like diamonds under the light of the bedside lamp.

The cloudiness of the glasses obscured the pale green color of the liquor, reminiscent of now-banned absinthe. Slightly thick, similar in heft to the thin, light sugar syrup used in making meringues. At the first sip, the Chartreuse coated my tongue, enlivening my taste buds. My brain flashed on an Alpine meadow, as in Savoie, where many of the 130 medicinal plants originated. The burst of herbal flavor in that sip imparted a taste unique in its breadth.

Words, at least in English, fall short when it comes to flavor and taste.

English is "color-blind" that way, flavor blind. So when it came to describing the nuances of the taste of Chartreuse, the word "grassy" popped up, but not like turf grass out on the front lawn. Instead, the grassiness resembles, more than anything, the smell of running through a freshly mowed field on a hot summer day, chewing anise seeds.

A feeling of freedom, a glimpse of what a carefree childhood might be.

Potato Pancakes Catursiani

4 medium russet potatoes

3 eggs

4 scallions, green part only, thinly sliced

2 garlic cloves, peeled and finely minced

2 tablespoons fresh parsley, finely chopped

½ teaspoon fresh rosemary, finely minced

2 tablespoons heavy cream, more or less

3 tablespoons clarified unsalted butter

2 tablespoons vegetable oil

Fine sea salt, to taste

Freshly ground black pepper, to taste

Bake potatoes until done, using a standard method. When done, cut open and scoop out pulp. Place in a 1-quart mixing bowl, mash but not too much. Add eggs, scallions, garlic, parsley, and rosemary. Add cream, again not too much–the mixture must be malleable enough to form patty-like mounds. Heat 3 tablespoons butter and 2 tablespoons vegetable oil in heavy 10-inch sauté pan. Form patties about ¼-inch thick and 2-inches wide. Carefully place patties in butter/oil. Fry until brown and crisp on both sides. Serve hot. Serves 4.

~~~~~~~~~~~~~~~~

A Rabelaisian World

Appetite comes with eating … but thirst goes away with drinking.
~ François Rabelais

The world of food constantly and consistently offers opportunities for discovering complex linkages between the darnedest things.

Take, for example, my goal of writing about melegueta pepper (*Aframomum melegueta*), a spice originating in Africa. The process of writing always led to new discoveries, for I never knew into what rabbit hole I would descend.

I hardly expected to end up in France via melegueta pepper.

I began this foray into the background of the spice … and ended up with belly laughs Chez François, Rabelais that is. Sixteenth-century Benedictine monk and priest, theologian, medical doctor, satirist, budding scatologist, and possibly the all-time champion thumber-of-noses at power and privilege, that was François Rabelais. I dimly recalled reading his work in French classes at university. Rediscovering him again after many years reminded me of finding a forgotten twenty-dollar bill in an old coat pocket.

Sudden riches to brighten a gloomy day.

Before I got to the heart of the matter, I paused and perused a few encyclopedic digressions into its genealogy: melegueta pepper—Guinea pepper, alligator pepper, Grains of Paradise, etc.—perfumed and livened up food in Europe during the Middle Ages. And beyond.

Grown primarily in what is now Ghana, and still grown there, melegueta pepper claims cardamom and ginger as botanical cousins. Depicting it tastewise is like a blind man describing an elephant. Think slow burn and Fire-Stick, that old movie-theater cinnamon-fueled candy with the broodingly hot aftertaste. Surprisingly, the slow burn extends to fingers and lips that touch this tiny, innocent-looking berry, the wrinkled fruit of a shrub called, well, *Aframomum melegueta*.

When, out of curiosity, I searched for mentions of melegueta pepper in various forms of literature, a book on translating prose popped up. Burton Raffel's *The Art of Translating Prose*. He discussed the difficulties of translating Rabelais's sixteenth-century works, who was—as he put it—"a cross between James Joyce and Laurence Sterne." Especially so in his bawdy, food-drenched *The Life of Gargantua and Pantagruel*, composed of five books.

Or "pentalogy," to be exact.

Raffel wrote:

"Before I leave the first paragraph, at long last, let me explain that although amomon *is clearly the French term [used by Rabelais], dating back to the thirteenth century, for the spice generally known as 'cardamom,' with the authority of* Le Petit Robert, *I have slightly (and I trust to its gain) expanded my translation of* amomon *to include another exotic spice, melegueta pepper. ... I hope there are no chefs outraged by the linkage [between cardamom and melegueta pepper]."*

Beyond that well-chewed first paragraph mentioned by Raffel, Rabelais treated his readers to a timeless kaleidoscope of sensations, smells, tastes, jokes, and allusions. Recalling the topsy-turviness—and stinkiness—of life during the sixteenth century, *The Life of Gargantua and Pantagruel* both shocks and surprises the modern reader, especially in Raffel's somewhat modernized version. Comedians David Letterman and Jay Leno could lift scatological material from Rabelais's book and make merry hash of it all, every night, for weeks.

Satire is satire, and *The Life of Gargantua and Pantagruel* oozed with it.

Suffice it to say that, in book 4, chapter 60, "How the Belly Worshipers Sacrificed to Their God on Fish and Fasting Days," Rabelais excoriated the rich and the pious by listing the immense amounts of food available to them:

"What," he [Pantagruel] said," will these rascals sacrifice to their belly-potent god, on fish and fasting days?"

"I tell you," said the pilot [of the ship]. *"For the first course, they serve him:*
caviar
pressed caviar
fresh butter
thick pea soup
spinach
sweet white herring
assorted other herring
sardines
anchovies
salted tuna

cabbage in oil
bean and onion salad ..."

Rabelais followed with a list of dozens and dozens of types of seafood. Ending with a reference to the privy, which I best not detail, the chapter railed against the moneyed and privileged classes with colossal bitterness.

Why did Rabelais feel the need for such derision? What was happening in his world, in his times? Consider the impact of the Renaissance and Reformation, the Age of Conquest and Exploration.

There was also the question of *fouaces* (also called *fouées*), a bread similar in concept to pita from the Touraine area of France, made famous by Rabelais's tale of a war between the bakers of Lerne and the shepherds of Seuilly.

From melegueta pepper to *fouaces* ... what a Rabelaisian world it turned out for me as I tumbled down that rabbit hole!

Fouées de Touraine (French Pita-Style Bread)

4 cups bread flour

2 teaspoons fine sea salt

1 tablespoon yeast

2 cups or more lukewarm water

Put flour and salt in a bowl. Measure out water into a small bowl. Add yeast to water and let sit until bubbly. Stir yeast mixture into flour and knead for about 5 minutes. Grease another bowl, make a ball of dough, place dough in bowl and coat all sides with grease. Cover bowl with a damp cloth. Let rise until doubled, about 2 hours, depending upon room temperature. Heat oven to 425°F. Use a baking stone for best results, but a heavy baking sheet works well, too. Heat oven with stone or baking sheet inside, on lowest oven rack. Punch dough down and divide into 12 equal-sized balls. Let dough rest about 10 minutes, then roll out into thin rounds, about 6 inches or so in diameter. Place 2 or 3 of the *fouées* on the stone/baking sheet. Within a few seconds, rounds will start puffing up. Bake 1-2 minutes. Cool on racks. Repeat with remaining rounds. Makes about a dozen.

Aix-en-Provence

By then I knew more about how to be a good ghost.

~ M.F.K. Fisher

One gloomy November night in Aix-en-Provence, I sat near a rain-drenched window, reading food writer M.F.K. Fisher's *Map of Another Town*, about her time in 1950s Aix. She spoke of the incredible loneliness she felt, the sense of being an "outlander," her precise word.

In other words, she pondered the question of exile. Whether voluntary or not.

She lived near where I sat, across the street. For a while, she rented a room at 17 rue Cardinale, with the unforgettable Madame Lanes. She detailed her thoughts and feelings in her book, writing bluntly about the French propensity for abrupt rudeness to strangers:

What was harder to take calmly, especially on the days when my spiritual skin was abnormally thin, was the hopeless admission that the people I really liked would never accept me as a person of perception and sensitivity perhaps equal to their own.

Now I understand what she meant. Completely.

What is it to be a stranger in a strange town? Displaced from most of what makes us, well, "us?"

I've often wondered how people—uprooted from their homes and loved ones—maintained their sense of who they faced events that stripped them of their usual identity markers. Think of the Jews during World War II. Or maybe we should go back even further to the 1492 diaspora enforced by the Catholic monarchs of Spain? Or even forward in time to the people of modern Syria?

Being a stranger in a strange land imbues a whole new meaning to the phrase from Genesis 18:2: "... he [Abraham] ran from the tent door to meet them and bowed himself to the earth" or the Benedictine admonition to greet strangers as if they were divine incarnations.

Being a stranger demands a sense of humility, as well as remembrance of what we needed most when vulnerable and alone, when an act of welcome came when nothing seemed secure.

Being a stranger means when we no longer are strangers, we remember those despairing feelings of isolation, when an extended hand meant so much.

Guests. Sojourners. Immigrants.

Exiles, all, in a way. What kind of welcome do we give strangers in our midst?

Granted, it is not fair to paint a whole people with a tarred brush, but the truth is that in many parts of France, townspeople greet a stranger with less-than-great enthusiasm. Graham Robb dissected this dilemma exceedingly well in *The Discovery of France: A Historical Geography.*

My room that night in Aix was about fifty yards from Saint Jean de Malte, built in the thirteenth century. At Vespers, the bells rang. For some reason, I threw on my woolen coat and walked down the dark street. The light of the nave shone through the opened wooden doors. Inside, I sat in a back pew, weeping, missing Mike and Erik with almost physical pain in my chest. After the service, I stood up to leave and felt someone move close to me. A young French woman patted my hand. And motioned for me to join her and others around a small table topped with plastic glasses filled with wine and a tray of sweets.

It might not have been the Body and Blood, but it was communion, nonetheless.

Steak Frites

½ cup unsalted butter, softened

1 large shallot, minced

2 tablespoons fresh parsley, minced

2 garlic cloves, peeled and minced

Fine sea salt and freshly ground black pepper, to taste

2 pounds boneless rib-eye steaks, about ½-inch thick

2 tablespoons vegetable oil and 1 tablespoon unsalted butter for cooking steaks

French fries, made in the usual way, or use frozen

Make shallot butter by mixing first four ingredients, set aside. Season steak with salt and pepper on both sides. Heat 2 tablespoons oil and 1 tablespoon butter in a heavy skillet over medium-high heat until bubbling. Sear steaks and cook about 3-4 minutes per side. Place steaks on warm plates, top each steak with some shallot butter, cover loosely with foil, and let sit for 5 minutes. Serve with *frites*. Serves 4.

The author at the Cathedral of Aix

A Whiff of the Middle Ages

Just speak very loudly and quickly, and state your position with utter conviction, as the French do, and you'll have a marvelous time!
~ Julia Child

The beefy smell of soup and wood smoke nudged its way into the night air. It was the hour of Vespers, or evening prayers, and the village began to lock up, settling down, lights going out one by one like fireflies blinking on a long, scorching summer night. Kitchen lights flickered over the cobblestone street as mothers and wives, widows and widowers, fathers and husbands, ladled their evening broth over thick crusts of stale bread and topped with grated Gruyère cheese.

A peasant meal, eaten in one form or another for centuries.

An occasional headlight cast an incongruous shadow through the narrow outer door onto the stone walls reaching nearly fifty feet above my head. I sat on a long narrow bench, in relative darkness, alone. Stamping my feet on the stone floor, I glanced around me again, marveling that not another soul breathed with me in the great narthex of the Basilica of St. Mary Magdalene. Built in the twelfth century in Romanesque style, gray, square, and foreboding, the church sits on a high hill overlooking tranquil Burgundian wine country and the village of Vezelay, France.

Eager to be rid of the numbing coldness creeping up my legs, I jiggled my feet again and stood up quickly. In the shadows, tiny holes—like pockmarks cratering the faces of long-dead pilgrims suffering from smallpox—indented the surface of each square of stone in the floor. Light from the sunset suddenly blazed through the stained-glass windows, cascading over the faceless statues carved into the enormous tympanum above the arched double doors leading into the pilgrimage sanctuary. Irate villagers smashed the features off most of the faces during the French Revolution of 1789. Or they completely removed their heads, a telling act at a time when the guillotine ruled.

His nose gone, Christ stands at the center of the multitude of figures, his robes swirling like the trajectory of stars in Vincent van Gogh's "Starry Night."

The odor of soup, laced with medieval hints of nutmeg and cloves, lured me out into the street. I followed the scent to a small café across from the church.

The waiter, an older man perhaps in his seventies and bent forward like a question mark, sensed my hunger and settled me into a seat at a table near the window overlooking the faceless saints.

Soon a bowl of orange-colored soup steamed beneath my nose.

Pumpkin.

Pumpkins as a soup ingredient only figured in European recipes after Christopher Columbus clambered onto the Santa Maria, bringing several new foods from the New World back to Spain, including squash.

I ate, but the pamphlets in my backpack played with my mind. St Bernard of Clairvaux called for the Second Crusade, right there in Vezelay, on a hillside just beyond the city walls. An act that reverberates throughout the world to this day.

History, in the mouth and everywhere … .

La Soupe au Potiron (Pumpkin Soup)

4 cups pumpkin or butternut squash, cut into 1-inch cubes

8 tablespoons unsalted butter

1 large yellow onion, peeled and finely chopped

1½ cups fresh white breadcrumbs, toasted

½ teaspoon ground nutmeg

½ teaspoon ground sage

2 bay leaves

Fine sea salt, to taste

Freshly ground black pepper, to taste

6 cups unsalted chicken stock

½ cup grated Gruyère cheese

½ cup heavy cream

Toasted slices of bread

Chopped flat-leaf parsley as garnish

Preheat oven to 250°F. Melt butter in a heavy Dutch oven over low heat. Sauté pumpkin until browned on the sides of the cubes. Add onion and cook until soft, about 10 minutes. Stir in breadcrumbs and cook for 2 minutes. Mix in nutmeg, sage, and bay leaf. Season generously with salt and pepper. Add stock. Remove from heat, stir in cheese. Bake in oven for about 1½ hours, covered. Remove from oven. Taste for seasoning. Before serving, stir in heavy cream. Warm through on top of stove, do not boil. Place a slice of toasted bread in the bottom of each serving bowl, fill with soup, and garnish with chopped parsley. Serves 4–6.

Notre Dame de Paris

NOVA VIRGINIÆ TABVLA

Virginia was home for a large part of my life. First for graduate school, and later after returning for good from life overseas due to Mike's position in the Office of International Research, Education, and Development at Virginia Tech. I worked as a freelance back-of-the-book indexer for several years. Briefly, I attempted to be a personal chef, but found it unrewarding. Historic sites abound in Virginia, and I soon gravitated to the Peacock-Harper Culinary History Collection at the Virginia Tech library, volunteering with a committee seeking to increase the size of the collection and encouraging its use by researchers.

Amstelodami, ex officina Henrici Hondii.

Hearth in a Colonial Virginia home

Mountain Pie

*In my South, the most treasured things passed down
from generation to generation are the family recipes.*
~ Robert St. John

I once lived at the edge of coal country. Many mornings, I'd stand on the
balcony of the house I'd built on the ridge, scan the horizon, miles and miles of
fog-licked mountains poking out from lace-handkerchief-white clouds, seeking
the sun like sunflowers on a scorching summer day. A romantic picture-perfect
postcard of a place that belied a sad truth. As a wise man once said when asked
why he left the heart-stopping beauty of Italy for the grimy steel mills of Pitts-
burgh, "You can't eat beauty."

Appalachia still suffers from poverty and isolation, both reasons for the
way cooking evolved in the log cabins and homeplaces that dotted the slopes.

Blackberries grew wild there, in the Blue Ridge Mountains. Bushes
plump with fruit covered whole hillsides, and in July cooks battled with crows
and bears for the jewel-like berries. But the fight was worth it, as a bucket of
foraged blackberries can take a soul to heaven and back.

Especially if there was a "Mountain Pie" cooling on the table.

The first night I slept in those mountains, a neighbor brought me a
"Mountain Pie" as a "welcome" gift.

With that name, I stumbled into an abyss called "the names of things."

One name just won't do. No.

"Mountain Pie" was kin to cobbler, grunt, slump, crisp, buckle, Brown
Betty, crumble, pandowdy, sonker. Not only a supper dessert in the pie-loving
South, these traditional dishes also tasted good first thing in the morning, too,
washed down with swigs of bitter black coffee. My Southern grandmother,
whose cooking I mostly don't remember, made berry cobblers and a carrot cake
that still makes my mouth water when I think of it.

My neighbor's pie in front of me, sitting on a packing crate, I sank my
spoon right into the oozing pudding-like center. Pure sweetness soothed my

tongue, while the tang of blackberries evoked the taste of blood, almost metallic.

That pie claimed no heritage other than that of poverty and scarcity.

"Mountain Pie" captured the essence of that history.

Take the basics: flour, sugar, milk, some blackberries, a pinch of salt, and a heaping teaspoon of baking powder. No vanilla. Not even a whisper of cream. From a kitchen so poor that the cook who invented this recipe lacked eggs, one part of the holy trinity of the kitchen: eggs, flour, and milk. Mix it up and set it in the oven, maybe even a wood-burning stove. That was it.

Inherited from English and Scottish and Irish forebearers, "Mountain Pie" sustained those who clambered over the mountains when things got too hot for them in the lowlands of the Atlantic coast. Or when too many people lived too close for comfort on the edge of the frontier.

The hollers of the Southern Appalachian Mountains offered a perfect place to stop and set down roots. Steep, sloping and rocky, veined with coal and old Native American trails, thick with old-growth forests and pure water seeping from untainted springs, the mountains the Native Americans called "Ahkonshuck" walled off the outside world.

Foraging seemed like such a romantic thing, with all the farm-to-table propaganda.

One summer, I tried to repeat the "Mountain Pie" of my first night in the mountains. Snaking my fingers under the long briars of the blackberry bushes on the slope behind my house, I nicked my flesh one too many times, sucked the blood, and noted that blackberry juice turned black-red, the color of blood that has pooled around a wound and dried.

"You can't eat beauty." A profound lesson.

Blackberry Mountain Pie

½ cup unsalted butter

1 cup granulated sugar

1 cup all-purpose flour

1½ teaspoons aluminum-free baking powder

Pinch fine sea salt

¾ cup whole milk

1 teaspoon pure vanilla extract

2 heaping cups fresh blackberries, rinsed and hulled

Heat oven to 350°F. When oven is hot, place a glass pie pan with the butter on center rack. Mix sugar, flour, baking powder, and salt together in a bowl. Stir in milk. Take hot pan out of oven, pour in batter, and smooth to edges. Top with berries and push them down into batter. Bake 45–60 minutes, or until set and bubbling. Serve with whipped cream. Serves 8.

The author and Mike in their house in Virginia

Moonshine!

Well, between Scotch and nothin', I suppose I'd take Scotch.
It's the nearest thing to good moonshine I can find.
~ William Faulkner

I know the smell of moonshine. I also know the taste.

And, oh yes, the jolt.

I drank some once when I was young and stupid, in a rather bare bachelor apartment, in the mountains of southwest Virginia. Five cousins from Wytheville County, superb banjo pickers, and even better singers, invited a group of friends over for a night of debauchery. Or at least all-out drunken abandon.

Before that night, I knew nothing about moonshine, except for stories of bootleggers and Prohibition-era Chicago gangsters.

The smell of moonshine—also known as white lightning, hooch, mountain dew, and a whole slew of other quite colorful names, including rotgut, bathtub gin, popskull, panther's breath, block and tackle, squirrel likker, creepin' whisky, pine top, corn squeezin's, splo, white mule, white dog, and—the best one yet—sweet spirits of cats a fightin'—filled the apartment, along with the aroma of some mighty good weed.

Cautiously sipping from a Mason jar, I recoiled like a snake had gotten a stranglehold on my lips when the transparent liquid stroked my tongue. It's not for nothing that Irvin S. Cobb, a Kentucky humorist popular in the 1930s quipped, "When you absorb a deep swig of it, you have all the sensations of having swallowed a lighted kerosene lamp."

The banjo music faded away as that sip of illegal "mountain dew" slipped into my stomach and hammered through my bloodstream to my brain. There's nothing shy about 'shine, or un-aged corn whiskey.

This drink, indelibly associated with the American South, is now legally produced commercially in some states. There's no dearth of customers, many too young to remember the lore that rose up around the moonshiners of Appalachia, their copper stills hidden in the "hollers," out of sight of excise men/tax collectors.

I might even say the story of moonshine was the story of America.

The name originated with the producers of "shine," who distilled it at night, to keep their activity secret from the revenuers or excise-men. Distilling had a long tradition among the Ulster Scots who settled in the Appalachian Mountains in the seventeenth and eighteenth centuries. To pay the federal debt racked up by the Revolutionary War, President George Washington approved a tax on distilled spirits in 1791. The tax led to the Whiskey Rebellion in 1794, when a group of irate Pennsylvania farmers had had enough. Some of them packed up and left for the Appalachian Mountains.

Moonshine became a symbol of resistance and independence from government interference when a tax was levied on alcohol in 1861 to pay for the Civil War. During Prohibition in the 1920s, many moonshiners became rich, but they spent years in jail when the excise men caught up with them.

Moonshiners hired drivers known as "bootleggers" to deliver their product to markets as far away as Chicago, New York, and Philadelphia. To elude the revenuers, these drivers drove souped-up cars on narrow winding mountain roads, developing such immense skills that they became the first NASCAR stars many years later, Junior Johnson being just one example.

The recipe for moonshine was simple:

Cornmeal (made from dried sprouted corn that is then ground)

Sugar

Yeast

Water

Starting with the mash, corn soaking in water, fermenting as it were, was easy. But cooking the mash and keeping the temperature steady at 172°F, well, that was the hard part.

Packaging the product often involved the whole family, according to Nancy Vance Hatfield, of Gilbert, West Virginia:

"Daddy bootlegged for years. It was our only income in the 1950's. Daddy said a man had to do what a man had to do to feed his family. Some of my greatest adventures were helping my daddy bottle moonshine from our bathtub when I was about 8 years old."

Sometimes children or women served as lookouts while the men operated the copper stills, usually located near streams running with clear, cold mountain water. Or they collected the clear, glass-like liquid from the "worm" protruding from the still. The emblematic Mason jars became a popular way of packaging when the need for metals during World War II caused a scarcity of the usual tin containers.

Living as I did in the heart of white-lightning country, a few years later I almost dropped a cookbook when I read the word "Moonshine." If it had been a Southern cookbook or a Foxfire book, I would have turned the page without a second thought.

This reference to "Moonshine" came from English food writer Elizabeth David's book, *Summer Cooking*. As my eye darted from the title of the recipe to the recipe credit and attribution below, I got an even bigger shock: the recipe first appeared in *The Accomplisht Cook*, by Robert May. In 1660.

"Eggs in Moonshine" had nothing to do with stills or hollers or bootleggers.

Astounding, how one word can signify many different things.

After all, "moonshine" *does* imply the light of the moon. And Greek yarrow, too.

Omitting the verjuice, or the juice of white grapes, "Eggs in Moonshine" was a way of cooking eggs *au plat*. In those days, that would have been a pewter plate.

Truth be told, a much more palatable way to enjoy "moonshine." But, happily, the eater feels a lot better in the morning, too!

Why call this dish "Eggs in Moonshine?" The roundness of the eggs, the onion slices, the color? That mystery, and the thrill of the hunt, made food and cooking all the more intriguing.

Every day, some new thing to learn, some tidbit or morsel of information appears.

But not always accompanied by dreamy young men picking banjos.

Eggs in Moonshine

Break them in a dish, upon some butter and oyl, melted or cold ; throw on them a little salt, and set them on a chafing-dish of coals ; make not the yolks too hard, and in the doing cover them, and make a sauce for them of an onion cut into round slices, and fried in sweet oyl or butter ; then put to them Verjuice, grated nutmeg, a little salt, and so serve them. [From The Accomplisht Cook, *by Robert May, 1660]*

She-Crab Soup

Have you ever watched a crab on the shore crawling backward in search of the Atlantic Ocean, and missing? That's the way the mind of man operates.

~ H. L. Mencken

Many places in my memory house no longer exist. I could list them, of course. And when those places sit on stilts high above some raging surf, their loss comes as no surprise. Hurricanes sweep away more than wood and glass. Memories go too.

Harry's, in Virginia Beach, Virginia, joined that long list of spots where food epiphanies occurred.

It was in Harry's wood-planked dining room that I first tasted she-crab soup. The creamy mouthfeel reminded me of lobster bisque. Indeed, the foundations of the two soups belong to the "family" of French flour-thickened sauces, based on roux made from a mixture of fat and flour. Utilized by French chefs in the young United States. Encouraged even by the culinary leanings of President Thomas Jefferson, a Francophile who saw to it that chefs working for him learned French culinary secrets. He brought one of his enslaved workers, James Hemings, to Paris for that express purpose.

What of the crabs in this soup?

Blue crabs—*Callinectes sapidus*, meaning "beautiful savory swimmers"—live along the Atlantic coast of the United States. Notorious scavengers, they eat nearly everything, the details of which might have kept me from ordering the soup had I known.

William W. Warner's Pulitzer-winning *Beautiful Swimmers: Watermen, Crabs and the Chesapeake Bay* appeared in 1976. Warner described in detail these crabs and their place in their habitat. Knowing something in depth about the crabs made cooking, and eating them, all the more precious. One thing I never knew concerned crab "aprons" or the underside of crab shells, signaling the sex of these crustaceans. One way of telling the difference between the sexes turned out to be the best example I ever read: Male crab aprons sport a Washington Monument-like image, while the female apron resembles the U.S. Capitol Building.

She-crab soup received its name from the addition of roe or eggs. In lieu of authentic crab roe, many cooks added crumbled, hard-cooked yolks of chicken eggs as a substitute.

When I cooked she-crab soup, I took the easy way out: I bought pre-cleaned crab. For I'd learned my lesson in Mexico. No crab cleaning for me, as it was too intimidating a task. Knowing what I knew about the crabs' questionable eating habits, I just trusted the fishmongers and purveyors to do the job right.

At least I didn't have to kill them myself.

She-Crab Soup

3 tablespoons unsalted butter

4 tablespoons all-purpose flour

1 bay leaf

2 cups fish or shrimp stock

Juice of one lemon

2 cups whole milk

1 cup heavy cream

Fine sea salt, to taste

Freshly ground white peppercorns, to taste

½ teaspoon paprika

½ cup crab roe, divided

1 pound blue crab meat, picked over and cleaned, divided

¼ cup dry sherry

Chopped flat-leaf parsley, for garnish

In a saucepan, dissolve flour in melted butter over medium heat. Add bay leaf and let cook for a few seconds. Pour in fish stock, simmer until thickened. Add lemon juice, milk, cream, salt, white pepper, paprika, ¼ cup crab roe, and ¼ cup crab meat. Simmer 10 minutes. Stir in sherry off the heat. Fill four soup plates and sprinkle with remaining roe and crab meat. Garnish with chopped parsley. Serves 4.

International meetings on Integrated Pest Management took Mike and me to Manado, in the Sulawesi province of eastern Indonesia for nine days. There I met Marlon Kamagi, referred to me by someone on a U.K. Facebook group. Marlon took me to many places, showing me a side of Indonesia and its food that I would never have seen otherwise. Palm sugar, nutmeg plantations, jackfruit, and a market selling dog and snake meat. The hotel chef served Indonesian dishes for the entire conference, always something different.

Sulawesi

Fishmonger, Manado, Indonesia

Sambals

Indonesia has vast region with so many islands, comprises so many ethnics,
tongues and cultures that make it so hard to be recognized as a single nation.

~ Toba Beta

An adage has it that the first view of a new place colors everything thereafter.

If that's true, then the verdant volcanoes I noticed as our plane circled Manado foretold everything. Looming up beneath the airplane as it swung left and headed for earth, their green velvet crests sparkling like emeralds in the noonday sun, the Mount Klabat and Mount Lokon volcanoes cradled that traditional and modern city, raised to the sky like two hands in namaste.

Known worldwide for its superb deep-sea diving and snorkeling, Manado was a city in predominantly Christian North Sulawesi. Sulawesi (formerly Celebes) was one of the furthest east islands of the immense Indonesia archipelago, which consists of 17,508 islands. To put some perspective on the distances involved, Manado lay 1,350 miles east of Jakarta (formerly Batavia), capital of Indonesia, situated on the island of Java.

The Dutch colonized Indonesia and ruled for close to 350 years, beginning in 1619. They introduced a number of cool-weather crops such as cabbage and carrots, along with baking traditions still visible: doughnuts, cookies, and cakes like the coconut-imbued *Klappertart*.

In 1859, the British naturalist Alfred Russel Wallace spent several weeks in the area, solidifying his theories about evolution, resulting in what became the Wallace Line, a hypothetical boundary between Asian and Australian fauna.

Charles Darwin beat Wallace to the finish line on evolutionary theory with the publication of *The Origin of Species* in 1859, even though they'd co-authored a paper the previous year on the subject of evolution.

But I wasn't in Sulawesi to probe Wallace's connection to the island nor his explorations.

I came to explore the food.

Preparing for a session with the Sintesa Peninsula Hotel's chef, I drank thick black coffee laced with a generous dollop of palm sugar.

Chef Ahmed Rofiq and his staff prepared Nasi Goreng (Indonesian fried rice), Satay (grilled meat with peanut sauce), Braised Ox Tails, and a delicious Soto, or soup, highly seasoned with the warm flavor of ginger. Sambals, similar to salsas, always turned up on the table, allowing diners to liven up their food should they wish to do so. Except for the oxtails, most of these dishes—more traditional on the island of Java than on Sulawesi—lack the local "*rica-rica*" treatment, the fiery red pepper paste so common in the Manado area. North Sulawesi enjoyed the reputation of serving the hottest food in Indonesia. Chef Rofiq, like many Indonesian chefs, worked on cruise ships after attending culinary school in Europe. Hailing from Bali, he assured me that his house would be open to us any time we found ourselves there.

"My house is your house," he insisted.

I wondered if the chef cooked the food of Bali because he was, after all, an exile in Manado.

A stranger. Like me.

Sambal Rica-Rica

5 medium shallots

10 fresh red chiles

7 fresh Thai chiles

2-inch piece of ginger, peeled

2 stalks lemongrass, thinly sliced

3 tablespoons vegetable oil

2 tablespoons dark brown sugar

1 teaspoon fine sea salt, or to taste

1 tablespoon freshly squeezed lime juice

In a mortar, grind shallots, ginger, lemongrass, and chiles. Or use a blender. Heat oil over medium-high heat, sauté chile paste until aromas are released. When paste turns dark red, it's done. Stir in sugar, salt, and lime juice. Continue cooking until thick and pasty. Makes approximately 1½ cups.

An Extreme Market

You have just dined, and however scrupulously the slaughterhouse is concealed in the graceful distance of miles, there is complicity.
~ Ralph Waldo Emerson

"It's over that hill there," Marlon pointed. A bus painted yellow and blue, people clinging to the ladder on the back, screeched around us, its tinny horn beeping, barely missing the front fender of the Jeep.

Marlon let loose with a few choice swear words in Indonesian. But maybe not. He and his family adhered to the philosophy of the Salvation Army. The first site he took me to was an enormous Christ figure north of Manado, over-looking the city.

We pulled up to the infamous Tomohon market, discussed in every guidebook I'd read before I boarded a plane in Singapore for the last leg of a very long trip to Indonesia. Actually, "discussed" was a bit tame.

Actually, "discussed with horror" would better describe it.

At the "extreme market," vendors sold dozens of varieties of dried fish, as well as dog meat, fruit bats, and jungle rats.

It began at the entrance.

Cages the size of banana boxes held squealing, barking, whining dogs, sometimes as many ten crammed into the small space. A few feet away, two men squatted on a step, blowtorches in one of their hands, a long metal skewer as thick as a crowbar in the other, a dead and scorched dog hanging on the end.

I recoiled, in shock and disgust.

"Marlon, I didn't think it would be like this!" I whispered. He nodded.

Inside, I saw vegetable and fruit vendors, their colorful arrangements looking like any other open-air market.

As I turned down another passageway, a more disturbing sight stunned me.

Hanging like a windsock from a rusty hook, a yellow and black snake quivered as the knife slithered through its living flesh. Blood cascaded down the smooth white belly skin, rich, dark, thick, like just-boiled pomegranate syrup.

Bleeding pigs' heads and scorched bat carcasses lay on tables within feet of each other. Chunks of splayed flesh and congealing blood covered still more tables.

An endless parade of vendors passed by, each carrying some bloodied bits of animal or reptile. I drew back.

The noise, the flies, and the screeching of the live dogs unnerved me. I sensed that my breakfast beating a hasty retreat as I stared at the eyeless skull of a flayed pig.

Marlon, too, seemed overwhelmed by it all. So did his 10-year-old daughter Amirah, who stared at everything. I expected her to cover her eyes, but she never did.

We dashed outside and sucked in the fresh air, gulping it as if we'd been underwater, holding our breaths. In a way, we had.

Women dressed in rainbow-hued batik-print sarongs sat near the other entrance to the market, selling live fish swimming in small metal buckets or large plastic tubs, and dead fish laid out in colorful mosaic-like patterns on wooden trays. Chickens pecked the ground, strings tied to their legs, vendors holding on to the strings like kids with helium balloons at a birthday party. Others carried scorched dogs on trays, as people haggled over the price and bought them.

In some parts of Asia, people considered dog meat a delicacy.

Wet markets like Tomohon are common in many parts of the world. They offer traditional, vibrant sites for people to buy food and socialize. Despite the prevalence of refrigeration in many urban areas, and often rural areas as well, wet markets continue to be popular. When I lived overseas, I shopped at these markets, but I usually called them "open-air" markets.

The word "wet" refers to the cleaning taking place at the end of the day, when cleaners hose down white-tiled countertops and floors. Drains and gutters allow the water to flow out, removing blood and bits of flesh and caked-on dirt, readying the market for the next day.

After another ten minutes, Marlon looked at me. I nodded.

It was time to leave the nightmare. Waking from it as from a long, hard night. We sat in silence for most of the two-hour drive back to Manado.

Mental images of Tomohon market stayed with me for years.

In the beginning, I found it barbaric, and it was.

But I thought, too, that starving humans eat anything, even each other, when survival is on the line.

Dog eat dog.

Peanut Sauce for Satay

1 tablespoon peanut oil—be sure it tastes truly peanutty

4 medium shallots, peeled and finely minced

3 garlic cloves, peeled and minced

1 tablespoon fresh ginger, peeled and minced

2 Thai chiles, or other fresh red chiles, seeded and finely chopped

½ cup crunchy peanut butter

1¾ cups coconut milk

1 tablespoon soy sauce

1 tablespoon dark brown sugar

1½ tablespoons fish sauce

2 tablespoons freshly squeezed lime juice

In a skillet, heat peanut oil over medium heat. Add shallots, garlic, ginger, and chiles. Fry, stirring, until shallots start to brown. Lower heat to medium low. Add peanut butter, coconut milk, soy sauce, brown sugar, fish sauce, and lime juice. Stir until smooth. Turn heat to low and simmer for about 10 minutes, ensuring the consistency doesn't become too thick. Add water, a tablespoon at a time, if necessary, to maintain thickness of a medium white sauce. Serve with grilled meats. Or mix into cooked noodles. Makes approximately 2 cups.

Palm Sugar

There is a specific difference in palm sugar naming in Indonesia: if it is made from coconut, it is called as gula jawa *or* gula merah *(red sugar), on the other hand* gula aren *(aren sugar) refers to palm sugar that is specifically made from the sap of aren palm flower buds.*

~ Wikipedia

After bumping along the narrow, traffic-congested roads of North Sulawesi for an hour, on the first day of my tour of northern Sulawesi, Marlon stopped the Jeep in front of a modest cinder block house, also a *dodol* factory. The owner of this twenty-five-year-old home-based business, Mrs. Polin Tanod, led us to a tiny smoke-filled room in the back of her property.

A wiry man of approximately forty years stood there. He made the *dodol*, or coconut candy, very much like soft toffee.

He first folded freshly grated coconut into a damp cloth, then squeezed its milk into a wide flat aluminum pan. Next, he slowly added rice, ground to a powder with a special machine. Jaggery, or cane sugar, went in next. Then came the most demanding part of the procedure. He stirred the mixture over a charcoal fire until the fire rendered it into a dark brown paste, close to the color of Brer Rabbit molasses.

Once the consistency looked and felt right, he spread the thick paste onto a flat surface to cool. Mrs. Polin Tanod carried a pan of it out to the patio, where her children sat, ready to help, a large pile of palm leaves cut into small squares on the table in front of them. First pinching off pieces of the cooling sugar mixture and rolling them in roasted peanuts, they then wrapped the small cylinders with fresh palm leaves. The candy tasted very much like a Tootsie Roll. The family sold these sweets in the local market, Airmadidi.

The next day, at the end of a rutted and muddy road, another treat awaited.

Palm sugar, crucial in many Indonesian recipes, counteracts the saltiness of the ubiquitous *trassi*, or shrimp paste. When we arrived at his small palm farm, Mr. Pandey Sibi had just finished cooking up a batch of palm sugar in the breezeway of his cinder block house, where his teenage son played online video games.

Mr. Pandey Sibi ladled the caramel-flavored sugar into empty coconut shells that give the sugar its distinctive shape. While the boiling hot sugar cooled in those shells on a large iron rack, Mr. Sibi demonstrated his method of gathering palm flowers for making the sugar, by climbing up a wide bamboo ladder using only his big toes to steady himself. I held my breath the whole time.

Mrs. Sibi squatted near the still-red hot earth oven and began removing sugar from the molds, plucking off the fresh nutmeg leaves used to block the "eye" holes in the coconut shells.

"Do you want to taste it?" Marlon asked.

"Yes, yes," I said, glad to be feeling better than I had the day before, when we'd visited a commune growing jackfruit.

After a lecture by the commune manager, we left, headed to another site, when severe abdominal cramps caused me to nearly faint. Faced with finding a bathroom in the middle of who-knew-where, Marlon pulled off at a friend's house, a very modern place, smack in the middle of a leafy green palm forest. The lady of the house took me by the hand, leading me through the kitchen.

Three women stood around a large square table, talking, slicing vegetables. Another woman, maybe a daughter, lingered at the bathroom door, her naked little boy, a mere toddler, clearly finishing a bath. She picked him up, his skinny torso wrapped in a thick red towel. I stepped into the bathroom, shut the door. And my heart sank. No way could I answer the call of nature here. Water covered the tiled floor, the walls, everything. In the toilet, water lapped at the rim. No.

I raced out, whispering to Marlon that I needed another place. Sorry.

Finally, we pulled up to an outhouse off to the side of yet another farmer's land. Sweating and nauseated by this time, I grabbed the box of Kleenex I'd brought and raced to the small cement room, the size of an airplane toilet.

I pulled the door shut.

I was alone at last.

I relaxed in the privacy granted by the four walls.

I returned to the Jeep, ashamed, but no one seemed to think a thing of it.

The call of nature, always a challenge in unfamiliar places.

Palm Sugar Coconut Pudding

¾ cup palm sugar, crushed

3 cups water

Juice of 2 limes

5 tablespoons pectin powder

1 cup coconut milk mixed with ½ teaspoon fine sea salt

In a saucepan, boil palm sugar and salt in 1 cup of water to dissolve. Add the remaining two cups of water, lime juice, and pectin powder. Cook for 5 more minutes. Stir in coconut milk. Pour into eight ½-cup molds and refrigerate for at least 2 hours. Serves 8.

Left to right: Marlon and Eran; Chef Ahmed Rofiq; Dogs doomed to die

The Fisherman

The fishermen know that the sea is dangerous and the storm terrible, but they have never found these dangers sufficient reason for remaining ashore.
~ Vincent Van Gogh

I cannot forget his face.

Soaked with seawater and sweat, grimacing with the physical effort of his daily labor, lines in his forehead telling of years spent waking in the light of dawn, the smoke of the cooking fire perfuming his hair.

He sank into the churning dirty water, leaving his flip-flops on the slippery cement stairs. Long, narrow boats glided closer, weighted down by large plastic buckets filled with silvery fish gasping in the sizzling tropical air.

Grasping the first bucket by the edge, he hoisted it up like a shepherd slinging a recalcitrant sheep over his shoulder and staggered as he moved toward the stairs.

As he approached the top step, he swung the bucket down as the market vendor reached for it, a crumpled 5000 rupiahs note (U.S. 50 cents) gripped in his right hand. The man took the money and then thrust a hand into the bucket, pulling out a few slippery fish, which he tossed down next to his flip-flops.

Then he trudged back into the choppy water as the next boat slid close to the shore. Again, he perched a huge plastic bucket on his shoulder. Again, he presented the bucket to the vendor, who paid him. Again, he took some fish in partial payment and tossed them next to his shoes. Red flip-flops. Worn and thin. The rubber soles bearing the imprint of his feet.

In the end, I counted twelve fish as his strong hands plunged them into a plastic bag, some still writhing.

By the sweat of thy brow … .

Indeed, this is a lesson I thought about as I traveled along the roads of North Sulawesi, Indonesia, where food production and food consumption hold hands, as it were, companions on a journey.

That fisherman, in the water all day, damp and salty, working for a few fish. Maybe a few coins.

I tried not to think of it, the life poverty condemns people to live.

Indonesian Fish Curry

2 pounds fish fillets, cut into 4 pieces (snapper, cod, grouper)

4 tablespoons yellow curry paste

1 stalk lemongrass, crushed

1 tablespoon tamarind paste, stirred into ½ cup hot water

1½ cups coconut milk

Fine sea salt, to taste

2 tablespoons freshly squeezed lime juice

Vegetable oil

Red Thai chiles and Thai basil, for garnish

Preheat oven to 400°F. Line a baking sheet with foil. Rub each piece of fish with about 2 teaspoons curry paste. Bake fish until done. Broil on high for a few seconds to achieve charred surface. Set aside on warm platter. Heat 2 tablespoons vegetable oil over medium-high heat, add remaining 2 tablespoons curry paste and lemongrass. When aromatic, add tamarind water. Let boil a few minutes, then stir in coconut milk. Season with salt and lime juice. Let sauce thicken until it coats a spoon. Ladle a few spoonfuls of sauce onto four warm plates, top with fish, and garnish with chiles and basil. Serves 4.

The fisherman's sandals and fish

Above: Ladling palm sugar into molds

Right: Demonstrating how to climb a bamboo ladder

Below: Preparing palm sugar molds

Train Tracks

At Home

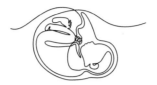

I live alone in the House of Memory, in one or another of the suites known as Youth, War, Love, Age, and Dreams.

~ John Freely

Life begins in isolation. That much is true.

Although a strong, blood-filled cord attaches a fetus to its mother, it is insulated from the greater world. As Puerto Rican poet Cindy Jiménez-Vera wrote, "Being born is the first exile," a profound observation.

And, depending upon life's circumstances, some people might subconsciously long to return to that state of being. Warm, cushioned, fed, safe. They go to great lengths to achieve those primal things, to acquire them, journeying far and near. Inside their heads. On the road. Sometimes forgetting the journey is the point, not the destination, as the saying goes.

Every person seeks something as their journey of life unfolds.

Wealth. Fame. Family. Knowledge. Safety. Peace.

The list is as endless as there are people.

My life, my journey began on a table in a delivery room where the nurses expected me to die soon after birth. I didn't. Six weeks in an oxygen-rich incubator, another form of exile, dragged me from the edge of death to life. But I paid a price for that. Not as high as other preemies paid, but a few coins changed hands, nonetheless.

Time soon revealed my price for survival: hearing loss, mostly in higher ranges, and retinopathy of prematurity, with low, uncorrectable vision in one eye, thanks to life-saving oxygen pumped into the incubator.

The struggle to hear turned out to be the greatest challenge of the two, partly because of the hearing aid technology available at the time and partly because of little familial support for me with that disability. Straining to hear, reading lips, pretending to be "normal" drove me to prefer isolation and aloneness. To cope, I first turned to books. Next, I added cooking and cookbooks to my quiver of arrows. Finally, I traveled, crossing borders, reveling in other cultures, especially all things culinary.

Here, I've strained out some of the debris, the struggles, the joys and the sorrows, so characteristic of anyone's life. I've buttoned my lips about things I wish I could say but shouldn't. And I've glossed over some of the choices I made, as well as ones I didn't make.

After all the books, kitchens, stoves, suitcases, and travels, can I say that I've found home, after all the years gone by? My true North?

Not really. If home is a physical place, then I am still on the journey.

But maybe, in the end, home is not just a physical space with walls, a town or, a country, but a state of mind.

And that is what exiles know.

Again I leave you here with the bones in the sieve.

We all long for Eden, and we are constantly glimpsing it:
our whole nature at its best and least corrupted, its gentlest
and most human, is still soaked with the sense of exile.
~ J. R. R. Tolkien

Bibliography

Antofi, Simma. "The exile literature of memoirs – debates, dilemmas, representative texts and their formative-education effects." *Procedia—Social and Behavioral Sciences* 93: 29-34, 2013.

Baldwin, James. *No Name in the Street*. New York: Dial Press, 1972.

Bell, Gertrude. *The Desert and the Sown: Travels in Palestine and Syria*. London: W. Heinemann, 1907.

_____. *A Woman in Arabia: The Writings of the Queen of the Desert*. London: Penguin Classics, 2015.

Bird, Isabella. "Notes on Morocco." *Monthly Review*. 1901.

_____. *The Hawaiian Archipelago: Six Months in the Sandwich Islands, amongst the Palm Groves, Coral Reefs and Volcanoes*. London: J. Murray, 1906.

Bowles, Paul. *Days: A Tangier Diary*. New York: Harper Perennial, 1991.

_____. *Points in Time*. London: Peter Owen, 1982.

_____. *Their Heads are Green and Their Hands are Blue*. New York: Random House, 1963.

Bradley, Vicki Alayne. *Finding Home: A Creative Journey on a Trip Around the World*. n.p.: Blurb, 2015.

Bryson, Bill. *Bill Bryson's African Diary*. New York: Broadway Books, 2002.

_____. *I'm a Stranger Here Myself*. New York: Broadway Books, 1999.

_____. *Neither Here nor There: Travels in Europe*. New York: Morrow, 1992.

Buck, Pearl S. *My Several Worlds*. New York: Pocket Books. 1960.

Burton, Sir Richard. *First Footsteps in East Africa*. London: Longman, Brown, Green, and Longmans, 1856.

Byron, Robert. *Road to Oxiana*. London: J. Cape, 1937.

Chatwin, Bruce. *Anatomy of Restlessness: Selected Writings 1969-1989*. New York: Viking, 1997.

_____. *In Patagonia*. New York: Summit Books, 1977.

_____. *What am I Doing Here?* New York: Viking, 1990.

Child, Julia, with Alex Prud'homme. *My Life in France*. New York: Alfred A. Knopf, 2006.

Cousineau, Phil. *The Art of Pilgrimage: The Seeker's Guide to Making Travel Sacred*. Berkeley: Conari Press, 1998.

Dante Alighieri. *The Divine Comedy*. Translation/Notes by Allen Mandelbaum and Peter Armour. New York: Alfred A. Knopf, 1995 (original manuscript 1320).

Dinesen, Isak. *Out of Africa*. New York: Random House, 1938.

Fermor, Patrick Leigh. "Haiti," in *The Traveller's Tree: Island-Hopping Through the Caribbean in the 1940's*. London: J. Murray, 1950.

_____. *Three Letters from the Andes*. London: J. Murray, 1991.

Fievre, M. J., editor. *So Spoke the Earth: The Haiti I Knew, The Haiti I Know, The Haiti I Want to Know*. CreateSpace, 2012.

Fisher, M.F.K. *Two Towns in Provence*. New York: Vintage Books, 1983.

_____. *Long Ago in France: The Years in Dijon*. New York: Simon & Schuster, 1991.

Flanner, Janet. *Paris Journal 1944-1965*. New York: Atheneum, 1965.

_____. *Paris was Yesterday, 1925-1939*. New York: Viking Press, 1972.

Gallant, Mavis. *Paris Notebooks: Essays and Reviews*. New York: Random House, 1986.

_____. *Varieties of Exile*. New York: New York Review, 2003.

Gellhorn, Martha. *Travels with Myself and Another: A Memoir*. New York: Dodd, Mead, 1979.

Greene, Graham. *In Search of a Character: Two African Journals*. New York: Viking Press, 1961.

_____. *The Comedians*. New York: Viking Press, 1966.

Haldas, Pauline. *Letters from Cairo*. Syracuse: Syracuse University Press, 2007.

Hemingway, Ernest. *A Moveable Feast*. New York: Scribner, 2009. (Restored edition, originally published 1964.)

_____. *For Whom the Bell Tolls*. New York: Charles Scribner's Sons, 1940.

_____. *The Sun Also Rises*. New York: Charles Scribner's Sons, 1926.

Kephart, Beth. *Handling the Truth: On the Writing of Memoir*. New York: Gotham Books, 2013.

Kingsley, Mary. *Travels in West Africa*. New York: Macmillan, 1897.

Lee, Laurie. *An Obstinate Exile*. Los Angeles: W. M. Cheney, 1951.

Lerner, Ben. *Leaving the Atocha Station*. Minneapolis: Coffee House Press, 2011

Liebling, A. J. *Between Meals: An Appetite for Paris*. London: Longmans, 1959.

Mantel, Hilary. *Eight Months on Ghazzah Street*. New York: Henry Holt, 1997.

Markham, Beryl. *West with the Night*. Boston: Houghton Mifflin, 1942.

Maugham, William Somerset. *Collected Short Stories* (Vols. 1, 2, 3, 4). Penguin Books: London, 1963.

_____. *The Summing Up*. London: William Heineman Ltd., 1938.

_____. *A Writer's Notebook*. Kingswood, Surrey: Windmill Press, 1949.

Mayes, Frances. *Under the Tuscan Sun*. New York: Broadway Books, 1996.

Mexía, Ynés Enriquetta Julietta. *Botanical Trails in Old Mexico: The Lure of the Unknown*. [Berkeley]: [California Botanical Society], 1929.

_____. *Three Thousand Miles up the Amazon*. n.p.: n.p., 1933.

Morais, Richard. *The Hundred-Foot Journey*. New York: Simon & Schuster, 2010.

Nabokov, Vladimir. *Speak, Memory*. London: Victor Gollancz, 1951.

Naffis-Sahely, Andre, editor. *The Heart of a Stranger*. London: Pushkin Press, 2020.

Niethammer, Carolyn. *A Desert Feast: Celebrating Tucson's Culinary Heritage*. Tucson: University of Arizona Press, 2020.

Ondaatje, Michael. *Running in the Family*. New York: Vintage, 1982.

Píchová, Hana. *The Art of Memory in Exile: Vladimir Nabokov & Milan Kundera*. Carbondale: Southern Illinois University Press, 2001.

Raban, Jonathan. *Arabia Through the Looking Glass*. London: Collins, 1979.

Said, Edward W. "The Mind of Winter: Reflections on life in exile." *Harper's*, September 1984, 49-55.

_____. *Reflections on Exile and Other Essays*. Cambridge: Harvard University Press, 2002.

Sereni, Clara. *Keeping House: A Novel in Recipes*. Albany: State University of New York Press, 2005.

Stark, Freya. *Dust in the Lion's Paw. Autobiography 1939-1946*. London: J. Murray, 1961.

_____. *The Valleys of the Assassins*. London: J. Murray, 1934.

Theroux, Paul. *The Old Patagonian Express: By Train Through the Americas*. Boston: Houghton Mifflin, 1979.

_____. *On the Plain of Snakes: A Mexican Journey*. Boston: Houghton Mifflin, 2019.

_____. *To the Ends of the Earth*. New York: Random House, 1990.

Thomsen, Moritz. *Living Poor: A Peace Corps Chronicle*. Seattle: University of Washington Press, 1969.

Time-Life Foods of the World series. New York: Time-Life, 1968-1970s.

Twain, Mark. *Innocents Abroad*. San Francisco: H.H. Bancroft and Company, 1869.

Watson, Jane Werner and the staff of Walt Disney Studios. *Walt Disney's People and Places*. New York: Golden Press, 1959.

Acknowledgments

Writing about the past, as I have done here, dredges up many memories, many good, but some bad and others frankly ugly. But memory can be spotty, often unreliable, and elusive, that's true.

So, to capture as much as possible about those bygone days and years, I've relied not only on my memory but also on that of others.

Thank you to my sister Paula for providing more furniture for the house of memory. And childhood friends Vickie Gamble Starbuck and Sarah Thonney Fortin came through with some choice gems, too. College classmate Bret Peaden's sharp recall of names brought several events into focus. My cousins Charles and Ruth Iott also helped me with remembering our grandparents' house. Over 20 years ago, I met my friend and colleague Janet Perlman when I worked as a professional indexer. I welcomed her insightful advice on wording and ideas for several passages.

I must also mention several friends whom I've never met face-to-face but with whom I have nonetheless enjoyed long friendships with through social media. Leo Racicot offered encouragement and wisdom on many days when I wondered if I were crazy for pursuing the writing. He also provided much assistance in the choice of a subtitle. Elatia Harris also stepped up with help in reviewing possible titles. Members of the Facebook group Writing the Kitchen shared terrific quotes about cuisine, especially Terry McKenzie and Sharon Peters.

There are no words in any language for how much I owe to the sharp-eyed first readers of the manuscript: Marcia Krause Bilyk, Kim Redlin, Janet Perlman, and Mike Bertelsen.

The M.F.K. Fisher Literary Trust granted permission to use several short quotes from Mrs. Fisher's work. Thanks are due to Kennedy Friede Golden and Michael Carlisle.

Scanned photos and old photo albums brought a greater sense of immediacy to the whole project, as did letters saved by many family members.

Cathy Gibbons Reedy deserves a huge "thank you" for the design and layout of this book, the fifth such book she has worked on with me.

My husband Mike and our son Erik pitched in with memories of our lives overseas, too. Thank you both for sharing the journey.

List of Illustrations

All photos not listed below came from the personal collection of the author.

Cover photo: Massonstock, istockphoto

Title page photo: Alexander Pokusay, istockphoto

Frontispiece: Suitcases (BrAt_PiKaChU, istockphoto)

Title Page: Stove (Jozsef Zoltan Varga, istockphoto)

Page 12: Choosing a Path … (Elena Schweitzer, Adobe Stock)

Page 19: **Washington/Oregon territory map**: Corporate Author Illman & Pilbrow. Title Oregon Territory [electronic resource]

Page 20: Wheat (Andrii Zastrozhnov, Adobe Stock)

Page 66: **Florida map:** Florida Center for Instructional Technology (FCIT) at USF, by Diego Gutierrez, 1562 *Americae sive qvartae orbis partis nova et exactissima description* Imprint [New York: Illman & Pilbrow, [1833]

Page 68: Stone Crabs (nyker, Adobe Stock)

Page 95: **Mexico map:** 1679, "Atlas minimus, or, A book of geography : shewing all the empires, monarchies, kingdomes, regions, dominions, principalities and countries, in the whole world", by John Seller.

Page 96: Skull, Day of the Dead (Diana, Adobe Stock)

Page 127: **Puerto Rico map:** A Map of Hispaniola and Puerto Rico, Joan Vingboons, 1639

Page 128: Cook Stove, Puerto Rico (nicolebleck, Adobe Stock)

Page 141: **Paraguay map:** Paz Soldan, Mariano Felipe, 1821-1886, 1888, David Rumsey Historical Map Collection, Mapa de la Republica del Paraguay.

Page 142: Gaucho-Style Barbecue (Marco Aurelio, Adobe Stock)

Page 181: **Wisconsin map:** (ruskpp, Adobe Stock)

Page182: Winter Road (mtatman, Adobe Stock)

Page 201: **Honduras map:** Central America (PicturePast, Adobe Stock)

Page 202: Sign in Honduran Open-Air Market (Presse750, Dreamstime.com)

Page 231: **Haiti map:** Matthew Carey, 1818, David Rumsey Historical Map Collection

Page 232: Haitian Women with Beans and Rice (Lorg52, Dreamstime.com)

Page 263: **Morocco map:** Society for the Diffusion of Useful Knowledge (Great Britain, 1836, Morocco)

Page 264: Moroccan Market (Dinogeromela, Dreamstime.com)

Page 289: **Burkina Faso map:** Perry-Castañeda Library Map Collection. Wikipedia

Page 290: Burkinabe Woman Cooking with a Child Strapped to Her Back (Djembe, Dreamstime.com)

Page 319: **France map:** Rigobert Bonne, Carte Generale de France divisee par Gouvernements, 1771

Page 320: Peeling Potatoes in France (Martin Bertrand, Adobe Stock)

Page 347: **Virginia map:** Nova Virginiae Tabula.1630, Henricus Hondius

Page 348: Hearth in Colonial Virginia Home (Antonio Gravante, Dreamstime.com)

Page 357: **Indonesia map:** Shutterstock.com

Page 358: Fishmonger, Manado, Indonesia (C. Bertelsen)

Page 370: Train Tracks (zefart, Adobe Stock)

Graphics emanated from many sources, including Adobe Stock, Wikicommons, and Freepik.

Recipe Index

About the Author

After years of living overseas and working with humanitarian aid projects, Cynthia D. Bertelsen now lives in Gainesville, Florida. There she writes and cooks and enjoys ice-free winters. Summers are another story. She is the author of *Mushroom: A Global History*, *"A Hastiness of Cooks": A Handbook for Deciphering Historic Recipes and Cookbooks*, *In the Shadow of Ravens: A Novel*, *Wisdom Soaked in Palm Oil: Journeying Through the Food and Flavors of Africa*, and *Meatballs & Lefse: Memories Recipes from a Scandinavian-American Farming Life*. *"A Hastiness of Cooks"* won the Gourmand World Cookbook Awards in 2020 for the Best in Culinary History category for both the U.S. and the world. And *Meatballs & Lefse: Memories Recipes from a Scandinavian-American Farming Life* placed as a Finalist in the 2021 Next Generation Indie Book Awards. She contributed numerous articles to various food encyclopedias, as well as book reviews for *The Roanoke Times*, *The New York Journal of Books*, *Library Journal*, and *The Digest of Middle Eastern Studies* (DOMES). Her columns for the *Cedar Key Beacon* in Cedar Key, Florida covered culinary history at a time when few writers and academics paid attention to the subject. She holds a B.A. degree in Latin American Studies, an M.A in History, an M.S. in Human Nutrition and Foods, and an M.L.I.S in Library Science. Read more of her writing on her blog, "Gherkins & Tomatoes," at gherkinstomatoes.com.